Also by John R Scannell

A Life in Formation:
The Autobiography of John J. Scannell
(editor)

Letters to Veronica, 1941 – 1944
(editor)

My Backyard Is Murder
(novel)

Babysitting Grandpa
(Illustrated by Leslie Sklar)

For Wendy Leigh Kelling

Wife, Friend, Lover, Advisor
&
Numbers Fiend, Personal GPS
&
Political Ally
&
Pet Rescuer, Culinary Genius, Back Scratcher,
&
Editor

Acknowledgements

When I retired, people asked me if I'd miss the travel. Now that a few years have passed, I realize I don't miss the travel—not at all—but I definitely miss the people.

Sure, I traveled alone, but at both ends of my journeying, I found myself in the company of so many wonderful, thoughtful, and caring people—people who made my work not only possible, but made it a joy as well. It's also true that they are "too numerous to mention," but that doesn't mean I shouldn't try. I actually have an anecdote I could tell about virtually everyone on the list, but decided that would entail an entirely different book. Maybe…someday.

The folks listed here are (were) my family, my friends, and my valued colleagues who helped me forge a career I never anticipated. A simple thank you feels massively insufficient, but it's all I have to offer.

I put the acknowledgements up-front—where they belong. They are the real preface and instigation for this book.

John Ade, Mary Jane Allbaugh, Pam Angotti, Karen Arensberg, Mary Jane Attwood, Ann Barefoot, Bill Barnett, Gretchen Bates, Gene and Anna Bindreiff, Mary Ann Bonner, Dr. Amanda and Nick Brender, Mannie Brodie, Bob Brooks, Tom Bruce, Joe Brumfield, Diane Busche, Vicky Bush, Luana Canty, Robert Carle, Dr. James Carlson, Bill Chapman, Nivia Claussen, Anita Clay, Cindy Coleman, Connie Cooper, Robert Cox, Jane Cressall, Traci Scannell Crowe, Sharon Cruikshank, Rick Culp, Jim Danielson, Charles and Mary Davis,

Chuck Davis [Idaho], Celeste DeCuir, Frank Delano, Dick Devine, Glenn Diedrich, Maureen and Charles Dimeck, Bob Doan, Mary Ann Dudzinski, Kevin Duffy, Pat Easterbrook, Bill Eastman, Dynva Edens, AJ Edwards, Heather Elko, Buzz Ellis, Dr. Judith Espinola, Judy Falen, Alex Federhoff, Diane Feldman-Schoen, Jayne Feuerbacher, Emily Flores, Ysau Flores, Trevor Fox, Vicki Gibbons, Ronnie Gill, Rick Glen, Jeff and Martha Golub, Davy Gontz, Paul Goralski, Eve Gordon, Don Gore, Al Gosney, Rebecca Graziano, Harold Gross, Cheri Guenther, Don Hackett, Jana Hamilton, Bob Harris, Dwight Heirendt, Tom Hernacki, Brett Hicks, R. Preston and Sue Hindmarch, Carol Hindmarch-Weiss, Glen and LeRae Hoggan, Claire Hollenbeck, Lori Holmes, Michal Howden, David Irons, Dawn Jenkins, Susan Johnson, Jim Jones, Lloyd Jordan, Shana Jukes, Jack Kapoor, Andy Keim, Carol and Verne Kelling, Chris and Camille Kelling, Jennifer Kelling, Sam Kelling, Rebecca and Ryan Kennedy, Kip Kennett, Larry Kershaw, Dave Knapp, Kimberly Koerber, Bonnie and Ed Kozlowski, Gary Kranc, Lynne Kraus, Dorothy and Bob Kulwin, Elisa LaRue, Don and Peg Lebo, Terry Leister, Bernice Levens, Melanie and Scott Leweke, Diane Lewis, Pat Lewis, Kathy Lewis-Stewart, Sharon Lipton, Marilyn Loop, Mary Lybrand, Joanna Lyle, Trudee Lynch, Jim Malcolm, John and Mary Markowski, Bob Mather, Ed Matuszak, Missy and Ray Mayes, Dr. E Annette Mazzaferri-Robertson, Steve McClung, Roger and Connie McColley, Doug McCollum, Tom McCrossen, Nancy McDonald, John McHale, Pat McHugh, Chuck McIlvaine, Dorothy McIlvaine, Glen McKee, Chuck McMillan, Michael McSweeney, Wayne Meadows, Laurie Merlo, Joe Micalizio, Mary Lou Michler, Peggy Miles, Jackie Mink, Patrick Momsen, Gary Moore, Mary Morrissey, Rick Moulden, Floyd and Kathy Murphy, Irene Murphy, Gary Nash, Dick Neff, George Newell, Debbie Nix-Carlson, Nancy Nordquist, Dewhanne Nyivih, Marie O'Callaghan, Frank O'Keefe, Steve Olsen, Tom Omli, Holly O'Neill, Brad Onken, Glen Osborn, Craig Osborne, Janay Page, Scott Page, Barbara and Jimmy Peck, Richard W. Peck, Rich Phelan, Dan Pier, Marisa Pier, Rebecca Powell, Cindy Powers, Tom Price, Bill Quinn, Molly Raine,

Dale Ream, Tim Reed, Kirsten Richert, Jean Ripple, Molly Roller, Ann and Rick Rubie, Jessica Rubie, Megan and TJ Rubie-Orthmeyer, Todd Rubie, Jeanne and Richard Rummel, Lindsay Samudio, Carole Sandefer, Jerry Santangelo, Rich Sayers, Ben Scannell and Caroline Leu, Bill and Marg Scannell, Faye Scannell, Jack and Vera Scannell, Mike and Shelley Scannell, Connie Scarborough, Conrad Schmitt, Don Schubert, Lou and Deb Serensits, Jan Shaw, Emily Shenk, Darin Shepherd, Richie Sherwood, Larry Shupe, Marie Sidun, Nick Sinnott, Sanna Skeffington, Scott Skene, Barb Smith, B.J. and Dorothy Smith, Carol Smith, Cheryl Smith, Margariute Smith, Marty Smith, Darla Snyder, Jessie Snyder, Neil and Sally Snyder, Dennis Spotts, Frances Spotts, Jack Stahl, Rick Steinkamp, Doug and Nancy Stone, Lea Ann Strand, Irene Strayer, Joyce Sutter, Jennifer and Brian Suwalski, Mary Tate Swecker, Garrett Thain, Tiffany Thissel, Julie Thorpe, Kay Thrasher, Tammi Thrasher, John Toft, John Toomey, Sue Troff, Jack Tucker, Brenda Underwood, Daryl Unruh, Bert VanDercar, Jeff Vierra, Todd Villotta, Lisa Vinson, Kirk Van Wagoner, Gary and Suzy Walker, Dave Watt, Jennifer Watterson, Judi Weaver, Jeannette Weber, Francine Weinberg, Dave Whiting, Joe Wieczorek, Cheryl Wierwille, Don Williams, Jack Witmer, Judy Witmer, Gail Witt, Chris Womeldorff, Vivian Wong, Gene Yokota, Ken Young, Mindy Ziegler, Tom Ziegler, Steve Zimmerman.

I'd be hard pressed to say where most of these folks are at this point in time. I simply don't know. Some have passed, and some may have different last names. And I'm sure I've missed someone—undoubtedly several someones. If I were looking at a list like this expecting to find my name—but didn't—I'd probably be disappointed. But for anyone who is certain they belong on this list, I'm sure you are right. So please accept my apology. And write me a letter. Memory fades. My gratitude never will.

Table of Contents

Road Warrior, A to Z
A Memoir

Preface

SPOILER ALERT. THIS not a "How To" Book. The title *Road Warrior, A to Z*, should not be construed as "How to Be a Road Warrior." If it were, I'd probably only need two letters. *T is for Time* and *P is for Patience*. I could probably have finagled a chapter on *W is for Waiting* or *S is for Sitting,* but I can assure you they would be as redundant and as boring as waiting and sitting often are.

The only chapter that might be considered a template to be emulated is the first one: *A is for Advice*. When I began traveling as a publishing consultant, the advice of several colleagues made it possible for me to survive as a national textbook consultant for more than 26 years, as I flew 4.7 million air miles, drove more than 600,000 rental-car miles, worked (and played) in all 50 states and five foreign countries, and spent more than 4,000 nights in hotels. I really cannot say how many take-off and landings I've experienced, but I suspect the answer is "too many." My wife suggested a chapter—*I is for Insanity*—but I expect the concept of insanity is inherent in the term "road warrior."

No, this book is a memoir, born of more than a quarter century of experiences, observations, and reflections on the road. A memoir crafted from the events and places that became stories of bidden and unbidden moments. Simply, a compendium of what I did, what I didn't do, and what I should have done; how I coped, how I didn't cope, and how I survived.

In 1988, I became that cliché of clichés—the traveling salesman. Ronald Reagan was president, George Michael sang about *Faith*, Roald Dahl penned *Matilda*, while Steven Hawking offered the world an almost understandable cosmology in *A Brief History of Time*. I began traveling when conversation was *de rigueur*—in a world with few cellphones, let alone laptops or tablets. I began traveling before September 2011, when the TSA made traveling an invasive waiting game—more a chore than a delight.

I began traveling the year the airlines finally banned smoking.

I was 40-years-old when I began traveling, and my four children were 18, 8, 6, and 4. When I retired from traveling, I was 66 and they were 44, 34, 32, and 30.

Perhaps if you realize I was a high school English teacher for 15 years before I took to the road, you'll better understand my impulse to write. Writing was an impulse my English students staunchly resisted,[1] complaining they had nothing to write about, as if their lives were totally devoid of interest, incident, or accident. Of course, that was not true—not then, and not now—but one of the truths most people recognize as they grow older is that every person's life is actually a series of anecdotes—a series of events where we are either the driver or the driven—the actor or the acted-upon. In my recollections, I am both.

After reviewing most of what I have written—the stories of my

---

1 I always said that there were two things my students disliked doing: reading and writing.

road warrior existence—I wondered if there was something I'd neglected, something I should have said. That's when I realized that for twenty-six years, I was the frequent beneficiary of unexpected help and good will from almost every quarter possible.

Glen Hoggan, my first boss in the publishing business, once remarked that if you want to connect with people, ask them to do you a favor. I thought he was crazy, but I quickly discovered he was right. For twenty-six years, I asked complete strangers for directions—to schools, to restaurants, to the rest room, to the nearest Radio Shack. For twenty-six years, I asked the locals to help a stranger in a strange land. Almost to a person, they did exactly that. They stopped what they were doing and helped me. Happily. Without question.

I have no idea who they were, or where they are today, but I am in their debt. Over the years I approached uncounted numbers of strangers at one time or another, and they helped me do or find what I was unable to do or find for myself. Most often they saved me time. Occasionally they saved me from making a fool of myself. But each helped me.

I always said thank you.

Growing up as I did on the banks of the Delaware River in the small city of Easton, Pennsylvania, I never anticipated the life of a traveling salesman—hereafter called "the road warrior life." "Road warrior" has so much more pizazz than "traveling salesman."

Looking back, I can see the range of my travels grew in concentric circles. As a youngster, my travels were confined to south side Easton, and Morgan's Hill, where I could ride my bike, catch salamanders, and climb trees. By the time I was seven, my Hoboken-born, New Yorker father had taken me to the Polo Grounds to see his favorite baseball team, the New York Giants, and their centerfield phenomenon, Willie Mays. My travels also included the New Jersey shore, and once or twice my parents vacationed on the shores of Lake Oneida in the Finger Lakes region of upstate New York. That's near Utica, New York, where we'd visit my grandparents during summer vacation. The only other trip of consequence was my high school senior class trip—when class trips were still part of the senior experience—to Washington, D.C.[2]

I expanded my geographical reach a few times as a college student. Kutztown State College sent me to Bowling Green State University, just south of Toledo, Ohio, and to Towson State College, just outside Baltimore, to perform at Reader's Theatre Festivals.

My first real trip, and the furthest I'd ever gotten from home, was during my summer vacation in 1970. My wife Faye and I had just finished our first year as teachers, and we decided to drive to Colorado with our six-month-old daughter to visit Faye's oldest sister, Jean. Her family lived in Leadville, the highest incorporated city in the United States. The silver-mining town of Leadville was built at 10,152 feet above sea-level, a fact made evident whenever I tried to breathe. Oxygen was at a premium.

My next longest trip was to Seattle, Washington, in the late summer of 1972, so I could begin my graduate studies at the University of Washington. We traveled to Seattle via Colorado, making the trip longer than it had to be. But the diversion south allowed us to see Faye's sister again while I tested my lung capacity.

Two years later, I left the UW, having secured a high school teaching position in the Bellevue School District on the eastern shores of Lake Washington. After that, my family and I would drive to Pennsylvania at least every other year—our first 6,000+ mile roundtrip occurring during the summer of 1974.

One long road trip—perhaps two—each year does not qualify for road warrior status. Before 1985, most of my traveling consisted of the daily twenty-mile commute to teach English, Drama, and Debate at Newport High School. Occasionally I would accompany my students to debate tournaments, but those trips seldom required more

---

2   Class trips seemed to be the norm when I was growing up. When I "graduated" from eighth grade, we traveled to NYC for the day.

than a 300-mile drive to a destination in Washington or Oregon.

Most of the time, my life was defined by the four walls of my classroom and the pages of a book.

Despite the "Road Warrior" title, I never carried a weapon sharper than a pen during my years on the road. And in the interests of full disclosure, I've appropriated the term "road warrior" because when traveling occupies as much of one's life as it has mine, it seems appropriate.

The reader has the right to ask: How much traveling is required to achieve "road warrior" status? Is it the distance traveled each year? Number of nights out? Amount of time spent commuting daily?

The truth is, I really don't know, but I believe the numbers provide critical context.

As I said, I was a "road warrior" for more than a quarter century (1988-2014)[3], traveling as a national textbook consultant for two publishing behemoths. Over twenty-six years, I averaged 180,000 air miles annually—a monthly average of 15,000 miles.

Spending 150 to 180 nights out annually, represented approximately 65% to 78% my work year. On average I spent at least 65% of my work year in hotels. May I round up to two-thirds?

Of course, there have been road warriors since the dawn of humankind. The earliest humans were hunter-gatherers, so they were road warriors by default—always picking their way across a valley or chasing down their next meal.

I really don't know who the first "road warriors" were, but they

---

3   I was a local sales representative—selling textbooks in Washington State for the first few years of my publishing career. I went on the road—i.e. became a road warrior—in July 1988.

were probably on foot, perhaps barefoot or wearing leather sandals. Putting Cro-Magnon and Neanderthal behind us, the Middle Ages gave us the Anglo-Saxon *scop*, the German *Meistersinger*, and the French *jongleur*, all of whom were part journalist and part entertainer—traveling from village to village to sing their songs, tell their tales, and spread the news. They were Middle Age road warriors.

Modern means of transportation have afforded the modern road warrior a unique perspective that earlier road warriors could never achieve. As a road warrior in the late 20th and early 21st centuries, I possessed a singular advantage that explorers like Marco Polo or Columbus or even Magellan never had. No ancient road warriors ever flew in an airplane. None ever saw the earth's astonishing beauty from 30,000 feet. None ever knew the joy of traveling 3,000 miles in a single day.

Of course, none knew the joys of waiting for hours in a Los Angeles traffic snarl, or ever waited in a Kenai, Alaska, traffic jam because a stubborn moose refused to move off the road. On second thought, woolly mammoths may have been a problem at one time.

Worst of all, none ever got any hotel points or frequent flyer mileage. Ah, well.

This book is a compendium of anecdotes, compressing millions of miles and thousands of days into the funny, frustrating, delightful, and aggravating journey that every road warrior encounters. I hope the reader finds it, by turns,

1. Enjoyable
2. Enlightening
3. Entertaining
4. Funny
5. Informative

6. Interesting
7. Thought-provoking
8. All of the above.

When you've finished, I hope you can check "all of the above."

John R. Scannell
February 2019

A is for Advice

The traveler sees what he sees.
The tourist sees what he has come to see.
—G.K. Chesterton

To travel hopefully is a better thing than to arrive.
—Robert Louis Stevenson

I HAD TWO careers before I retired. Good advice kept me from having three, and good advice also helped me find incredible enjoyment in my second career. As my father always said: *A smart man listens to good advice, but a wise man acts on it.*

My first career was as an English teacher in junior and senior high school—and briefly as a graduate teaching assistant in the University of Washington's Department of Speech.

My second career is the one that gave birth to this book. I worked as a "national consultant," selling textbooks and training teachers for two publishing behemoths—Macmillan/McGraw-Hill for twelve years, then Pearson/Prentice Hall for fourteen years.

My childhood friend, Sterling "Jimmy" Carter, an advertising executive in southern California, always joked that I'd left teaching to become the cliché of clichés. "You're a traveling salesman, Red[4]," he'd say, shaking his head in amusement. "Imagine that! A traveling salesman." He'd size me up with a dubious look. "National consultant?" he'd say. "That's gilding the lily."

---

4   My childhood nickname was "Red." So was the color of my hair.

My third career was an almost—happily.

Never Corps to the Core

Following college graduation in the spring of 1969, I taught twelfth-grade English at the only high school in the town of Nazareth, Pennsylvania,[5] until June 1970. I would have continued teaching at Nazareth High School, but in mid-April 1970, I accepted a teaching assistantship at the University of Washington's graduate school. I'd be joining the Department of Speech-Communication in the fall. Unfortunately, two weeks after I promptly said "Yes" to my acceptance in the UW graduate program, and three days after my resignation had been reluctantly accepted by the Nazareth Area School Board—complete with a lovely "good-luck-in-all-your-future-endeavors" letter—a Marine Corps recruiter called me at home.

"Mr. Scannell?" asked a voice with a syrupy Southern accent.

"Yes?"

"Sir, I'm Sergeant William Grady, recruiter for the United States Marine Corps. How are you today?"

I was caught quite unawares. "I'm fine, Sergeant." I imagine my voice was filled with hesitation.

"I am pleased to hear that, sir. I'm calling because we have your name on the August draft list. We'd like to invite ya'll to come on down to the office and talk about your future."

I was stunned. "My future?" I asked. "What are you talking about?"

"Mr. Scannell, your two brothers saw fit to join our country's finest fighting team—the United States Marine Corps. We're hoping ya'll consider doing the same." His drawling articulation was clipped and full of enthusiasm. He'd done this before.

It was true. Both my older and younger brothers joined the Marine Corps after high school, and both eventually served in

---

5   Nazareth, Pennsylvania, is home to Martin Guitars and race-car driver Mario Andretti.

Vietnam, but I had a teaching degree, a wife, and a four-month-old daughter.

"Sergeant Grady, I'll be attending graduate school at the University of Washington later this year. For my Master's degree. My family and I will be moving to Seattle sometime in August. I'll be a teaching assistant there. I expect my draft deferment will be extended until I complete my Master's degree."

"I beg your pardon, son,"—he'd switched from "sir" to "son"—"but ya'll need to understand that deferments are only for college undergraduates." He emphasized the "under" part of that word.

Now I was reeling. I could feel my uncertainty growing. "Sergeant, I appreciate your call, but I have no plans to join the military."

"I understand, Mr. Scannell. But I expect your draft number will certainly be called. By the end of the year you'll be wearing khaki."

Khaki was the last word I remember hearing in that conversation. I can't recall saying "thank you" or "good-bye." The next day, my own local Draft Board confirmed the recruiter's khaki comment. When I resigned my Nazareth teaching job, I also lost my draft deferment. I wouldn't be reclassified 1A until early July, but then it was only a matter of time until I received my invitation from Uncle Sam. I knew the only way to avoid "the wearin' of the green" was to find another teaching position. Immediately.

I did.

For the next two years, I taught eighth grade English in the small town of Lykens, Pennsylvania—about 100 miles west of Nazareth and 30 miles northeast of Pennsylvania's capital, Harrisburg. I kept my draft deferment, and during those years, opposition to the Vietnam War grew and the draft rolls shrank, making it possible for me to finally attend graduate school without the threat of khaki.

In the fall of 1972, I commenced my graduate studies at the University of Washington. After grad school, I taught for another dozen years at Newport HS and then, in 1985, I joined the text-book publishing industry. I'd successfully side-stepped a military career. For the record, lest someone thinks I blithely shirked my military obligation, I offer an excerpt from a 1968 letter that my oldest brother, Bill, wrote to me from Da Nang while stationed with the 1st Marine Division.

While still in college, I'd written Bill that I was considering joining one of the branches of the armed forces after graduation. His response was that of the typical loving brother.

Jesus, John, you'll have a college degree. Use it! If you even think about joining the military, I'll kick your ass from one end of the country to the other. Don't you know they're trying to kill us over here?

That's brotherly love. I took Bill's good advice...no...I took his excellent advice.

Good Advice

My teaching career lasted a total of fifteen years—first high school, then junior high school, then college students, and finally back to high school. I can unhesitatingly affirm that the teaching landscape is dominated by four walls. Every day. Morning 'til evening. That may have changed to some extent with the advent of technology, but it was true when I began teaching in 1969. Before I left teaching and began working as a national consultant, I'd never realized the true dimensions of the word "travel."

Travel proves the adage: *You don't know what you don't know, until you have traveled.*

Reading books about distant places may satisfy a thirst for information, but only by traveling, only by being there, can you satisfy your thirst for experience. When you've arrived some place new, you take its pulse, listen to its sounds, and inhale its aromas. Only when you feel it in your bones can you really say you've been there. Otherwise you are just passing through.

In 1988, *Macmillan Publishing* made me their very first national language arts consultant. That's verbal shorthand for "Former English teacher sells textbooks to currently-employed English teachers across the United States."

I'd always had the wanderlust, the itch to travel. Now I could scratch that itch.

Fortunately, I had a colleague, Jeannette Weber, who'd been a high school Home Economics teacher before she became a national consultant for *Butterick*, selling clothing patterns and instructional manuals to high school Home Economics departments. Jeannette came to *Macmillan Publishing* when *Macmillan* purchased *Butterick's* extensive catalogue of Home Ec instructional materials. Baby-boomers remember the post-World War II schools with their emphasis on life skills—Home Economics for girls and Industrial Education, usually called "shop," for boys.

Jeannette pulled me aside during my inaugural National Sales Meeting in Denver to offer me some advice—her personal philosophy for "road warriors." As my friend, Rick Rubie, used to say. "Giving advice is the easy part...but listening to advice...that's where all the problems are. The tough part is knowing if it is good advice. If it is, then what are you gonna do?"

It never occurred to me to have a philosophy for traveling. What was there to know?

Travel to work. Do the work I am supposed to do—selling Literature books and Writing books to English teachers. Return home. Repeat.

"I've been a national consultant for more than a dozen years," she said to me over coffee. "I expect you'll be traveling almost every week. You'll be on the road 150 nights each year, give or take. That's a lot of away time. If you just go to work, you'll miss everything that this job has to offer."

She could see I wasn't clear about what she meant.

"If you stick around long enough, you'll get assignments that will take you to every major city in the country—Chicago, Boston, Miami, Houston, Los Angeles, all of 'em—and to a bunch of itty-bitty burgs that barely appear on a map."[6]

The prospect of travel excited me, but I still wasn't sure what she was trying to say. She read the confusion on my face.

"It's very simple, John. First, you plan your work. Then, you plan your play."

"Okay, Jeannette," I said. "That makes sense."

"No, John. I don't think you get it." She leaned toward me. "I know you'll plan your work. That's a given. But national consultants who only plan their work never last. They burn out. This job—this really attractive job—becomes an endless parade of airports, hotels, and restaurants. Which is why most national consultants quit after a few years. They leave because their jobs become like every other job...except theirs comes with a three-thousand mile commute." She leaned back.

Her advice was beginning to sink in.

"But you like your job, right?" I asked. "You still like it. You aren't burned out."

"No, John, I don't like my job," she said, her dark eyes beaming. "I love my job. I can't believe they pay me to do what I do."

I'd frequently said the same thing about teaching theatre, so I knew how she felt. "So, after more than a decade, you still love your job." I was curious. Her enthusiasm was infectious. "Tell me why."

She chuckled to herself. "Let's start with going everywhere on somebody else's dime. I live in northeast New Jersey, and three weeks ago I worked for three days with San Antonio teachers. If you've never been there, you'll discover San Antonio is a fun city. I went to the Alamo, had dinner at the Riverwalk.[7] A week before that, I worked

---

6   This was 1988. Large, tri-fold, paper maps proved indispensable to navigating the states and cities. The better city maps also printed a small schoolhouse logo wherever a school was located. My traveling preceded any kind of digital navigation system. No Siri giving cell phone directions. No in-car GPS. The human brain's capacity for interpreting a map was still a requirement.

7   I won't spend time explaining any of these places here. Most people have heard of the Alamo, but the San Antonio River Walk is a network of walkways along the banks of the San Antonio River, lined by bars, shops, and restaurants. Newcomers might not know about it. NOTE: If I'd written this in 1988, I couldn't have said, "Google it." But these days, "Just Google it."

in New Orleans and spent my evenings in the French Quarter." Her face radiated a quiet look of satisfaction. "You've got to plan your play, just like you plan your work. Find out what's special about every place you go. Discover the things unique to that place, something only that place has to offer. Or do what you like to do best in a brand new place."

I thought for a moment. "I like history."

"So when you go to Boston or Philadelphia…or find yourself near the Little Bighorn Battlefield…" Her voice trailed off.

"I really like baseball," I said. "I don't go to a lot of Mariners' games, but I really enjoy going. My father used to take my brother and me to see the Allentown Cardinals when I was growing up."[8]

"So go," Jeannette said. "Go! Better yet, take a teacher to the games with you."

"I can do that?" I asked.

"It's called 'selling,' John, and yes, you can do that."

I could tell she was amused by my question. "And the company will just pay for that?" I'd spent fifteen years cloistered in the classroom.

She pointed at me with her coffee spoon. "I can see there's a lot you need to learn about selling." She leaned across the table as if she were divulging a state secret, lowering her voice conspiratorially. "Listen, John, not only will they pay for the ballgame, they'll be particularly happy if you take a teacher or a curriculum director along."

I began laughing—flashed Jeannette an "honest-to-God?" look—and she laughed along with me.

"Now you get the idea. Plan your play, something you think is fun…and then find someone who wants to share that fun with you."

"I love musicals, too," I said.

"History, baseball, musicals? If that's what you like, if that's what

---

8   The Allentown Cardinals played in Allentown, Pennsylvania. They were a Class A farm team for the St. Louis Cardinals. My dad had been a hardcore New York Giants fan, but the New York Giants broke his heart when they headed for San Francisco after the 1957 season. He still loved baseball, but now the Allentown Cardinals would have to do.

makes you smile, take a teacher along, and you'll have fun without ever once talking about books. You'll begin creating relationships, forging friendships, and end up selling a ton of books. Take it from me, John, people—and teachers are people, you know—buy from their friends." She finished her coffee. "You're going to be new at this for a while, so give me a call if you want to talk about doing the job."

It was clear we had to get to our next session, but as we pushed back from the table, she stood up and hugged me. Holding me at arms' length as if she were my mother, Jeannette offered me her assessment of her job.

"We all get tired when we travel, John. Traveling is hard work. Don't ever let anyone tell you differently. The plane-car-hotel routine gets to be really monotonous. We're away from our families way too much. Sometimes we just want to sleep in our own beds. But if you really understand how this national consultant's job gives you opportunities that other people would kill for, then you'll understand why I think this is one of the best jobs in the world."

We began walking into the conference center. "There's always the work, John. That'll never change. But plan your play, find the fun, and you'll always look forward to your next trip."

I think that's what Robert Louis Stevenson meant when he wrote "To travel hopefully is better than to arrive."

Taking Good Advice

I remember once reading a quote from Oscar Wilde: "The only thing to do with good advice is pass it on. It is never of any use to oneself." But—and may the literary gods forgive me—Oscar Wilde was wrong. Jeannette's advice clearly made her love her job, and her advice changed the entire trajectory of my life in sales.

I found the fun.

In twenty-six years of traveling to all fifty states, from the Canadian border to the Mexican border, from sea to shining sea—and occasionally over the shining sea—I was able to find the fun, often just by savoring the scenery and the breathtaking vistas—driving through the Rockies, cruising the Blue Ridge Mountains, craning my neck while driving the Turnagain Arm south of Anchorage, admiring the autumn leaves in the Adirondacks, pausing along the Pacific Coast's Big Sur, or walking to the water's edge at North Carolina's Outer Banks. My spirit was always renewed at the sound of the eternal, crashing surf.

The thought that most often occurred to me was, *They pay me to do this. They actually pay me to be here.* Those thoughts occurred non-stop on each of the five occasions I worked for the Department of Defense schools in Germany, Italy, Guam, and Saipan. While working at the United States military base in Wiesbaden, I visited Germany's storybook Heidelberg Castle and its lovely *Weihnachtsmarkt*—Christmas Market. That same trip took me north on the train to Cologne's ancient cathedral, Der Dom, whose foundation stone was laid in 1248.

In 1995, I called my father from a pay phone outside the cathedral, and said, "You'll never guess where I am, Dad." I waited a moment. "I'm calling you from Germany. I'm in Cologne, standing next to *Der Dom*, an incredible cathedral."

"You know, son," my Dad said, "the last time I saw Cologne, we were flying at 20,000 feet. We used *Der Dom* as a sighting point for dropping bombs."

"Well, Dad, times have changed."

Indeed they had.

Natural beauty and man-made wonders always commanded my attention, but I also indulged my favorite—more mundane—passions. For instance, I managed to see baseball games in every major league ballpark. My favorites were "The Jake" in Cleveland and the Orioles' Camden Yards in Baltimore.[9] [See: B is for Baseball] Over the years, I took an informal poll of ballpark fare—of course, I only polled myself—and the brats at the Oakland A's stadium won the wiener war.

---

9   Let me apologize in advance. Of all the comments I could make, this one is sure to stir arguments. There are many wonderful stadiums—old and new. Boston's fabled Fenway Park, the Cubs' historic Wrigley Field. I love them all. I just love some more.

Milwaukee was a close second.

When I wasn't in a major league town, I'd see if one of the farm teams like the Chattanooga Lookouts were playing. I attended a Lookouts' game when they were playing another double A baseball team—the Jacksonville Suns—on a warm June evening. The Jacksonville players had a large JS emblazoned on their jerseys. As I ate popcorn and sipped a beer, one of the teachers I'd invited to watch the game pointed out that the team's logo were my initials—JS.

"I'm impressed. That's your team," he said. "Selling books must pay pretty well."

Throughout my traveling career, I watched many Triple A and Double A ballgames, and most of the time I had a teacher or two enjoying the evening with me.

If baseball games were unavailable or the weather disagreeable, I might take in local theatre. For two and a half decades, I delighted in scores of musicals and plays—usually with teachers in tow. I know I saw *Show Boat*, the Jerome Kern/Oscar Hammerstein musical, at least five times. I saw *Les Misérables* in at least five different cities— probably with five different casts.

So planning my work and planning my play became my *modus operandi*. With the growth of the internet, planning my play became much easier. Before the internet became ubiquitous, I'd phone to ask the local sales representative what was fun in their territory, or I'd consult the local newspaper once I hit the ground. That's how I ended up visiting every Civil War battlefield in the United States. From Vicksburg, to Shiloh, to Antietam. That's how I ended up exploring the absolutely incredible Stark Museum of Art in Orange, Texas.

Orange, Texas, was one of those "itty-bitty burgs" that Jeannette was certain I'd encounter on my travels. This "itty-bitty burg," however, has a world class art museum, an unheralded gem filled with western art from Albert Bierstadt, Thomas Moran, C.M. Russell, and Frederic Remington, and its *pièce de résistance*, a rare John James Audubon elephant folio. I was astonished, amused, and incredibly happy that I'd been wise enough to take Jeannette's advice.

I found the fun.

Over 26 years, I've munched on funnel cake at State Fairs; enjoyed dressage and jumping events at California horse shows; eaten my way across the annual Strawberry Festival in Plant City, Florida; cheered for the racing chestnut bays at Churchill Downs; ridden the rides at Disneyland and Disneyworld; and toured the stunning Chateau-esque Biltmore mansion in Asheville. I visited the Biltmore Estate between Thanksgiving and Christmas, and the memory of a Biltmore Christmas remains with me still.

I stood on the parapets of Fort Moultrie near Charleston, South Carolina, where American patriots beat back the British in 1776 while British cannon balls bounced off the palmetto logs that armored the palisades. I served on a mock jury in Colonial Williamsburg. Once I rode the cramped elevator pod up the St. Louis Arch for an unparalleled view of the mighty Mississippi. On one trip, I stood atop the Twin Towers in New York City and surveyed the vastness of the greater New York City metropolitan area. I'd often seen the world from the observation deck of the Empire State building, but this viewing vantage dwarfed even that...until the Nine-Eleven attack. [See: N is for Nine-Eleven]

I rode a cable car up the face of Sandia Peak to a restaurant aptly named *High Finance* in Albuquerque; walked Boston's Freedom Trail; sipped wine in the Napa Valley; toured the SS Jeremiah O'Brien, a WWII Liberty ship moored at San Francisco's Fisherman's Wharf. Ships like the O'Brien carried troops and supplies to the battlefields of WWII.

One year I'd be at the Rose Bowl with my childhood friend, Sterling, watching Washington State University[10] play UCLA, and the next year I'd be inhaling the sultry swamp breezes as my airboat danced over the gator-filled Everglades.

Sometimes I'd be by myself, but most of the time I had teachers with me, who helped me relish the moment. They were the locals who knew so much about whatever it was we were doing. I soon

---

10 My daughter Amanda was attending Washington State University at the time.

realized that baseball, history, and musicals were only the tip of the iceberg in the sea of fun that the world offers.

Best of all, the teachers I spoke with were more than happy to help me participate in the fun they found in their own worlds. On Presidents' Day 1993, two Rapid City teachers and I found ourselves at Mt. Rushmore in the Black Hills of South Dakota, staring up at the faces of Washington, Jefferson, Roosevelt, and Lincoln. It was a bit foggy that day, but then the sunshine burned away the residual haze obscuring our enjoyment of Gutzom Borglum's chiseled masterpiece.

A teacher once invited me to the roof of his high school in Orlando, and we watched a space shuttle launch from Cape Canaveral about fifty miles east. Despite the distance, the shuttle's tail-flame glowed with a brilliant diamond light—like a welder's torch—as it arced into the upper atmosphere. We burst into applause as the noise of the distant rocket reached us. We were reduced to "oohs" and "aahs" as the space shuttle grew smaller and smaller.

Plan your work, but find the fun.

Good advice…no, excellent advice.

B is for Baseball and Battlefields

Baseball is ninety percent mental and the other half is physical.
—Yogi Berra

There are only two seasons—winter and baseball.
—Bill Veeck

Any fool can be brave on the battlefield when it's be brave or be killed.
—Margaret Mitchell

BEING ALONE AND on the road is a voyage of self-discovery. I discovered many things, but two things stand out. First, I realized what I genuinely liked to do. Second, I realized that Bruce Springsteen was right: *The past is never the past. It is always present.*[11]

I loved attending major league baseball games and touring American battlefields—Revolutionary, Civil War, and Indian Wars—because they afforded me a chance to talk with teachers. I was selling textbooks, after all. But after twenty-six years of baseball and battlefields, I realized I didn't go there to talk, I went there to listen. The past speaks. We just have to be quiet.

---

11   As a former English teacher, I wanted to quote William Faulkner. "The past is never dead. It's not even past."

It was 1954. I was six years old; Dwight David Eisenhower was president; *Father Knows Best* was primetime television; Marlon Brando won his first Oscar for *On the Waterfront*;[12] Bill Haley and the Comets kept teenagers hopping with *Rock Around the Clock*; and baseball's New York Giants were still in Upper Manhattan, and the Dodgers were still in Brooklyn.

The summer of 1954 was also when my father took me to the Polo Grounds for my first major league baseball game. We sat in the centerfield bleachers and watched his favorite baseball team, the New York Giants, take on the Cincinnati Redlegs. I can't remember who won, but I remember my father's delight as we soaked up the summer sun and the stadium noise. Best of all, the Giants starting centerfielder was Willie Mays, the Say-Hey Kid, who would wave to the fans in centerfield as he took his outfield position. Willie Mays won the Rookie of the Year in 1951, and the arc of his career was still headed straight up.

"Remember this day, son. You're watching a legend," my Dad told me. "Soak it in. Remember you saw him when…"

I fell in love with big league baseball that day.

Sure, I played little league baseball—for a team called The Fleas—and I also played what everyone called "teener" ball. My time in organized baseball, however, expired during the spring of my ninth-grade year when I was cut from the team during tryouts. That was the first and last time I'd ever been cut from a sports team, but in defense of Notre Dame High School's baseball coach, I admit I was mediocre player.[13]

I may have been an indifferent baseball player, but I became a fervent fan. Only decades later would I realize how my love of baseball could help me survive my years on the road while helping me forge relationships with teachers.

Akin to my Dad's love for the New York Giants was his love for the Civil War's Gettysburg Battlefield in south central Pennsylvania.

---

12 Filmed on the Hudson River in Hoboken, New Jersey, my father's hometown.
13 I could field, but not hit. Ah, well. Apparently football was my game.

From the time I was eight or nine, we made regular pilgrimages to the Pennsylvania battlefield that historians call "the high point of the Confederacy." Our excursions there were usually quiet walks, letting the sacred silence and the "honored dead" speak to us.

Soon after beginning my life on the road as a consultant, I discovered that my travels frequently intersected with America's major league stadiums as well as its Civil War, Revolutionary War, and Indian Wars battlefields.

Alliterative as baseball and battlefields are, they would seem to have little in common—except metaphorically. Occasionally sporting events are described in military terms, a war between teams being played out on a battlefield—the stadium. However, it's far less complicated than that for me.

Whenever and wherever I traveled, I loved attending baseball games and walking American battlefields. Both activities—watching a baseball game and touring battlefields—permitted me to relax and enjoy the company of the teachers I was working with. We seldom talked about the textbooks I hoped they'd buy. There was no need. Of all the major league sports, I believe baseball provided the best opportunity for conversation and for silent contemplation.[14] And there's no better place to take a Social Studies teacher than a battlefield.

I actually got to visit every major league team at home at least once during my 26-year tenure as a consultant. Best of all, I could take teachers with me. A few of those stadiums where I enjoyed bratwurst and beer along with hits, runs, and errors, are now gone—replaced by newer, snazzier digs[15]—but I got to see every American and National League team, plus a dozen or so Double-A and Triple-A teams, too.

---

14 When you read *H is for Horse Racing*, you might find that horse-racing is the most conversational sport.
15 Like the new Yankee Stadium. I became gun-shy when I saw the ticket prices.

One of the last Double-A games I attended was in Chattanooga, Tennessee. The Chattanooga Lookouts were hosting the Jacksonville Suns. I'd invited several teachers to enjoy an evening of baseball with me—and I told them the tickets were so incredibly cheap that'd I buy them dinner at the park, too—meaning I'd splurge for a hot dog and beer. I concluded that Triple-A and Double-A ticket prices are all about building a fan base, because every seat at Chattanooga's stadium was literally a "cheap seat." Our "cheap seats" were only four rows behind the home team dugout.

During the early innings, one of my teachers asked me if I happened to be rooting for the Jacksonville Suns. "Look at Jacksonville's jerseys," he said. "They're wearing your initials." He laughingly pointed at the pitcher warming up on the mound. "I'm impressed. That's your team," he said. "Selling books must pay pretty well."

Sure enough, the Jacksonville Sun jerseys all bore a large "JS" stitched on the upper left breast.

I laughed when I realized what the teacher was saying. "I think that's copyright infringement," I said. "They've stolen my initials… without my permission, mind you. By the way, I would never root against the home team. Tonight, Chattanooga has my heart," I assured my guests.

Interestingly, the Jacksonville Suns have since changed their name to the Jacksonville Jumbo Shrimp—a far different and more humorous name. However, the initials JJS are exactly those of my father—John Joseph Scannell. Dad may have passed away in 1999, but his baseball karma lived on.

When I called on teachers, I met them in their classrooms, in their offices, in their libraries, and occasionally at restaurants--sometimes for breakfast, sometimes for dinner. But I'll admit, much of my success with teachers often revolved around the three "B's": baseball, beer, and bratwurst—a triple play that is happily found at every local baseball stadium.

On one trip, I found myself working in the greater Cleveland area. The local baseball stadium was Jacobs Field—*The Jake*—a field I hadn't yet visited. The Jake opened in 1994, and everyone who had ever visited the ballpark sang its praises. I was working the southern reaches of Cuyahoga County—Cleveland is the county seat—and staying in a suburban hotel when I asked an English teacher named Cal if he'd be interested in watching the Indians play that evening.

He jumped at the chance. "Absolutely! They built 'The Jake' a dozen years ago, and I still haven't gone to see a ballgame there."

I've always responded positively to a positive response. "Great. Weatherman is talking possible thundershowers tonight," I warned, "but I'd love to go anyway."

"We should take the train into town," Cal said. "It's faster and we won't have to worry about traffic or parking."

"Okay. You'd know better than I would. Game starts just after 7:00 p.m. Can we leave early enough to get some dinner first?"

"We sure can."

Cal picked me up at my hotel, and after a quick ride to the train station, we hopped aboard the train and headed north. It was clear that this train was bound for a baseball game because most of the passengers in our car sported Indians' gear: caps, sweatshirts, sweatpants—one even wore a beige, red, and dark-blue leather jacket with a smiling Chief Wahoo over the breast pocket.

Without waxing rhapsodic about my father's great love of trains, I'll say only that my Dad always wondered about "...the wisdom of getting Americans out of trains and into their cars, so they could spend countless hours stuck in traffic jams. Trains have always been better than cars," he'd say. Spoken like a true New Yorker.

Immediately across the aisle from Cal and me were two women, who appeared to own every possible piece of Cleveland Indians gear, far beyond the typical hats and sweatshirts. One had an Indian decal on her left cheek, while the other had a Cleveland Indians blanket carefully folded and draped over her lap. They seemed incredibly

17

happy and energized.

When we made eye contact, I asked, "You ladies wouldn't be Indian's fans by any chance?"

They burst into laughter.

"We were trying to be inconspicuous," said the blanket lady.

It was our turn to laugh. "Well, you've failed the test for inconspicuousness," said Cal.

"Cal's right," I assured them. "He's an English teacher, and I bet he knows a lot about words like inconspicuous...and conspicuous, too...with synonyms like 'evident'..."

"And 'visible'," said Cal.

"And 'obvious'."

They introduced themselves as Maureen and Jane, explaining that they were devoted Cleveland Indians' fans and long-time season ticket holders.

"Been a season ticket holder for more than fifteen years," Maureen proudly said. "Once the kids were out of the house, and my husband and I actually had some time and money for ourselves, I got season tickets."

"But her husband doesn't much care for baseball," Jane confided. "So her best friend—that's me—decided that husbands are quite unnecessary to enjoy an evening of baseball."

"Husbands are superfluous?" asked Cal.

"Eight-one days a year, anyway," chimed in Maureen. "Even more if we make the playoffs."

Cal was impressed. "You guys go to every game?"

"Pretty much. We can't get to all the Wednesday games—they start at 1:00 p.m.—but we get to most of the others. I love my Indians."

Cal seemed curious. "So what do you talk about 81 days a year?"

"Sometimes we don't talk at all," Jane admitted. "We really don't have to. We just sit and listen to the crack of the bat and the smack of the ball in the glove. Listen to the crowd."

"And wait for the song of the beer vendor," Maureen reminded her.

"Right. Can't forget the beer," said Jane. "It's all very relaxing." She paused and looked at us.

"Are you two going to tonight's game?"

"As a matter of fact, we are," I assured her.

"Are you Indians fans? I don't see any gear."

"Wasn't any left after you two left the store," I said, gesturing at the head-to-toe regalia they both wore.

Jane leaned forward with an impish grin. "Since you're going to the game tonight, I'll be happy to escort you to the team store. I bet they've restocked since Maureen and I were there." She tugged at the brim of her ball cap, like a pitcher getting serious about the next pitch. "You still didn't answer the big question. You gotta be an Indians' fan to ride this train."

"Then we are definitely Indians' fans," I declared. "Pretty sure Cal's a fan. He's local. And tonight, I'm an Indians' fan, too. I always root for the home team, unless they are playing my Seattle Mariners. Then I just fall into respectful silence," I said in reverential tones.

Maureen and Jane started laughing again. "Yeah, I bet you do," said Maureen. "You from Seattle?"

"Yep. I invited Cal because anyone who teaches novels like *The Natural* or *Shoeless Joe* or watches *Field of Dreams* should see at least one major league baseball game every year, right, Cal?"

Cal nodded.

"Besides, we've both heard that The Jake[16] is a great place to watch a baseball game."

"None better," Jane said. "None better."

"Aren't you two getting an early start tonight?" I asked.

"Having dinner at the Hard Rock Café," Maureen said with a big grin. "You guys want to join us?" She gave her head a flirty toss. "We let strangers dine with us from time to time when our husbands aren't around, don't we, Jane?"

Our first stop was the Hard Rock Café. I bought dinner. Expense accounts are wonderful things.

---

16   Short for Jacobs Field.

Turned out that their tickets were directly behind home plate. *Pricey*, I thought, *but half the fun at a game is in the stands…not on the playing field.* So I bought two tickets behind home plate—I never thought they'd even be available—and Cal and I watched the Indians' come-from-behind victory up-close and personal. Maureen and Jane sat almost directly in front of us, and just to our left was the baseball speed gun—the device that registered the speed of CC Sabathia's fastballs that chilly night. Unlike the weather, they were sizzling. CC Sabathia won the Cy Young Award later that year.

Sometime around the third inning, there was a brief rain delay. That's when Maureen and Jane took us to the newly-restocked Indians Team Store.

"Men," Jane said in a tone that assured us we were about to hear some universal truth. "You'd sit there and shiver the whole game, wouldn't you?" In just a few moments, she and Maureen presented Cal and me with our own official Cleveland Indians sweatshirts. "Didn't your mothers ever teach you to dress for the weather?"

"Yeah, she did," I said. "You're not going to be a tattle-tale and tell her, are you?"

"I'll make you a deal," Maureen said. "You wear this beautiful Indians sweatshirt to the next Mariners' game and I'll never, ever, ever say a word to your Mom about you failing to take her advice."

This is how to have a great evening 2,500 miles from home.

Every baseball game was different. Different stadiums. Different teams. Different people. But I always found folks ready to be friendly—to sit and talk, or just sit and watch—even with a stranger who was a Seattle Mariners' fan. An important part of traveling was finding the fun.

One of the funnier outings occurred when a teacher from the San Leandro School District joined me for an evening of San Francisco Giants baseball. The funny part all happened on the way to the game.

Chris and I had taken BART into San Francisco and decided to get off on Market Street and walk straight down 2nd Street to the stadium—a twenty-block walk or so, maybe a mile. As we walked toward PacBell Park,[17] a young man—late twenties, maybe—approached us, holding up Giants' tickets. Typically, I buy my tickets at the stadium, but he stepped into our path and asked if we needed tickets for today's game.

"Yes, we do. How much?"

"Hundred ten dollars," he said.

"For two tickets?" I asked. My face often reveals too much. This was one of those times.

"No. Hundred ten each."

I'm sure my expression changed. "Really? Really? Those must be great seats. What's the face value?"

He had to look at the tickets to check. "Fifty-five."

I don't mind paying a bit more, but I've never liked paying a lot more. Double the price was a lot more. It was time to dicker.

"Tell you what. I'll give you a hundred twenty…for both."

Now it was his face's turn to say, *Really?*

"I'm guessing that's a no," I said. We resumed walking. "Okay, thanks. You have a good one."

A few blocks later, Mister Hundred-Ten-Each showed up again. Neither Chris nor I had seen him get past us, but here he was. We stopped to talk a second time.

"Alright," he said, "a hundred fifty…for both."

I wondered what I should say to this young man. "That's seventy-five each. And I'm betting the face value hasn't changed in the last five or six blocks. So, no thank you."

---

17 It's now AT&T Park, but it's still the same stadium.

I turned to Chris. "We'll buy the best seats available at the box office. That way we'll be getting our money's worth."

Again, we walked past the young man, and again he showed up, this time about two blocks from the stadium. He was nothing, if not persistent.

"A hundred forty."

I pointed to the stadium about two blocks distant. Pedestrians were hurrying toward the gates.

"There's a box office right there," I said. "I told you a hundred twenty. That's ten dollars for you. In about five minutes, you'll be selling those tickets for less than face value…or eating the whole hundred ten dollars, and wondering why you didn't take my offer."

His determination faded and his face collapsed into grudging agreement.

I asked to see the tickets. After I was satisfied that they were *bona fide* tickets to today's game—and that the face value was, in fact, fifty-five dollars—I gave him $120.00 in cash.

That day Barry Bonds hit his 711th home run to tie the game in the bottom of the ninth inning. I turned to Chris and said, "Oh, thank heaven, for 7-11." But the Giants lost to the Pittsburgh Pirates in the tenth inning.

I probably attended eight to ten big league baseball games every year.

My other fascination was with battlefields, and I always loved walking a battlefield with someone who knew what had happened. I once walked the Shiloh battlefield with a U.S. history teacher from Corinth, Mississippi, who was also a descendant of a Confederate soldier. He had invited me to drive with him to Shiloh, only 23 miles north, on the banks of the Tennessee River. He briefed me on his family's military history. His great-great-grandfather served in the Confederate Army under General Albert Sydney Johnston at the Battle of Shiloh (April 6-7, 1862), and died a year later and hundreds of miles from home in the Civil War's most famous battle—Gettysburg. From war records, he'd discovered his ancient ancestor had died in an attack on Cemetery Ridge on July 2nd, 1863, the second day of the battle.

"One historian described that engagement as 'a feeble, disjointed attack that was repulsed'," my teacher friend explained. "I've often wondered how the world would be different if my great-great-grand-father had lived." As we walked the battlefield, he mentioned that he couldn't remember a year passing without him and his dad coming to visit the Shiloh battlefield.

"Every man in my family served in the military except my great grandfather. Dad used to say that great grandpa didn't serve because there were no wars to fight. Unless you count the Indian Wars. Great grandpa was born right here in Corinth in 1862 and died in the late 1890s. No one knows how. All anyone would ever say was that he got sick and died. My grandfather served in WWI, and my dad fought in WWII. Me, I did one tour in Vietnam, in the infantry, and went to college at Ol' Miss on the G.I. Bill."

"I think I became a Social Studies teacher so I could talk about my relatives," he said. "My students love it when I make the wars personal."

When we stopped at a place known as The Hornet's Nest, he spoke with great reflection. "I know I became a soldier so I could talk to the 23,000 men who were killed or wounded here." He shook his head as if he were trying to comprehend the incomprehensible. "Two days. Twenty-three thousand."

His calm voice spoke in measured tones with a reverence for the past. "Here at Shiloh…and Bull Run and Antietam and Fredericksburg and Chancellorsville and Gettysburg and Vicksburg and Chattanooga and Chickamauga—I contemplate the terrifying carnage—trying to imagine the depth of commitment and bravery that has soaked into this soil. In these places, the past is always present."

I bet his students loved him.

While I loved Civil War battlefields, civilization had already encroached on the ground where many of those battles were fought. Often only pieces remained. Perhaps that's why I loved the Little Big Horn battlefield in southern Montana. Except for the Visitor Center, the battlefield is still a windblown, arroyo-pocked rise above the meandering Little Big Horn River. Populated by scrub brush and rattlesnakes, the battlefield remains largely unchanged.

Because I was also a Social Studies consultant, my company permitted me to take a class called "The Unquiet Shades of the Little Big Horn." The focus would be on the Indian Wars of 1876, but we began our study of those encounters in northeastern Wyoming where the *Wagon Box Fight* occurred on August 2, 1867. Then we drove further north into Montana and walked the grounds where the U.S. Cavalry clashed with the Lakota Sioux and Cheyenne tribes at the *Battle of the Rosebud* on June 17, 1876.

I was there with seven U.S. History teachers, all of us curious to understand the hearts and minds of the soldiers and warriors who fought and died here. We were all in the capable hands of Don Rickey, a grizzled author and scholar who had dedicated his life to the study of the American West. He had written *History of Custer Battlefield* (1967) as well as *Forty Miles a Day on Beans and Hay: The Enlisted Soldier Fighting the Indian Wars* (1963).

We benefitted from both his knowledge and his spirit because, as it turned out, Don Rickey was something of a mystic. As we stood surveying the Rosebud battlefield, one of the teachers mused "it would be nice if these rocks could talk."

Without any hesitation, Don turned and said, "Oh, they do, young man. They do."

When we bivouacked that night, eating beans and breaking our molars on hardtack, we wondered why anyone would stay in the cavalry. The food was terrible and the sleeping accommodations were uncomfortably hard. Nevertheless, Don Rickey wanted all of us to have a genuine 7th Cavalry experience, which included bad food and pup tents on rocky ground.

"When we walk these battlefields," Don pointed out as we sat around the campfire, "remember that momentous things happened here. Important things. Terrible things. Wherever men have gone into battle, something remains. You can feel it. You can hear it."

Don Rickey looked at all of us. "There's plenty of history here. If you stop and listen, you'll find that the past is still with us." He spoke with quiet intensity and conviction.

That evening, one of my fellow teachers offered a succinct analysis. "How great is it when the man teaching the course not only knows where all the bodies are buried, but he talks to them, too?"

The next day, we walked the Little Bighorn Battlefield (June 25, 1876). Don, walking ahead of us in a tan, broad-brimmed hat, used a gnarled, wooden walking-stick to keep rattlers at bay, and the rest of us did our best to listen to the quiet spirits of the estimated four hundred[18] soldiers and Indian warriors who had died in battle here more than a century ago.

So, for twenty-six years, baseball stadiums and battlefields were among my favorite destinations—usually with teachers but sometimes alone. Don Rickey, our guide to the Indian Wars, said that battlefields were his favorite haunts—the emphasis on haunts because "the past is always present." When I retired, I knew that I would probably never return to many of these places except in memory.

Shortly after retiring, I mulled over the possibility of becoming a guide at a Civil War battlefield. Then my wife reminded me that we

18   Naturally, sources differ as to casualties. Cavalry records show 268 soldiers dying on the battlefield, and six dying later from their wounds. Indian death numbers are more problematic, ranging from 36 (Sitting Bull) to 136 (Red Horse) or more.

lived in Seattle, and the closest Civil War battlefield was thousands of miles away. She put the whole business in the simplest of terms. "It would be a terrible commute and uniforms aren't your best look."

Ah, well.

C is for Credit Card

The handy thing about credit cards is that they
are a great way to pay off your credit cards.
—Anonymous

I had plastic surgery last week. I cut up my credit cards.
—Anonymous

DEPENDING ON WHOM you ask, either love makes the world go round, or credit cards do. As a person constantly on the road, I can attest that credit cards helped me get around the world—to all fifty states, and to foreign destinations like Germany and Guam. My mother, who was born in 1919, never liked credit cards, and regularly grumbled, "What ever happened to cash?"

The truth is, not having a credit card—or not having available credit—could quickly bring my road warrior life to an abrupt halt. This is why I was painstakingly punctual about submitting my Travel and Entertainment Reports (T&E)—aka Expense Reports. My colleagues coined a playful name for me—Mister-File-On-Time—because I fastidiously filed my T&Es every two weeks, as if my work life depended on it. And it did.

Expense reports are easy and straightforward documents. Every two weeks, I'd complete my T&E. I'd drop the finished T&E (with all receipts) in the Saturday mail. My boss, Steve McClung, received my T&Es and receipts by Tuesday and approved them. Once approved, my company sent payment to American Express for all the expenses

I'd incurred against my company credit card. They also electronically reimbursed my personal checking account for all non-American Express cash expenses. It was a great system...most of the time.

My tardier colleagues—even one who often failed to file his T&Es for months—regularly teased me about my neurotic punctuality. However, being out-of-pocket for thousands of dollars in expenses was simply not possible for me. At a consultant meeting, one colleague laughingly commented, "Rumor has it you're anal about your T&Es." I could offer no argument.

Still, submitting my T&Es punctually didn't always have the effect I hoped it would, a truth I discovered during one of my East Coast trips in February 1991. I'd been selling Literature books in North Carolina for several consecutive weeks, requiring a weekly commute from Seattle. Typically, I'd fly to North Carolina on Sunday, and fly home either Thursday night or Friday morning, depending on the flights available.

The cost of flying me 6,000 miles roundtrip each week wasn't cheap, and when the cost of rental cars and hotels was included, it behooved me to file my expenses in a timely fashion. Something I *always* did.

Just Give Me Credit

One Thursday afternoon I was returning my rental car at the Hertz counter at the airport in Charlotte, North Carolina. My fellow consultant, Rebecca Powell, and I had traveled together all week, and now we were headed home. She was flying home to Fort Lauderdale, and I was catching a 5:00 p.m. flight from Charlotte through Cincinnati to Seattle. I expected to walk in my front door about 10:00 p.m., eight hours after departure.[19]

The Hertz agent behind the counter took my rental papers, studied his computer screen and said, "Mr. Scannell, there's a hold on

---

19 Whenever anyone flies East Coast to West Coast, they experience an especially long day—27 hours.

your American Express card."

"A hold? For what?" I asked.

I was concerned and my colleague, Rebecca, shared my concern.

"I don't know. But I have an 800 number here that you can call." The Hertz agent picked up his desk phone, dialed, and handed the receiver to me.[20]

A young, female voice answered. "This is American Express customer service. Belinda speaking. How may I help you?"

"Hi Belinda," I said. I wasn't certain what to say next. "Belinda, there's been a hold placed on my American Express card. I'm calling you from Charlotte, North Carolina, and I am standing at the Hertz rental counter trying to pay for the car I used this week. Can you tell me what's going on?"

Belinda asked me for my credit card number, and then we waited for her computer to tell us why there was a hold on my card. "It appears that your bill is past due. You haven't paid anything against your American Express account for more than sixty days."

Bullshit, I thought. *I've been sending in my T&Es on time every two weeks. And my checking account has always been reimbursed for out-of-pocket cash expenditures.*

"There's gotta be some mistake, Belinda. I file my expenses every two weeks."

"I'm sorry, Mr. Scannell, but no payment has been made against the outstanding balance in your account for more than sixty days."

"But that's not possible," I insisted. "Besides, I don't pay the American Express bill myself. My company does. I work for McGraw-Hill. I send them my expense reports with my receipts, and they pay you."

"I'm sorry, Mr. Scannell, but your balance is in arears."

I thought for a moment. I could feel myself getting angry. I took a deep breath.

---

20 I trust it's clear that this was all before cell phones became the norm. If the Hertz agent hadn't offered to help, I would have gotten to a pay phone and made the call to the 800 number.

"Alright, Belinda. But let's deal with the immediate problem. I'm here at the airport, trying to catch my five o'clock flight to Seattle. I need to pay for the car I used this week. What can I do?" I felt a growing desperation.

"Mr. Scannell, I can remove the hold on your card if you promise that you'll send us a check for the amount that is in arears."

"How much is that?" I asked.

I could hear her fingernails tapping on her keyboard. "Three-thousand, five hundred and sixty dollars."

I swallowed hard. "Look, Belinda, I'm not gonna lie to you. I don't have that kind of money in my checking account. I wish I did. But even so, my company owes you that money. Not me. They're supposed to pay you, not me."

"Mr. Scannell," Belinda said in a very practiced voice, "I must have assurances that you'll remit that amount of money to American Express this weekend, or I cannot remove the hold that's on your credit card."

Unbelievable. I was wondering what the Hertz agent and Rebecca thought, hearing only my end of the conversation. "Let me see if I understand what you're saying, Belinda. If I lie to you and tell you that I'm sending you three-thousand five hundred and sixty dollars this weekend—money that I don't have—you'll remove the hold on my card."

"No, Mr. Scannell, I simply need your assurance that you'll send that amount of money to American Express this weekend."

I might as well have been talking to the wall. She was saying, *Lie to me and I'll remove the hold.* I know she was trying to be helpful.

"Jesus, Belinda. Come on. I'd love to pay you guys, but I don't have that kind of money. I need your help here. I'm on my way home to Seattle. It's late Thursday afternoon. I'm not gonna send you a check, but I'll look into the problem tomorrow or this weekend." I heard myself pleading.

"Then, I'm sorry, Mr. Scannell, I cannot remove the hold from your American Express account."

That was that. I thought: *The truth will set you free? Bullshit. A lie will set you free.*

Now I was angry.

"Belinda?"

"Yes, Mr. Scannell?"

Angry and rude.

"Go fuck yourself."

Rebecca and the Hertz agent looked surprised as I reached over the counter and hung up the phone. I pulled out my personal VISA card and handed it to the agent. We weren't supposed to use our personal credit cards for company business, or our American Express company cards for personal business. Unlike many of my colleagues, I never used my personal credit card while I was on the road. I would have loved to, because there were rebates and rewards that came with it, but I tried to obey company policy...until company policy put me behind the eight-ball that Thursday afternoon. My experience that day led me down the wayward path to persistent and unrepentant fiscal disobedience.

I paid for the Hertz rental with my credit card, said goodbye to Rebecca, boarded my flight, and arrived home on schedule. On Friday morning, I called my boss at his Columbus, Ohio, office. Steve McClung and I had a solid relationship, and I was certain he could find out why my American Express payment was overdue. The credit card debacle was my first order of business.

"Steve, I was standing at the Hertz counter last night with Rebecca Powell when I found out that there is a hold on my American Express card. Apparently my account is more than sixty days overdue. Sixty days! What's up with that? I had to use my personal VISA." I didn't mention my impolite sign-off.

Steve was solicitous and understanding. "I'm sorry that happened, John. I'll look into it for you. I'm sure it's just some glitch."

"I'm on time with submitting all my expense reports, right?"

He laughed. "I wish everyone got their expense reports to me the way you do, John. You're completely up-to-date."

"Good," I said, "because unless I hear that the hold is removed from my American Express card by Saturday evening, I won't be flying back to North Carolina on Sunday. I mean it, Steve."

I'd actually drawn a line in the sand. I worried how Steve might react to my threat.

Steve paused for a moment before quietly replying. "Okay, John. I hear what you're saying." The concern in his voice was real. "I'll get back to you today before noon your time, okay?"

"Okay. I'll be here working on my T&E. Call me when you have some news."

Barely an hour passed before Steve called. "We've doubled your credit limit to $15,000, and the hold has been taken off your credit card. American Express said you were at your credit limit, so we asked for a higher limit."

"Thanks, Steve, I appreciate that." I was still wondering why my bill hadn't been paid in over sixty days, but I didn't ask.

"So you're good to go to North Carolina?"

"Yep. All set to fly to Asheville. Thanks for your help."

I flew to Asheville on Sunday, and after an early dinner and planning session, I returned to my hotel room. The ringing phone interrupted my watching *60 Minutes*.

"John Scannell," I said. I tried to let my tone say "Hello" for me.

"Hey, John, this is John D'Antonio from McGraw-Hill."

I didn't know any John D'Antonio, but there were lots of people at McGraw-Hill I didn't know. It wasn't unusual for a representative to call me out of the blue because I was one of only two national language arts consultants serving over one hundred representatives in all fifty states. John D'Antonio was probably a rep I didn't yet know.

"What's up?" I asked.

"John, I know you don't know me, but I'm the corporate liaison between McGraw-Hill and American Express. I'm the person who sets up all the T&E accounts and makes sure we maintain a positive relationship with American Express. It's an important relationship. I'm sure you realize that."

His final phrase, "I'm sure you realize that" put me on full alert. It's a sales phrase. It's a phrase calculated to lead you somewhere, maybe even somewhere that you don't want to go.

"Yes, I do," I said. Without missing a beat, I asked, "So let me ask. Why hasn't my American Express bill been paid?"

It appears I caught him off-guard.

"I don't know," he said hesitantly. "That's not the reason for my call."

"Oh? Really? It ought to be. It's a question I sure would like to have answered. I bet you're just the person that can answer that question. I'm glad you called."

Mr. D'Antonio's silence told me that he apparently didn't share my gratitude. Now I was curious. "So why are you calling me on a Sunday evening?"

"Well, last Thursday, you spoke with an American Express customer service representative named Belinda. Do you recall that?"

I knew where this was heading. There's magic in the word "fuck" when "gosh darn" or "heck" or any form of polite discourse simply won't serve. Insert "fuck" into any angry or excited utterance, and you immediately command people's attention. They know something is serious.[21]

"Yes, I recall that conversation."

"And you ended your conversation by saying something vulgar and inappropriate to that customer service representative."

"You mean when I told her to go fuck herself?"

I cannot say what was happening on his end, but it took him a moment to reply.

"Yes...that's what she reported you as having said and..."

---

21 The word "fuck" has probably lost some of its punch in the 2ist century, but back in the early 1990s, it was a word that stopped the conversation when appropriately...or inappropriately...applied.

"And nothing, Mr. D'Antonio. Yes, I told her to go fuck herself. I'm at the Charlotte airport trying to get home to Seattle. It's four o'clock on a Thursday afternoon, and I'm trying to make my five o'clock flight, and she tells me that if I don't promise to send her a check for three thousand five hundred and sixty dollars over the weekend—money I don't have…money that someone at McGraw-Hill was supposed to be paying in a timely manner—she won't remove the hold on my credit card. So unless I lie to her and say 'Sure thing, Belinda, I'll get that personal check in the mail first thing tomorrow,' I'm screwed. She was willing to hang me out to dry three thousand miles from home."

I was pissed off and on a roll.

"One more thing. When I'm in front of customers, I'm the model salesperson. I try never to say or do anything inappropriate, even when I'd like to punch them silly. That's what's expected of salespeople. If they tell me my textbooks are garbage, or that our service is shit, my job is to listen and respond…kindly. I don't have the liberty of telling them to go fuck themselves because they're my customers."

I paused, hoping to quell my pique. I failed. "But with American Express, I'm the customer. Me. So yeah, this customer told Miss Belinda of American Express to go fuck herself."

"Mr. Scannell," I could hear a new formality in his voice. "John" had become "Mr. Scannell." "McGraw-Hill wants to maintain a good relationship with American Express…"

I interrupted again. "So pay my goddamn bill, Mr. D'Antonio. Pay the goddamn bill. Belinda told me that my account was more than sixty days overdue, and McClung told me that I'd maxed out my credit limit. How can that be? I send in my T&Es every two weeks. Without fail. But someone hasn't been paying American Express and I'm the one getting screwed."

I emphasized someone.

"Mr. Scannell, there has been some problem in paying American Express, but…"

"So, is it your fault that American Express put a hold on my card?"

Even I wasn't sure if my question was a rhetorical one.

"In a manner of speaking."

What the hell does that mean? I thought. *Okay, I know what that means.*

"Mr. D'Antonio?"

"Yes?"

"Go fuck yourself." I hung up.

Yeah, that was rude. Strike two.

I wanted to know why McGraw-Hill was so tardy in paying its bills. More to the point, why were they so tardy in paying *my* bill? American Express wanted money from *me*. Money that they said *I* owed. I was on the hook even though my company was supposed to pay the bill.

So what was going on? At least two parties wanted to know: me and American Express.

It wasn't thirty minutes later when my phone rang again.

"John Scannell."

"Hey, John." It was my boss, Steve.

"What's up, Steve?"

"I just got off the phone with John D'Antonio."

As I said, I had a positive relationship with my boss, but now he was trying to referee the tiff between John D'Antonio and me over the use of "inappropriate and vulgar" language. Or was it "vulgar and inappropriate?"

"What did you say to him?"

I didn't hesitate. "I told him to go fuck himself."

"That's what he said you said." What did I hear in Steve's voice? Amusement? Frustration?

"Well, that's what I said."

"Look, John, you can't tell a VP in the finance division to go screw himself." Steve adroitly avoided the "F" word. "If John D'Antonio calls again, tell him you're busy and hang up."

"Look, Steve, I didn't cause this problem, but I'm feeling the fallout. I file my T&Es just the way I'm supposed to, don't I? Every two weeks? You sign'em and send'em to D'Antonio. And he pays

American Express, right?"

"That's right," Steve admitted.

"Not quite, Steve. Mr. D'Antonio's *supposed* to be paying American Express. But he's not. I don't care why he's not, but someone at McGraw-Hill should."

We lapsed into silence.

That moment helped me calm down. "I'm just angry that somebody's being paid to do a job that he's not doing."

"I understand."

"I hope you do. Anyone who makes me the bad guy when it's not my fault, anyone who hangs me out to dry three thousand miles from home..." I stopped before I called D'Antonio a four-syllable word that starts with *mother*.

"I call'em like I see'em, Steve," I explained.

Suddenly, the whole episode struck me as comic. I wondered if it was appropriate to chuckle. "Alright, Steve, I promise you this. If D'Antonio calls again, I'll make some excuse. Okay? I'll tell'im I'm busy. Tell'im I'm with a customer. I'll tell'im I'm with the Pope. I promise I won't tell him to go fuck himself...again. Promise. Cross my heart."

"Okay. Okay. Thanks, John," Steve said. Again, we lapsed into silence.

"Have a good week, Steve."

I worked the rest of the week in North Carolina—apparently my credit had been magically restored—then I flew home to Seattle on Thursday night. Sometime Friday afternoon, I got a call from Belinda, American Express customer service representative. I presumed my home phone number was part of my American Express account.

"Mr. Scannell, I hope you were pleased to see that the hold on your credit card was removed." Her voice was bright and cheery. Always a red flag.

"Yep."

I figured I couldn't go wrong being terse. Being chatty would be counter-productive.

After a notable pause, Belinda asked, "Are you still there?"

"Yep."

"Oh," she said in a hesitant voice, "it got quiet. I thought maybe you'd hung up."

"Nope."

"I was speaking to Mr. D'Antonio earlier today," she said, pausing as if this should evoke a comment from me. It didn't. "I know you had the opportunity to speak with Mr. D'Antonio earlier this week, about your delinquent account."

"Yep."

"I'm sorry about what happened a week ago, when you called from Charlotte."

"Okay."

I could tell that she was working up the courage to say something. I didn't know what that might be. Then she just said it.

"Mr. D'Antonio said that I could expect an apology from you for the comment you made to me last week."

"Did he?"

"Yes, Mr. Scannell."

"An apology?"

"Yes."

I laughed, and I am sure she heard my laughter on her end.

"Did D'Antonio really tell you that?" I asked.

"Yes, Mr. Scannell, he did."

"Let me ask, Belinda. Who's the customer here? Me or you?

She took a moment, but said, "You are, Mr. Scannell."

"I just wanted to be sure you understood that," I said. "So let me make this simple. You'll get your apology when pigs fly, Belinda. I'll apologize when hell freezes over."

I felt the need to explain myself.

"Please understand, Belinda, I don't need American Express. My company issues your credit card to all its reps and consultants, and they want us to use it, exclusively. But the truth is, I don't need it. I proved that when I used my personal VISA to pay my Hertz bill in Charlotte. You remember. When you refused to remove the hold on my card? I gotta tell ya, Belinda, I'm the customer here. So you're outa luck if you're looking for an apology."

"But Mr. D'Antonio is the vice-president…"

"Mr. D'Antonio is not my boss. So I don't give a damn what he thinks I owe you. He's the person at McGraw-Hill tasked with paying the American Express bills—including *my* American Express bill. But apparently he hasn't been paying my bill. I don't know why not. But here's the thing. You should be giving Mister D'Antonio grief for making American Express wait for its money. He screwed me *and* he screwed American Express. Do you understand what I'm saying? You want an apology? Call Mister D'Antonio."

"But he is the liaison…"

I interrupted. "Belinda? Go fuck yourself."

I hung up. Strike three?

Ten minutes later—practically the speed of light at McGraw-Hill—Steve McClung called me and asked me what was going on with American Express.

"Is there a problem?" I asked.

"John D'Antonio just called me, and he's not a happy camper. He said you repeated your comment to the American Express representative. Is that true?"

"You mean the vulgar and inappropriate one?"

"Yes."

"That's true. But she called me, I didn't call her."

"So what made you say…?"

"Go fuck yourself?"

"Yes. John, what's going on?"

"D'Antonio told her she could expect an apology from me. Honest to God. That guy's got big brass ones, Steve. He causes this problem, and then he wants me to apologize. Well, it ain't gonna happen. She called and kept insisting I apologize, so I reprised my one-size-fits-all comment for people who hang me out to dry."

Steve surrendered. I could hear the frustration in his voice. "Just don't talk to any of these people again, John. Alright?"

"Fine. I promise not to call either of them, but make sure they don't call me. If they do, all bets are off." After a moment, I added, "I'm sorry you're in the middle of this, Steve, I really am. I appreciate you raising my credit limit and all. But if D'Antonio had paid my bill, none of this would ever have happened. He'd better get on the ball and pay American Express. I'm pretty sure that I'm not the only one getting screwed."

One week later I was reminded that credit cards do make the world go round.

I met Rebecca Powell at the Raleigh-Durham airport on Sunday evening to begin our work week. As we checked into our hotel, the hotel clerk handed Rebecca's American Express card back to her and said, "I'm sorry, Miss Powell. There's a hold on your card."

I smiled.

D is for Don't

Don't inhale your food.
—Mom Scannell

The world is full don'ts—don't let the don'ts control your life.
—Kenneth Gable, professor, Kutztown State College

Don't judge me by my past. I don't live there anymore.
—Anonymous

When I considered writing a chapter about the things people did that annoyed the hell out of me as a traveler, I worried about being too negative. I considered revising my "Don't" sentences into "Do" statements—as the song says "accentuate the positive, eliminate the negative." But I just couldn't. After reading this chapter, my wife said I'd successfully indulged my tyrannical tendencies inherited from twelve years of Catholic school. For instance, the nuns taught me many things: on time is late; early is on time; don't make a fuss; pay attention; obey the rules; remember, you're not alone; and wait your turn. We'll see how well I did by the end of the chapter.[22]

AS I SAID in my opening chapter, this is not a "how to travel" book. I'm not certain there is the "one best way" to travel. Some people pack light; some people pack as if they may never return to their point

---

22 After reading this Don't chapter, let me warn you that the *R is for Rules* chapter appears to contradict everything I'm saying.

of origin, taking multiple bags that require three men and a mule to carry. I call them "turtles." Some people make last minute airline reservations or show up at hotels hoping there might be room at the inn, while others plan well in advance, and have every flight, hotel, and car rental carefully scheduled. I have no advice for either group because, as my father would say, "People travel the way they travel. Just find someone who travels like you if you hope to be a happy traveler."

I never had to worry because, as a business traveler, I traveled almost exclusively alone. Occasionally, I had a colleague traveling with me—and there are interesting stories there—but not often. If I have one recommendation it would be this: Put travel issues on your pre-nuptial questionnaire. And be sure to marry someone who travels like you.

If you travel enough, you'll learn the truth of the adage, "There's always *someone* in the crowd." Always someone who is sure they need special attention. Always someone who needs to cut in line because they're late. Always someone who talks on their phone as if the rest of the universe had disappeared. Always someone who endlessly complains, even though they know their flight is being delayed by maintenance issues, tornado warnings, icy conditions, or a plague of locusts—always someone who thinks any reason for delaying *their* flight is unreasonable. This chapter is about those someones.

Don't be the one who decides the rules don't apply

The world lived on tenterhooks immediately after the 9/11 attacks. We worried. *When might the next attack occur? For those of us who have to travel, how safe are we?* These were genuine concerns.

I don't know how other companies handled the problem of consultants who were hesitant—even reluctant—to board the next airliner. For many, the fear was palpable. Few images were as vividly persuasive as the Twin Towers burning and collapsing. Marjorie Scardino, the CEO of Pearson, told all consultants that none of us had to get on a plane until we felt comfortable doing so. Her permission was extraordinarily kind and thoughtful, and I took her at her word.

The week following the 9/11 attacks [See: N is for Nine-Eleven], I changed my plans for working in North Carolina because too much was ambiguous; too many unanswered questions about safety hung threateningly in the air.[23]

When I boarded my next plane two weeks later, it felt like all conversations inevitably moved to the topic of terrorism. Heightened airport security was everywhere. For the first time since 1988, the year I began traveling weekly—hell, for the first time in all the years I'd been traveling since I was a kid—khaki-clad soldiers armed with M-15 automatic rifles patrolled the airport concourses. All the rules governing air travel had changed, and they were about to change even more.

Oh brave new world, I thought.

The fearful mindset characterizing that "brave new world" was brought into sharp relief on Friday November 16, 2001, when I flew Delta Airlines from Seattle to Baltimore via Atlanta on my way to the annual NCTE conference—that's the National Council for Teachers of English. That's the day the story of an Atlanta passenger, worrying about being late to a football game, joined the lore of truly stupid moves at busy airports.

Let me see if I can summarize what happened when one person—one unmitigated idiot—breached security at Atlanta's Hartsfield International Airport on that November afternoon. A man named Michael Lasseter from Gainesville, Georgia, was running late for his Memphis flight to attend Saturday's football game between Georgia and the University of Mississippi. He had already gone through security and was at his gate when he realized he'd left his camera bag somewhere in the airport. He didn't know where, but he had to find it. He left the secure side of the airport, coming up the escalator to the main terminal, to look for it.

He finally found his camera bag, but panicked when he realized his flight was leaving in ten minutes. There was a long line at the security checkpoint, so naturally, he didn't want to wait. Who does?

---

23 What seems almost silly now is that presentations can easily be handled via digital conferencing.

Instead, he decided to dash past two security guards at the top of the escalator and run down the up escalator—returning to his gate the way he came.

The guards sounded the alarm.

Atlanta's Hartsfield International Airport went into shutdown mode.

All planes still at their gates were emptied. Arriving planes were parked on the tarmac short of their arrival gates. The world's busiest airport—yes, the busiest in whole world—was evacuated. Ten thousand would-be passengers and employees were not only inconvenienced, they were pushed outside the airport. It's not often that you read articles using words like pandemonium, or bedlam, or mayhem, to describe a major airport. But all those words fit.

As luck would have it, all of this happened as my Delta 757 was touching down at Hartsfield International. Normally we would have rolled to our gate and deplaned. Then I'd be off to catch my connecting flight to Baltimore. Normally.

However, Mr. Lasseter's actions cancelled normal. Instead of proceeding to the gate, we were quarantined aboard our plane until Mr. Lasseter was found. As I looked out the window, I could see we had plenty of company, as plane after plane taxied to a halt on one of the taxiways, far from the gates where the jetways awaited our deplaning. It was clear we were not going to the gate.

No one knew what was going on, not even our captain. He decided to reach out to his passengers for help.

"Well, folks, you can see that we are parked on a taxi way. We've been in touch with the company, but they aren't telling us anything, except that we're expected to stay parked here until further notice. I'm not sure what's happening, so feel free to get on your cell phones and find out. Let a member of the flight crew know when you have some information to share."

Suddenly the plane was alive with cellphones—everyone calling husbands, wives, significant others, mothers, fathers, and children—to find the answer to a single question: What the hell is going on at Hartsfield International Airport? We didn't have long to wait. Almost every television news network was running the story of someone breaching security at Atlanta's Hartsfield Airport. The airport—with its thousands of waiting and stranded passengers—was being evacuated as authorities searched for the potential terrorist.

In moments, the paucity of information transformed into a glut of televised speculation, and the captain was wise enough to give us just the broadest outlines of what was going on.

"It seems," the captain began, "that someone breached security, so they've evacuated the airport until they're certain that there is no threat of any kind." He paused for a moment. "But…it looks like we will be here for a while. I'm turning off the seatbelt light, so feel free to get up and move about. I'll let you know when I get word that we will be heading to our gate." The captain thanked everyone who had gotten information to the flight crew.

Questions about connecting flights couldn't be answered because everything had ground to a halt. We were in one of those moments that my wife calls "a wait state"—an informational vacuum when "nobody knows nothin'."

But the flight attendants could answer questions about liquor— and those of us lucky enough to be in first class decided to make a dent in Delta's liquor cabinet. As the liquor loosened our tongues, some of my fellow passengers suggested that whoever had caused the delay by breaching security ought to be brought into the terminal to confront the thousands of inconvenienced travelers. The general sentiment was that the angry mob would render appropriate, if rough, justice. It's always interesting when one hears liquor talk.

Time passed—news articles say three hours, and maybe that's right—and Hartsfield resumed operation. I deplaned, found my Baltimore flight was still on the ground, and flew to Baltimore-Washington-International fairly late that night. All because some jerk thought the rules didn't apply to him.[24]

---

24 Lasseter was sentenced to five weekends in jail, 500 hours community service, and was banned from attending any Georgia games the next fall 2002. Many felt that his sentence was way too lenient.

Don't act as if you're the only one on the airplane. You ain't.

My father's humorous advice about personal conduct was quite simple: "Act as if your mother is watching." I call that the Santa Clause corollary—"She sees you when you're sleeping, she knows when you're awake."

I discovered that people's behavior changes when they travel. Why else would waiting passengers crowd the narrow area leading to the jet way, making it difficult for others to board? Passengers have assigned seats, so no one will be left behind—unless they don't happen to be there. So why jostle to get a small advantage in the boarding queue?

As a status flyer who frequently boarded early, I realized these passengers were not worried about being left behind, they were worried about space for their carry-ons in the overhead bin.

Anyone who has flown knows that there is simply not enough room in the overhead bins to accommodate everyone's carry-ons. I knew this and simplified my travel life by always checking my luggage. The truth is I never owned any luggage that would have fit into the overhead, except for the small bag that carried my electronic equipment—a computer, an LCD projector, and cables. My clothes were always riding in the belly of the plane.

Many of my colleagues used only carry-on because they hated waiting at the baggage carousel after landing [See: L is for Luck], but picking up my luggage became part of my regular routine. In many ways, I felt as if I were doing my part for my fellow passengers. But, as I said, there's always someone…

Almost everyone had boarded. Along with all the other passengers, I had settled comfortably in my aisle seat and was reading the dust jacket of the Pat Conroy novel I'd just purchased. A late boarder came down the main aisle, looking for an open spot in an overhead bin for his suitcase. I place only my smaller carry-on bag—the one with my technology—in the overhead bin. That bag can often fit under the seat—depending on which kind of plane I'm on—but on some planes it occupies all the under-seat space, and I really need some room to stretch out my left leg. I've had a bad knee for years, and it aches when I can't flex my knee. Putting my small bag in the overhead solved that problem.

As I said, the man was looking for space in the overhead bin. He opened and closed several overhead bins as he made his way down the aisle. He stopped and opened the bin over my head.

"Whose bag is this?" he asked.

Since I couldn't see what he was seeing, I wasn't sure if he was talking about my smaller carry-on or not. When he took my bag out of the bin, I knew.

"Hey, what are you doing?" I asked.

"This bag will fit under your seat," he said, placing my bag in the aisle.

It bothered me enormously that he felt he could do whatever he wanted with my bag in order to accommodate his bag.

"That may be, but I need the space under my seat."

"Well," he said boosting his bag up into the bin, "I need this space for my bag."

I couldn't believe it. I rose from my seat and stood in the aisle. Then I reached up and grabbed his bag by the handle.

"I'm sorry," I said, as I began pulling his bag out of the bin. I stepped up into my seat to get better leverage. "I need this space, too. And my bag was already here. You might try checking your bag next time."

He was considerably taller than me and he began pushing his bag back even as I worked to pull it out. I don't know what my face betrayed, but he was livid. His face said, *What the hell do you think you're doing?* I was thinking the same.

The tug-of-war proved we'd reached impasse.

"Tell you what," I said, pausing in my effort to remove his bag.

"You can keep your bag up there if you put *my* bag under *your* seat." I nodded to my bag he had placed in the aisle.

"My legs are too long," he growled, as if that should somehow persuade me to give him my space in the overhead bin.

There's a strange dynamic that happens when strangers observe an argument in a public space. Passengers close enough to hear what was being said remained quiet. Rude-Man-Who-Wants-My-Bin-Space was tall and wearing a tailored suit. I was wearing jeans and a sweater.

"I can't help that," I said. "I have a bad knee. And my bad knee trumps your long legs." I resumed pulling his bag out of the bin. "My bag was up there first, and it's going back up there."

There was probably something in the tone of my voice which prompted two nearby passengers to hit their flight attendant call buttons. Two dings brought the flight attendant down the aisle.

"Is there a problem, gentlemen?" she said looking at us both.

I suppose the fact that I was standing in my seat didn't particularly help my case.

"My bag was tucked away up here," I said looking at her from my perch. My hand was still pulling on the handle of the bag belonging to the anonymous Rude-Man-Who-Wants-My-Bin-Space. "And this gentleman walks down the aisle and removes it. I don't know who made him God..."

"I need the space," he interrupted. His anger was clearly directed at me.

"Too bad. It's my space."

"Enough," said the flight attendant.

If she had said "children," I would not have been surprised.

She'd assessed the situation and decided on her course of action. "Will both of you please come with me," she said in a no-nonsense tone. She motioned to the rear of the plane. "And please," she said to Mr. Anonymous, "take your bag down and place it in the aisle."

We followed her to the back. Other passengers turned to watch the unfolding drama.

As soon as we arrived at the rear galley, she took absolute control. "Gentlemen, we have to get under way, and this problem needs to be resolved immediately." She turned to me. "You say your luggage was in the overhead bin?"

"Yes, ma'am"

Then she turned to Mr. Anonymous—aka—Rude-Man-Who-Wants-My-Bin-Space. "And you removed this gentleman's luggage?"

"Yes, but the reason…"

"I really don't care why you did it, sir. If there is no bin space, then you check your luggage. This is *shared* bin space…not *your* bin space. You have no right to disturb anyone's luggage."

He foolishly persisted. Clearly he didn't know who was in charge. "You don't understand," he began. "When we land in Chicago, I need to…"

She held up her hand like a traffic cop as she interrupted him. "When we land in Chicago, you'll pick up your bag at baggage claim." There was nothing tentative in her voice. "Unless you're connecting to another city." Authority filled her voice. "Is Chicago your final destination?"

"Yes."

"Good. Now," she turned to me, "you put your bag back in the overhead bin, and you," she pointed at the tall gentleman, "you return to your seat. I'll take your bag up front to be checked through to Chicago. I'll bring you your baggage claim tag after we've taken off. Alright?" Her tone declared the discussion over.

We both went to our seats. No fists were thrown, and there were no growling walk-bys during the flight.

I know it sounds anti-climactic, and I suppose it is. If he had politely asked me to accommodate him, would I have helped? I'm not sure. But I do know that it incensed me that he presumed he could have that space without asking. Was I angered by his arrogance and sense of entitlement? Damn right.

Once again, he's that one guy. The guy who thinks he can remove someone's bag to make room for his own. The guy who thinks he can shortchange someone else to accommodate himself. We've all met him, and usually we say nothing because it feels impolite to say something, or he's doing it to someone else. When he's doing it to you, it feels very different.

Don't share your dangerous behaviors

I confess; some airline rules seem capricious...especially when those rules revolve around technology. They probably seem capricious—perhaps even stupid or needless—to everyone. But since I don't know enough about airliners or airliner electronics, or the particular effect that one piece of gadgetry might have on airliners and their electronics, my attitude is "Okay, I'll do what you say." When the flight attendant tells me that all cellphones must either be in airplane mode or switched off, I don't complain. Just like I don't complain when I see *No Smoking* signs atop gas station fuel pumps.

Once I was actually refilling my rental car at a gas station in Fresno, and a man pulled up to the gas pump behind me. While I immediately noticed his slight build, scruffy beard, and dirty clothes—I guess he was about thirty, pencil thin, with greasy jeans and a torn black t-shirt—my attention was attracted by the lit cigarette hanging from his lip. I watched with growing concern as he inserted his credit card and made his selection of gasoline grade, removing the cigarette twice to exhale and crack his neck.

As he pulled the nozzle off its seat, I decided I needed to ask him to get rid of the cigarette.

"Hey, man, would you do me a favor and throw that cigarette away. We're both pumping gas here."

He glared at me. That's all. Just glared. Not a word. I suppose other people at other gas stations had asked him the same question, and now this sullen glare had become his stock response to assholes like me who suggested that open flames and gasoline don't mix.

When I realized he wasn't going to do as I asked, I stopped gassing my car and quickly reseated the nozzle in its holder. I decided that departure was wiser than confrontation. I didn't wait for the receipt even though I was on company business. Survival trumps receipts.

Since I didn't see the gas station blow sky-high as I drove north, and since I didn't hear anything on the news about a terrible gas station tragedy where some skinny son-of-a-bitch blew up a small corner of the world by smoking while he filled his gas tank, I wondered if my fears were groundless. My answer to myself was, "No. I wasn't being stupid or out-of-line by asking him to get rid of the cigarette." Sometimes, everyone gets lucky, even stupid people.

It is beyond debate that combining gasoline and lit cigarettes poses a real danger. But are we just as sure about keeping cellphones on when told to turn them off? Probably not. Nevertheless, I don't think the FAA sat around a conference table, wondering what regulations they could devise that would simply drive people crazy. Imagine that conversation.

"Hey, let's make a rule that all cellphones have to be off," says one highly-placed FAA mucky-muck.

"Why would we do that?" asks a less-highly-placed FAA mucky-muck.

"Just because."

"Won't that make people mad?"

"Maybe. But we'll make it sound like cellphones will interfere with the planes' avionics, and that's probably all that will be necessary."

"But *will* cellphones screw with the avionics?"

"Probably not, but we'll make it a rule, and everyone will just have to follow it."

Now I don't believe this particular conversation ever happened. And I don't believe the FAA made its cellphone rules just to be difficult. Nevertheless, some passengers seem to feel otherwise. Those that feel "otherwise" also feel they've got tacit permission to disobey the rules. That would be fine if they were traveling on the plane alone, where no one else could possibly notice or be affected by their behavior.

On one flight from Seattle to Newark, a young woman in the aisle seat of my row decided the cellphone rules didn't apply to her. From the moment that I plunked myself into my window seat, she'd been busy texting. Texting is fine until the flight crew announces that all cellphones need to be turned off or placed in airplane mode. If you fly often enough, you recognize the required, but boilerplate, FAA announcements that always precede push-back and take-off.

The flight attendant had walked past this young woman, stopped, and said, "Miss, time to turn off your phone."

The young lady—probably mid-twenties—said, "Sorry," and tucked the phone into the seat pocket in front of her. No sooner had the flight attendant moved forward than Miss I-Gotta-Text-Or-I'll-Die pulled out her phone and resumed texting.

I leaned over the empty middle seat. "You need to turn off your phone."

She looked up, surprised. "What?"

"You need to turn off your phone. Just as you told the flight attendant you would."

She ignored me and kept on texting.

Wow, I thought. *This calls for vocal escalation.*

"Turn off your goddamn phone," I growled.

This time she paid attention. She looked up, clearly annoyed.

"What are you, deaf?" I asked sarcastically, my volume building. "How many times does someone have to ask you to do what you're supposed to do?

What she did next surprised me. She hit her flight attendant call button.

The flight attendant arrived, and immediately Miss I-Gotta-Text-Or-I'll-Die blurted out, "This man is harassing me. I need to be re-seated." Even as she spoke she undid her seat belt and moved into the aisle.

That's the last I saw of her, but the flight attendant returned after take-off. "What happened here?" she asked.

"I asked her to turn off her phone. That's what happened."

"Why?"

"Because you had just asked her to turn it off, and the moment you were gone, she pulled out her phone and acted as if she'd never been told to turn it off. That's why."

"Sir, that's not your job."

I didn't like where this conversation was going.

"No," I said, "my job is to get safely to Newark. And either cellphones pose a threat and need to be turned off…or they don't. If they do, then I did us all a favor. If they don't, this whole conversation is happening for no reason."

The flight attendant flashed me a frustrated look. I'm betting the cellphone argument is one that flight attendants have had to deal with quite a bit. But the real issue was quite simple: Unless it's crazy or unreasonable, do what you are told by the flight crew. Don't be a jerk. Don't be that guy…or gal.

Don't live in a techno-bubble

Airport concourses are not private spaces. Nor are hotel lobbies, restaurants, or rental car shuttles. Just because you can carry a cellphone in any of these spaces shouldn't allow the owner of the phone to talk as if they're yelling across a football stadium.

Do you remember when cellphones came into vogue? I don't remember the year, but I do remember moving through a variety of airports or hotel lobbies thinking, *There's a guy over there by the window talking to himself. Is he crazy? Schizophrenic?*

Nowadays we know he's probably using a wireless headset with his cellphone. And for all the wonderful things cellphones have wrought, they've invaded and destroyed privacy in ways few of us would have anticipated. At least the now-extinct phone booth had glass doors insuring the privacy of both the caller and the outside world.

I traveled more than 4.7 million air miles between 1988 and 2014. With every passing year, I noticed that more and more people decided that they could say anything they wanted to the person on the other end of their phone conversation, and simultaneously to everyone else within earshot.

I became privy to a great many overheard conversations while idling away the hours in airport concourses, rental car shuttle buses, hotel lobbies—even restaurants. I was the unintentional eavesdropper on all kinds of private conversations—intimate, angry, joyous, laughing, trivial, and tearful conversations. My colleague once said, "They talk as if they're in the middle of a Saharan sandstorm."

These callers behaved as if they thought there was an invisible bubble surrounding them, making it impossible for bystanders to hear what was being said. Sometimes I'd chuckle to myself, as if I had found myself on an episode of *Get Smart*, watching the caller beneath his *Cone of Silence*. But usually I just found loud cellphone calls rude and annoying.

There were times when I just wanted to assure the offender, there wasn't any *Cone of Silence*.

Sitting at my departure gate in Atlanta's Hartsfield Airport, a man seated just opposite me raised his voice and shouted over the phone, "I don't care what she says she wants! The bitch can't have it!" I looked up—as did several other folks. The caller drilled me with a hard look and said sharply, "You shouldn't be listening to this conversation."

As if I had a choice.

There are probably a list of marginally appropriate responses when a moment like this occurs.

1) Look away and return to the book I was reading. 2) Stand up and move away to another seat in the gate area. 3) Say, "You shouldn't be shouting into your phone here, either. This is a public space, not your living room."

I did none of these. It had been a long week, so I chose the fourth option. I returned his hard stare while giving him the finger. He seemed surprised by my lack of civility.

Was it rude? Perhaps. Was it satisfying? Definitely.

There are rules that govern behavior in private and public spaces. At least, my mother says there are, and I believe my mother is correct. For instance, if I were in this man's living room—a private space—and I eavesdropped on his conversation, his rebuke would have garnered an immediate apology from me. I'd probably have said I was sorry and moved into another room. But the boundaries between the private and public arenas have clearly evaporated, allowing (but not condoning) people to loudly conduct private phone calls in public spaces.

This confusion of private and public can be carried to extremes. In 2011, a first-class passenger traveling from Salt Lake City to Boston decided he could watch a porn movie on his laptop. Yes, he was arrested in Boston, but the real issue is this: How did this man decide he could push his private behavior into the public arena? What made him transgress that boundary? What made him think he could be that guy?

Let me finish by saying that the importation of erstwhile private behaviors into the public space, combined with a growing heads-down addiction to our mobile electronics, has had a decidedly negative effect on the public space. The quiet, neighborly conversations that once flourished in airport concourses, on rental car shuttle buses, or in hotel lobbies, have been replaced with the silent inspection of the digital screen—with everyone emailing, texting, working, or gaming. Or the overloud cellphone call that is inflicted on any and all nearby individuals. Digital overload has led to the virtual abandonment of human intercourse between strangers greeting one another, or sharing common road-warrior stories. The once casual comments—"Where are you headed?", "Where are you from?", "Isn't this weather beautiful/heavenly/awful/God-awful?"—have all evaporated, like rain in hot weather. That's too bad. Our social fabric is stronger, and healthier, when its threads are woven into the cloth of conversation—a genuine act of connecting.[25]

---

25 I expect this comment puts me on the Old Fogey list —that somehow I have failed to embrace change like so many people before me. We are told that our technology promotes greater "connectivity" than ever before. I assert that there is genuine "connectivity" and counterfeit "connectivity." Talking to one's traveling neighbors is better than following an insular, solipsistic path mapped out by the newest drivers of techno-gadgetry.

E is for Et Cetera

The simple act of paying attention can take you a long, long way.
—Keanu Reeves

Pay attention. It's all about paying attention. Attention is vitality.
It connects you with others. It makes you eager. Stay eager.
—Susan Sontag

Consider this chapter as a self-interview potpourri. I like interviewing myself because I always know the right questions to ask, and I usually have the right answers for those questions. Amazing!

How many air miles did I fly during my twenty-six years as an educational consultant?

After reviewing my T&E's, the closest approximation is 4.7 million air miles. On Delta Airlines alone, I accumulated 1,749,061 miles, and I exceeded one million miles on Alaska Airlines during my last week as a consultant. My total on Alaska Air is 1,007,788 miles as of May 28, 2018. I am about 60,000 miles shy of a million miles on United Airlines. Tallying up the miles I flew on American, Continental, US Air, Southwest, and a few smaller regional airlines, 4.7 million is pretty close. [See: M is for Math]

How many miles did I drive during twenty-six years?

600,000+ miles, and that's in rental cars while on the road. I averaged 25,000 miles annually in my company car during those same years. That's another 650,000 miles. What exactly does such mileage mean? If I drove continuously at fifty miles-per-hour for 625 forty-hour work-weeks—that's without stopping for any reason, no food, no bathroom breaks—I could drive that distance. That's more than thirteen full work years—at 46 - 48 work weeks in a typical work year—just driving.

How much time did traveling entail for me over twenty-six years?
Traveling 4.7 million air miles means the following:

1. *Average flight.* Assume 2,000 miles each way. 4.7 million miles translates into 2,350 trips. Many trips were shorter, and many longer. Let's say I averaged 90 airline trips per year.
2. *Average airspeed and air time.* Assume 500 mph. That's 9,400 hours in airplanes.
3. *Departure time.* Assume that each of those 2,350 trips required at least 1½ hours at the airport. Waiting. That's 3,525 hours. Waiting.
4. *Arrival time.* Assume that retrieving luggage and renting a car took only forty-five minutes on each trip. NOTE: Except in rare cases, I always checked luggage through. We'll cut the trips in half because I had my own car at home. That's another 881 hours.
5. *Average driving speed and time.* Let's assume that all my rental car and company car mileage was driven at fifty-miles-per-hour. Most of it wasn't. Remember, I drove in school zones a lot. That's 25,000 hours in cars.
6. *Here is the summary of hours,* excluding time for checking into and out of hotels.

Flying time:	9,400
Departure time:	3,525
Arrival time:	881
Driving time:	25,000
TOTAL	**38,806**

7. *Assuming a 40-hour work-week,* that's 970 work weeks, and this is ALL travel time. I haven't done my real work yet. Since there are about 46 - 48 work weeks each year, I spent 20 - 21 work years traveling. When I consider that I spent twenty-six years as a consultant, I spent only five or six years working—if I only worked 40 hours per week. Now that's the way to make a living.

8. *Indisputable Fact:* I *never* worked just a 40-hour work week. I'd get up at 3:00 a.m. for a 6:00 a.m. flight to the East Coast. I loved the early morning hours because there was NO traffic.

How many nights did I spend in hotels during twenty-six years?
About 4,000 nights. I favored hotels that served breakfast and offered free and easy parking. I usually chose a Hampton Inn or a Holiday Inn Express.

In the cities I worked, which had the most unusual names?
I live in a state (Washington) that has a town with the fancy name of Plain, and a location named Point No Point. A local joke concerns a town on the Washington coast named Humptulips—suggesting that's something perverted bunnies do. But in my travels, I have worked in two small towns whose names fascinated me: Peculiar, Missouri, and Accident, Maryland.

One fine day, the good 19th century, pioneering folk of Peculiar—before it was named Peculiar—needed to name their town as a prerequisite to having a post office. Members representing the unnamed town sent three possible names to the postmaster, and they were duly informed that post offices with those names already existed. Finally, they sent a letter to the postmaster general saying, "We don't care what name you give us, so long as it is sort of 'peculiar.'" So be it. On June 22, 1868, the United States established its one and only Peculiar Post Office. It sounds apocryphal but apparently that is the story.

As for the town of Accident, Maryland, no one knows the origin of the name for certain, but it appears the name derives from a surveying "accident" during the Colonial era. In this instance, accident means miscalculation. Brooke Beall and William Deakins, Jr., were surveying large tracts of land when Deakins "accidentally" surveyed land already belonging to Mr. Beall. They were friends, so no harm, no foul. The twice-surveyed tract came to be known as the Accident Tract. Clearly, the early settlers' sense of humor prevailed because they kept that name—Accident—for their new town. To add to the humor, residents of the town are "Accidentals."

Was I ever afraid of flying?
No, flying always agreed with me...but I was afraid of crashing. Perhaps having a father who had been a World War II bomber pilot helped. I was never a white-knuckle flyer, but I did have a few white-knuckle experiences. For instance, I once had some shaky moments when I flew into Roanoke, Virginia, for the wedding of my friend and colleague, Melanie Leweke. [See: P is for Prayer]

What aspect(s) of my job did I enjoy the most?

1. Uninterrupted reading time. While spending hours waiting at the gate in every airport, or sitting for hours on end flying coast-to-coast, or idling in my hotel room, I would read. I frequently told teachers I had finally gotten the job I'd always wanted: one where I was essentially paid to read terrific books. (If I read trashy novels, they'd still pay me, too.) That's pretty much what happened. The novels I read helped me speak thoughtfully and intelligently to my fellow English teachers, who struggled for time to read good books. Good English teachers all speak novel fluently and enthusiastically. I needed to speak their language, so I read everything. [See: V is for Veritas]

2. Visiting members of my family—particularly my brothers and sister—and their families. Bill in Easton, Pennsylvania; Bonnie in Tampa, Florida; and Mike in Phoenix, Arizona. And visiting

my mother and father in Easton. My father passed away in March 1999, but my mother still lives there. She'll turn 100 on June 25th, 2019. [See: F is for Family and Friends]

3. Visiting friends. My best childhood friend, S. James Carter, lived in Trabuco Canyon just northeast of Mission Viejo in southern California, and I would drop in to see him whenever I traveled his way—which was quite often. [See: F is for Family and Friends]

4. Watching major league baseball games on the company dime. [See: B is for Baseball]

5. Touring American battlefields of the Revolutionary and Civil Wars as well as the Indian Wars. [See: B is for Battlefields] I particularly liked Shiloh, Vicksburg, Gettysburg, and the Little Bighorn.

What kind of books do I enjoy the most?
Novels. When I first became a consultant, I realized I had the time to read. I began filling what I called "the holes" in my reading background—classics like *For Whom the Bell Tolls* and *David Copperfield*. But I soon launched into contemporary authors, too: John Irving, Pat Conroy, and Barbara Kingsolver, among many. The next book I would choose was often recommended by a teacher with whom I'd worked.

If I didn't live in Seattle, where would I choose to live?
I've actually given this question a great deal of thought. Perhaps western North Carolina—the Blue Ridge. New England would be a close second.

Where in the USA would I choose NOT to live?
Geography plays a role. I'm a city person who also likes water and mountains. I'm not partial to land-locked states, so I suppose that eliminates the prairie states. Actually, there are twenty-three states that have a saltwater coastline, and another seven have one or more of the Great Lakes as coastline.

Attitudinally, I'm not partial to the South whether landlocked or not. They tend to be very conservative, and I'm a progressive—some say "bleeding heart liberal"—so I find Seattle much to my liking politically.

I also don't want to live in any prison. [See: I is for Incarceration]

Who were the happiest teachers I ever worked with?
If we are talking in the USA, then it would be North Dakota. I worked in ND three or four times, and the teachers always seemed more than just satisfied. I'm not sure why, but they seemed to be a happy group of teachers. When I consider all teachers, it would be the Department of Defense teachers who worked overseas. Without exception, I never heard DOD teachers say anything bad about their situation. I know they loved the travel opportunities that the DOD offered, because the military provided their transportation.

What sights remain with me after twenty-six years?

1. Storm lightning illuminating the innards of distant thunderheads as I watched from altitude.
2. Watching an intransigent moose block traffic on the main highway on the Kenai Peninsula, Alaska.
3. Standing on a narrow bridge in downtown Ketchikan, Alaska, watching hundreds—maybe thousands—of spawning salmon struggling upstream while a black bear dined leisurely beside the stream. We were no more than forty feet away.
4. Seeing the snowfields atop Mt. Rainier reflect moonlight as my plane descended into the Seattle area.
5. Seeing the Missouri River overflowing its banks as I watched from 30,000 feet. I could actually see where the main river usually flowed—the area was darker—but I could also see the watery overflow invading towns and spreading across endless acres of fields and roads.

6. Watching space shuttle take-offs just because I was working near the Florida coast. One from a high school roof in Orlando. The second from the beach eight miles north of Cape Canaveral. And a third while driving to Cocoa Beach. I stopped my car—like hundreds of other people—and watched in awe.

7. The mile-wide swath of complete destruction caused by a tornado in Joplin, Missouri. [See: T is for Tragedy]

What pleasant surprises did I experience during those twenty-six years?

1. Meeting my second wife, Wendy Kelling. In 2005, while attending the Seattle Pops at Benaroya Hall in Seattle, I saw a familiar face—a face from decades ago—walking across the lobby of Benaroya Hall. Wendy had been a high school student at Newport HS when I was teaching there in the late 1970s, and, while she was never in my classes, she sang and acted in my musicals. After high school and college, she went to London to study opera at RADA—The Royal Academy of Dramatic Art. She'd returned to the USA in 1990, and it was pure serendipity that we met that evening. I approached her, and when I announced myself, she delightedly cried out, "Mr. Scannell!" We married in May 2011. Whenever she calls me "Mr. Scannell" now, I'm in trouble.

2. The Stark Museum of Art in Orange, Texas. It's a phenomenally incredible museum with a John James Audubon elephant folio, paintings by Remington, Russell, Moran, and Bierstadt, as well as a Steuben glass collection. I'd made the mistake thinking that Orange, Texas, was "just another itty-bitty burg," when one of the teachers asked me if I'd been to The Stark. We went, and my estimation of "itty-bitty burgs" was forever changed.

3. Yellowstone National Park on my day off, simply because it was sunny and I was nearby. I oohed and aaahed at Old Faithful, and drove at my leisure around the park visiting paint pots and fumaroles. I had a similar Yosemite experience, shepherded by a local book rep, Janay Page.

4. Mount Rushmore on Presidents' Day. I would be working the next day in Rapid City, so two teachers and I decided it would be the perfect way to celebrate Presidents' Day.

5. Visiting the birthplace—now also a restaurant—of John Steinbeck in Salinas, California. I'd fallen in love with *The Grapes of Wrath* in high school and taught *Of Mice and Men*, *The Pearl*, and *The Red Pony*. I read *Cannery Row* the same week I knew I'd be going to Salinas, and read *The Winter of Our Discontent* when my personal life was falling apart. Steinbeck was a frequent companion.

6. Frequent flyer mileage. I was able to fly family members to two daughters' weddings in 2003. Yes, two daughters in one year. Michelle married on March 1st, and I flew my mother and other members of our families to Seattle. Then, on July 12th, Amanda married in eastern Washington, and I flew a total of sixteen people from the northeast, from Florida, and from Arizona to be at her wedding. All because I had the frequent flyer miles available.

7. Touring the Biltmore Estate in Asheville, North Carolina, just after Thanksgiving. Decorated for Christmas, the Biltmore was open for tours. Choirs and brass ensembles performed Christmas music in the atrium, and as I viewed the various rooms, I thought, *This is what heaven is like*.

8. Sometime in the mid-1990s, I rented a Hertz car at LAX—Los Angeles International Airport—that had a GPS system called *NeverLost*. One of the Hertz folks took a moment to show me how it worked, and I asked him what would happen if I didn't do as it suggested. He replied, "That's when the nice lady's voice will tell you, 'Don't make me pull this car over.'" Later that year, I was taking two nuns to lunch on Long Island when

the female voice on *NeverLost* told me to make a right-hand turn. "If that's the voice of God," one nun commented in a surprised voice, "God is a woman."

What change did I find most remarkable over twenty-six years as a consultant?

That's easy. Technology.

When I first started traveling as a consultant, our most important presentation tool—other than our brain, of course—was the overhead projector. Untold hours were spent creating beautiful overheads to accompany the narrative we'd use to attract and hold the attention of the teachers.

At the start of my career, when we presented our programs to teachers, we used overheads, cassette recordings, and VHS videotape. As time went on, we abandoned cassette recordings for CDs, and then in the mid-nineties, overheads were replaced with PowerPoint presentations shown via LCD projectors.

I don't remember when McGraw-Hill gave us all Blackberry cellphones, but it changed the entire face of travel.

As an English teacher, the biggest eye-opener for me were Student Writing software programs. It was startling in so many ways. Imagine a program that could evaluate a student's writing and suggest changes. Complete with plagiarism checkers. Egads! Incredible!

When I finally retired, publishers had reached the point where everything—literally, everything—was available on-line. Books could be sampled via the internet, cutting sampling costs to almost nothing. Some districts had declared they were "digital districts," and wanted every piece of the program they were purchasing to be available online.

As one teacher happily explained, "Think of the advantages to online books. Online textbooks are never late because they've been back-ordered. A student can never lose his or her online text. We don't have to spend time distributing books at the beginning of the year or collecting them at the end of the year. We don't have to scold students for writing in their books. And we don't waste space storing them over the summer."

What unpleasant surprises did I experience during those twenty-six years?

1. Waking at 3:00 a.m. on a bitterly cold January night in a Kansas hotel and being told by the local fire department that we all had to vacate our rooms because a water pipe had broken in one of the hotel walls. There was no fire, but the pipe fed the sprinkler system. That's why the fire department was there. We were not outside long, but with the temperature hovering near 0° F, how long would "standing outside" have to be?

2. Being rear-ended one rainy morning by an inattentive courier in Salem, Massachusetts, as I was driving to my next appointment. I was in a bronze Ford Taurus, and I was sitting at a stoplight waiting for the green, when I looked in my rearview mirror and saw a small pickup truck heading heedlessly toward me. At the last moment, she hit her brakes, but the wet pavement and her speed make collision unavoidable. She wanted to know if I'd simply accept cash for the damage to my car. She said her boss would fire her if she had an accident. Then I told her it wasn't my car. It was a rental. She was inconsolable.

3. Three parking tickets in Philadelphia. Philadelphia was the ONLY city where I ever got a parking ticket. Twice while I was having copies made.

4. The sheer poverty of many southern school districts.

Did I ever find small things simultaneously aggravating and amusing?

Yes, I did. After 9/11, everything changed. Everything had to be secure, making getting to the plane more difficult than ever. New informational signs for passengers cropped up every week. One week, probably months after the 9/11 attacks, I saw a chrome-plated, free-standing sign that declared:

> All passengers moving threw the security
> checkpoint are subject to additional search.

The meaning was clear, but the grammar—actually, the usage—was deplorable. How could anyone who offered signage services confuse "threw" with "through?" But they had. I stood stock-still in front of the sign, wondering why the TSA couldn't hire competent proofreaders. A TSA agent approached me and said, "Sir, you must keep the line moving."

"Have you seen this sign?" I asked. "Look at this sign."

He gave it a quick glance. "It means we can search you after you've passed through security," he said.

"I know what it says." I paused. "Don't you see the error?"

He looked befuddled.

"'Threw' should be spelled T-H-R-O-U-G-H. That's a usage error."

He glanced at the sign again and shrugged. "No big," he said. "You need to keep the line moving."

I wanted to say, "What cave did they find you in?" but instead I started walking and asked if I could see his supervisor or "whoever is in charge."

As soon as I passed through security, I was introduced to his supervisor. I asked if we could go and look at one of the signs posted on the other side of security. "You'll want to see it, I'm certain."

The supervisor accompanied me back through security, and we stopped directly in front of the sign. I pointed at it without comment.

When his face collapsed into disbelief, annoyance, and frustration, I knew that he knew. He slowly shook his head and gave me the look that says, "I got nothin'."

"Yeah," I said. "That's what I thought, too."

"What are you?" he asked. "An English teacher?"

"Yep," I said. "We're a sneaky bunch. We're everywhere."

"And so are these signs," he replied, the trace of a smile crossing his face. "Just my luck."

We both began to laugh.

"Somebody wasn't paying attention," I said. "Ah, well."

Without a word, we walked back through security.

"Thanks for pointing that out." he said. "That sign's gotta go."

I cannot say what happened, but that was the first, last, and only time I ever saw that sign. It's not easy to find good help.

F is for Family and Friends

Friendship is a slow ripening fruit.
—Aristotle

I would rather walk with a friend in the dark,
than alone in the light.
—Helen Keller

If I had a flower for every time I thought of you...I could walk
through my garden forever.
—Alfred, Lord Tennyson

CLASSROOM TEACHING HAS many advantages: a daily routine, a set of well-known colleagues, and a set of far-too-well-known customers—called students. For the first fifteen years of my professional life, I was a teacher. Each year, I went to the same classroom every day, and came home to the same house every night. Changes were infrequent, usually coming at the beginning of new semesters. I was seldom alone.

In contrast, I quickly discovered that the road warrior life lacks routine. Sometimes my day would begin at 3:30 a.m.—sometimes my day would end at 3:30 a.m. Sometimes both. Each day was unlike the day before—except that each day involved a mixture of airplanes, rental cars, hotels, dinners out, and meetings with educators. I seldom met regularly with the same company colleagues except over the phone. My clients were a parade of unfamiliar faces—new teachers, new curriculum directors, new state evaluators. I once likened road warriors to astronauts on a spacewalk because they needed a tether to keep them safe, a tether that prevented them from drifting away and becoming irretrievably lost. For road warriors, daily change is the only routine.

And I was frequently alone.

For me, that tether proved to be family and friends. Family—primarily in Seattle—also included a brother and his family in Phoenix, a sister and her family in Florida, my older brother and his family in Pennsylvania, as well as my mother and father and a whole flurry of cousins and in-laws in the northeast. Friends—those folks who would drop everything to go to a movie, celebrate a birthday or holiday, or just come over for a beer, a hot dog, and some idle chat—proved equally necessary for my sanity. For twenty-six years, my family and friends kept me tethered—to my home, my past, my self.

Home Away from Home

My first wife and I both resigned our teaching positions in June 1972, and then we left Pennsylvania that September for Seattle, with our infant daughter Michelle. I never anticipated NOT returning to Pennsylvania after graduate school, but, like so many things, it just happened that way. Whenever someone asks me why I didn't move back to the East Coast, I simply say, "Life got in the way."

Life—that wonderful amalgam of family, friends, and work—can easily do that. Whatever I might have planned, life got in the way. I am reminded of Robert Frost's, *The Road Not Taken*.

> *Knowing how way leads on to way*
> *I doubted if I should ever come back.*

I ended up teaching high school English for a dozen years. And then I accepted a job as a textbook representative for Washington State before becoming a national language arts consultant selling textbooks to English teachers much like me.

The major difference between being a teacher and a consultant was this: my consultant's job allowed me to visit all my relatives several times a year, something that teaching never did. Even better, traveling on company money meant I could take Mom, Dad, and my other relatives to dinner. My brothers and sister would let me sleep at their homes, so the money normally spent on a hotel was put to use at local restaurants.

As a national consultant, a year never passed without me being summoned to work in the northeast—New Jersey, Pennsylvania, New York, Ohio, Maryland, Delaware, or DC. These trips provided me opportunities to "drop in" on my relatives and say hello, frequently unannounced.

Whenever I traveled to Florida, my sister Bonnie invited me to stay with her. My youngest brother, Mike, lived in Phoenix, and I worked in the southwest virtually every year. In truth, I was frequently home—even while thousands of miles away from home.

This was a terrific perk.

There were other perks as well. Visiting Bonnie, I'd end up attending the Strawberry Festival or the Florida State Fair—places I probably wouldn't have gone on my own. Best of all, my evenings could end with a serene sunset over the Gulf of Mexico's shimmering waters or enjoying the dying light over the desert.

Leaving home to work was always easier when I knew I'd be spending time with family elsewhere.

Dad...Is There a Sweeter Word?

My extensive traveling also allowed me to be unexpectedly at my father's side when he was dying.

I had been working with English teachers in Cleveland, Ohio, and it was March 11, 1999, a Thursday, and three days after Dad's 83rd birthday. Dad had been in a nursing home for six months, and his health was failing. I thought I should see him and my mother before

I returned to Seattle. My Mom always insisted, "Make sure you stop by when you're only a hop, skip, and a jump away. We'll go see your father."

My flight landed in Allentown, Pennsylvania, in the early evening, and I drove to my mother's apartment in Easton, Pennsylvania. Mom was happy to see me, and we talked through the evening about my four kids—her grandchildren—and my travels. Before we retired for the night, we agreed to go see Dad the next morning.

We didn't have to wait. Somewhere around 2:00 a.m., my mother's phone rang and I jumped off the sofa bed to answer the kitchen extension. The caller was someone from Easton Hospital, and she was explaining that Dad had just been admitted. He was in the emergency room. A lung infection. Could someone come to the hospital?

I woke Mom and told her the little that I knew. The only thing Mom knew was that her husband of 54 years—the man she adored—was in Easton Hospital's emergency room. She'd fretted about Dad's health for months before she had finally agreed that he needed constant care in a nursing home.

This late-night call demanded her immediate attention.

"I'll be dressed in five minutes," Mom said.

So, in the middle of a chilly March night, Mom and I went to see Dad.

He was unconscious and on a respirator…and looked terribly alone on the far side of the emergency room. As we walked with the doctor to Dad's side, he explained that Dad had a lung infection, one that would probably kill him within 72 hours if they didn't attack the infection aggressively. Two young doctors, who my mother later said, "Looked young enough to be my grandsons," were on emergency room duty that evening. They directed us into a small glass-enclosed room to confer.

The doctors sat side-by-side directly opposite us. "We need your help in order to proceed, Mrs. Scannell," one of them said gently. "Mr. Scannell's condition is terminal, if left untreated. What would you like us to do, Mrs. Scannell?" they asked.

Mom burst into tears. "I don't know," she wept. "I just don't know."

Mom had told me how unhappy Dad was at the nursing home. Life had become a waiting game, with only a feeding tube and a pacemaker keeping him alive. We both worried that Dad had no quality of life, a realization that gnawed at us because we had known him as a vibrant human being—a man of laughter, a delightful punster, a gifted piano player, and a gentleman extraordinaire. On our way to the hospital, Mom had said, "I just want your father to be at peace."

My Mom and Dad at the Polo Grounds, 1941

Now we sat in a quiet hospital conference room. I spoke up carefully. "Tell them, Mom." I could see the reluctance in her face. "Mom, tell the doctors what you told me as we drove here tonight. Tell them."

As she cried, one of the doctors moved over and put his arm around my mother's shoulder. "Tell us what you want, Mrs. Scannell. We don't have to treat this infection. We can make your husband comfortable, and let it take its course. Mr. Scannell won't feel any pain. He'll stay on the respirator, and we can look in on him…" His voice drifted off.

I said the unspoken words to myself. *We can look in on him… until he dies.*

"I just want him to be at peace," Mom said. "Can you make Jack comfortable?"

"Yes, Mrs. Scannell. I assure you, we can."

Mom looked at me, but I don't think I was much help. Tears filled my eyes. I'd suddenly realized my Dad was dying. I sadly nodded my head, "Yes."

I sat vigil with my Mom at Dad's bedside the rest of the night, and my brother Bill and his wife Marg joined us in the early morning hours. I took my leave to fly home to Seattle late Friday afternoon, knowing with sad certainty that my family and I would be returning soon.

Bill and I embraced as I left Dad's bedside. "Call me, Bill," I said. I couldn't say aloud what we both knew was coming.

Bill hugged me and said, "I love you, John. I'll call."

While I was above the clouds somewhere between Pennsylvania and Seattle, Dad died. He was at peace.

I am eternally grateful for frequent flyer miles. I used them to fly my own family from Seattle and my Brother Mike's family from Phoenix to my Dad's funeral. We could all give my Dad the warm and loving send-off he deserved.

My Irish father was laid to rest on St. Patrick's Day 1999.

My vagabond road warrior life made it possible for me to be at my father's side during his last hours and to bring my entire family together to say good-bye.

Old Friends

As important as visiting my far-flung family around the United States was, having friends at home proved equally invaluable.

For a long time, I relied on the friendship of Chuck Davis, one of my first and closest Seattle friends. I met him at Our Lady of the Lake Catholic Church in 1972, just after we arrived.

Over time, his family and my family became closely entwined, and his oldest daughter, Ann Marie, and my oldest daughter, Michelle, were classmates for eight years at Our Lady of the Lake's elementary school.

I eventually became president of Our Lady of the Lake's Parents Club, the school's chief fundraising agency. In my first fundraising effort—a dinner theatre production of *Arsenic and Old Lace*—Chuck's wife, Mary, starred as the love interest, Elaine. Chuck's daughter, Megan also had a small part in that production, playing the dead body in the window seat. She had no lines.

Chuck was our unofficial, but very capable, photographer. He took photos at *Arsenic* as well my second fundraiser that we did the following year, a musical production of *The Sound of Music*. Parishioners filled all the roles as they had with *Arsenic*, and Mary Davis played the Baroness Elsa Schräder.

Professionally, Chuck was an IRS agent—or as he mockingly commented, "Everyone's best friend"—but he also coached my daughter Michelle's soccer team.

So for years—at church, on the soccer sidelines, in the theatre, or just socializing as we so often did—Chuck was companion, friend, and confidante. He was someone I could talk to about anything, and his counsel was always welcomed. Best of all, Chuck's quiet, thoughtful demeanor contrasted with my more impetuous and impulsive personality. I could rely on Chuck to say, "Now let's just think about this a moment, Johnny, boy." Whenever Chuck calls me Johnny, his sage advice is sure to follow, whether I accept it or not.

That friendship solidified during my years at Our Lady of the Lake, years while I attended grad school and taught high school. Two years after I joined the publishing ranks, however, my growing family moved to the Seattle suburbs—to a brand new house and a different parish.

During my first two years in publishing—and after then as

well—Chuck kept my feet on the ground even though the rest of me was somewhere in the sky. For instance, in the year 2000, I was considering taking a job as a marketing manager at a publishing competitor whose offices were in Chicago.

"I know it's in Chicago," Chuck said. "But that's an office job, isn't it?"

I simply nodded.

"Johnny, Johnny, I know you." He folded his arms and gave me an appraising look. "You wouldn't be happy in an office. You need an audience. You know that, don't you? You love performing for groups of teachers, because you, my friend, are a performer at heart. Not a paper pusher. Why would you get a job in an office, when you already have the job that gives you the satisfaction you crave?"

I didn't argue. Chuck was right.

He added, "Always ask yourself: what kind of work makes me happy?"

Chuck's advice—and his constant friendship—proved invaluable. Kept me tethered.

Meeting Rick Rubie

In 1990, I met the Rubies. Rick and Ann Rubie. They proved to be tethers, *par excellence.*

"You wonder how these things begin," says the narrator, El Gallo, in the musical *The Fantasticks.* Well, this friendship begins, as so many do, with children. When we met, Rick and Ann had three children: Jessica 11, Megan 9, and Todd 6. My three youngest children, Mandy 11, Becky 9, and Ben 7, attended Crystal Springs Elementary School with the Rubie children. Serendipity and Ann Rubie intervened one day when my daughter, Becky, arrived home with a note from Ann suggesting that the Scannells and the Rubies get together for a barbeque.

Proof, yet again, that your best friends often come via your children. Mandy and Jessica were already classmates and friends, as were

Becky and Megan, and Ben and Todd. Because of Ann's thoughtful invitation, their parents would join them in that circle of friendship.

It was a Saturday evening in late summer—school had just begun—when the Scannells convened at the Rubie home for hotdogs, hamburgers, conversation, wine, and laughter. The template for decades of future gatherings was set that evening. After dinner, all the kids ran outside to romp in the large open fields surrounding their home, and the adults gathered around the dinner table to continue the wine and conversation.

I'd be lying if I even attempted to recreate what was said that night. Whatever it was, we immediately felt comfortable with each other—two transplanted families, the Scannells from Pennsylvania and the Rubies from Montana, finding familial connections that exist to this day. In the fading summer light, we relaxed and spoke of jobs and children and days past, unaware that we were about to get an entomological lesson on the behavior of *Vespula pensylvanica* or western yellowjacket.[26]

Somewhere between sips of wine and shared stories, we became aware of children's voices growing louder and closer. Clearly, our children were running toward the house, and at first we thought it was all laughter and frolic. But then it sounded like screams. Our kids arrived in a panic with Becky and Megan bursting through the back door.

They were waving their hands wildly as they shouted. "There's bees. Bees everywhere."

We were just beginning to ask "What do you mean?" when Mandy and Jessica burst into the house, flailing at an invisible menace and brushing madly at their hair. They screamed the same urgent message: "There's another one," and "Oh, get it off, get it off!" The chaotic situation took only seconds to assess. We saw the yellowjackets caught in their hair and spotted several crawling beneath the sleeves of their

---

26 The western yellowjacket is a Nearctic species of wasp in the genus *Vespula*. It is native to regions of North America, largely in areas with northern temperate climates.

blouses. The girls slapped frantically at their own heads, screaming while trying to get the wasps away from their scalps without getting stung.

All the adults jumped up to help the children eradicate the wasps that had attached themselves to the girls. We surrounded the girls in an attempt to help. Amid a rain of slaps and brushing motions, yellowjackets fell to the table top and floor where they were crushed beneath napkins and shoe soles.

Then the boys burst into the kitchen with their own swarm of wasps in tow. Ben and Todd had inadvertently kicked a subterranean yellowjacket nest. Apparently these wasps are both defensive and unforgiving. The two boys, closest to the nest, had the furthest distance to run to escape the wrath of the yellowjackets. Unfortunately, wasps fly faster than boys run. By the time they'd made it home, Todd's head was covered with yellowjackets. I don't remember how long the wasp slaughter lasted, but they lost.

Nevertheless, before the evening was over, no fewer than seventeen stingers had been removed from Todd's scalp. Yellowjacket carcasses littered the floor—*Vespula pensylvanica* had been vanquished. Our children settled down in the living room to relax and recuperate from *The Great Bee Adventure*.

This was our first date with Rick and Ann and the entire Rubie family. It was as eventful as any we'd ever have. The Rubie's home provided a bit of nature for all our children to enjoy. That evening, nature reminded us all that the idyllic can quickly become the horrific. Fortunately, everyone survived thanks to quick legs, numerous swatting hands and benadryl. All's well that ends well.

As Faye and I and the kids left for home, I hugged Ann and said laughingly, "Next time we'll go to the dentist's office."

Memories being imperfect—but inventive—adventures like these take on lives of their own in the retelling. Distilled to its essence, the following may be said: We had dinner. We had great wine and wonderful conversation. Our children played outside until the yellowjackets intervened. The yellowjackets attacked our children. Our children ran home. The adults killed every goddamn yellowjacket that had the nerve to cross the threshold with our children. There were no survivors among the yellowjackets. The Rubies and the Scannells became fast friends.

Yellowjackets tend to do that.

Innumerable gatherings followed over the next quarter century. We celebrated Thanksgivings, Christmases, New Years, and Fourths of July. Choose any holiday, we celebrated it. We celebrated sunny days and rainy days. We celebrated for no reason whatever—celebrating "just because." Our two separate families became one genuine family.

Rick became my best friend.

Rick Reaches Out

Like all best friends, Rick and I kept in touch even while I was on the road. Seldom knowing where I was, he'd often call.

"Hey, stranger," a familiar and happy voice would say. "Where the hell are you?"

"Hey Rick, it's good to hear your voice."

I always loved hearing from him. "Let's see, if I'm on I-40, I must be in Tennessee."

"Well, are you on I-40?" he'd ask.

"Yes, I am."

"Well then you're in Tennessee."

"So how are things at home?" I'd ask.

"It's 85 degrees and sunny," he'd say.

Whenever we'd call one another, whatever the season, whatever the time of day or night, it was always "85 degrees and sunny." Meteorological impossibilities be damned.

Once I called him from Winslow, Arizona. When he asked me where I was, I sang, "I'm standing on a corner here in Winslow, Arizona."

"I'll bet you're a fine sight to see," he said, making musical banter among close friends.

"Hey, Rick…Rick…it's a girl, my Lord…"

"Is she in a flat-bed Ford?" he asked.

"Yeah, and she's slowin' down…to take a look at me."

"Her eyesight must be pretty damn poor if she's got to slow down to look at you," Rick said. "Hey, did I mention, it's 85 degrees and sunny here in Seattle?"

"Well, it's 102 degrees here…and sunny," I added.

If I happened to be in New York when he called, I'd respond by singing,

Start spreading the news, I'm leaving today
I want to be a part of it, New York, New York

And so it went. Once, when I was in Des Moines, Iowa, I began singing the song, *Iowa Stubborn* from *The Music Man*. There was a song for almost every place…and it was always, "85 degrees and sunny," even at midnight.

Rick supported me and advised me when I changed jobs. He comforted me when I divorced. He stood up as my best man when I remarried. He was everything a true friend should ever be—and a culinary genius to boot. That is why, when Rick died on the 16th of November 2014—sixteen days after I retired—it felt as if the sun had set. I felt as if I'd lost a part of myself.

Sterling Silver

Travelers also need friends awaiting them at various destinations to ameliorate the loneliness when distance from home shrivels the soul. Sterling James Carter did that for me.

Named Sterling by his parents, his puerile elementary school friends shortened his name to Sterl—which too often sounded like "sterile"—a name he grew to dislike. Sterling and I met at St. Joseph Elementary School on Easton's south side when we began first grade in September 1953. All the class photos, regardless of grade, confirm that Sterling was big, occupying more space vertically and horizontally than any other student in the room.

You remember those class pictures, don't you? The black and white ones with the whole class seated at their desks, each student's hands folded neatly, each student's feet flat on the floor, and each student sitting rigidly erect with each bright, shining face smiling at the photographer who apparently stood on a ladder somewhere in the front of the room. You've seen those pictures.

Sterling and I shared a long history together. We were altar boys; we were crossing guards; we were friends who played tag during recess, and who played hours-long games of Monopoly and Risk on rainy weekends. When we went to Notre Dame High School, we agreed to try out for the football team together as we entered our junior year in the fall of 1963. After sewing our varsity letters onto our shaker sweaters, we enjoyed the vaunted status of football heroes—members of Notre Dame High School's only undefeated football team.[27] We certainly picked the right year to join the team. When seniors, we were starters on the varsity squad.

Whenever we played our football games, both home and away, my dad was in the stands cheering for us both. Sterling's father had disappeared when Sterling was still in diapers, so my father made it his mission to be a surrogate father to this tall (6'2") broad-shouldered young man who played both offensive and defensive tackle.

Sterling and I also bowled in the same league together, and we double-dated to the senior prom. I took my girlfriend, Carol Hindmarch (pictured here), while he drooled over his date, Barbara.

---

27 As of 2018, the 1963 football team remains Notre Dame's only undefeated season.

After high school, Sterling attended the University of Scranton and got a degree in Social Work. For a brief time, he moved to Wilmington, Delaware, where he worked in a boys' group home. He worked there at the same time that I had gotten my first teaching position in Nazareth, Pennsylvania.

Sterling's post-graduate job in a boys' home was simply his "next job." Nothing more, nothing less. Sterling had spent his whole life— from about age ten from what I can surmise—supporting his mother and sister. His earliest job was as an assistant to Mr. Herkorn, the janitor at St. Joseph's Elementary School. Sterling would help clean the bathrooms, sweep the classrooms, and buff the tiled hallways that 200 students scuffed up every day. He also stoked the furnace on cold winter mornings and shoveled the sidewalks when the snow made them impassable.

I relate this because one story illustrates Sterling's life so well.

It's late June 1970. I had just finished my first year of teaching at Nazareth High School. My wife, Faye, and I had just had our first child, Michelle, in January. On this Saturday afternoon, Sterling was our guest, having driven north from Wilmington to visit his sister. He had stopped by our apartment so we could catch up. As we sat around the kitchen table drinking beer, the conversation turned to what Faye and I planned to do with our summer since we were both teachers.

"Now that there's no chance that I'll be heading to boot camp anytime soon[28] [See: A is for Advice], we are thinking of visiting Faye's sister out in Colorado," I told him. "We'll have to find a place to live near Halifax later this summer, so we can both start our new jobs. It'll be near Faye's Mom's farm. But our lease here isn't up until the end of August."

Up to that point, Faye's furthest trip west had been to Chicago—in 1968, at the same time as the Democratic National Convention— and my furthest trip had been to Bowling Green University just south of Toledo, Ohio. Both trips had been brief journeys with classmates

---

28 I'd found a new teaching job in central Pennsylvania when I was informed that I would not have a deferment while attending graduate school. That meant I'd be drafted.

from Kutztown State College. Now we had the whole summer in front of us. We had time to indulge our *wanderlust*.

"Sounds like fun," Sterling offered. "You know, you ought to stop just thinking about it and do it. Too many people just think about doing things and never do them."

"We have a six-month old daughter, Sterling," Faye said.

"Okay...and that means she'll never be easier to take care of than right now," Sterling replied. "I know what I'm talking about."

Sterling was probably right. Our six-month-old Michelle was completely portable.

"You're lucky. You know that, right? I've never had a vacation," he said without a trace of self-pity.

I'd known Sterling since elementary school, and I was astonished. "You're kidding me, right?"

"No, I'm not kidding," Sterling said. "Here's the nugget. I've worked my whole life. First at St. Joe's, then a bunch of part-time jobs all through high school. The only time I didn't work was during football season," he remarked. "I worked my way through college, too. You remember me driving that Jewel Tea Company truck for a few summers? That put me through my first three years." He paused. "Mom's insurance policy paid for my senior year." His mother had died tragically and unexpectedly from a pulmonary embolism during outpatient foot surgery during the spring of his junior year. Sterling had been devastated. "So...no...I've never had a vacation."

I mulled over what Sterling had just told me. "Why don't you come with us to Colorado?" I asked.

"Now who's kidding?" he said, looking at both Faye and me.

"I'm not kidding," I said. "You should come with us. I figure we'll be gone about two, maybe three weeks. Jean and Rich live up in the Rockies in Leadville, Colorado, about 120 miles west of Denver." Then I dug into my chamber-of-commerce trove of memorized information: "Leadville is the highest incorporated town in the United States, situated 10,152 feet above sea-level. You'll have to bring your own oxygen."

"Boy, I'd love to go," Sterling admitted.

"I doubt that Sterling has enough vacation time to go on this trip, John," Faye pointed out.

I found myself agreeing with her and feeling bad for Sterling. But only for a moment.

Sterling looked at Faye and me, pressed his lips together, and then broke out into his trademark grin. "Can I use your phone?" he asked. "It's going to be long-distance."

"Sure," I said, unsure of what was going on in Sterling's mind. Sterling looked through his small pocket phone book and dialed the number. We waited at the kitchen table.

"Hi, Phil," Sterling said. "This is Sterling. Yeah. I'm sorry to disturb you on a Saturday afternoon." There was a brief pause. I don't know if Phil was saying something or if Sterling was composing what he was going to say next. "Listen, Phil, I'm in Easton, but I called to tell you that I quit." There was a brief pause. "No, I'm not going to change my mind. I appreciate all that you've done for me, but something has just come up, and it won't wait. Yeah, it's personal. Yeah. So, I have to quit. Effective immediately." A few more comments were exchanged—mostly about where to send Sterling's last paycheck—and then Sterling hung up.

"Okay," Sterling said, "I can go."

I don't remember who spoke next, but someone asked, "What about your job?"

Sterling resumed his seat at the kitchen table. He took a deep breath, pulled out a cigarette and tapped it on the table. "Ah," he said, "I can always get a job. Finding a job is easy."

"But your draft deferment...you quit this job and they'll reclassify you, won't they? What's your draft number?"

"Mine? Dunno." He fished through his wallet until he found a slip of paper. "My number is ninety-five."

"Jesus. Ninety-five. Mine is one hundred and sixty-two, and I'm worried."

"Come on, Red," he said.[29] "I've already quit, and the earliest they'd reclassify me is the middle of July. It'll be another six weeks after that for the paperwork."

"You've got it all figured out, don't you?"

"Government paperwork's a bitch, isn't it?" He chortled. "By the time they get to my name, we'll be back from our vacation, right? And they'll have to figure out where to send my draft notification. I wish 'em luck with that. Even I don't know where I'll be two months from now."[30]

"Yeah, sure, but they'll find you sooner or later. You don't want your next vacation to be to Southeast Asia, do you? Or to Leavenworth?"

"Hey, a vacation sponsored by the Uncle Sam? All expenses paid. Three meals a day, a clothing allowance..." He saw that I was serious. "Don't you worry about me, Red, I'll be just fine." He pushed back from the table. "I'd better get back to Wilmington right away. I've gotta pack and say goodbye to my landlady. I can be back here tomorrow by noon. When do we leave?"

We left the next day. More than anything else, that story illustrates Sterling's *carpe diem* philosophy—a philosophy many of us envied but never understood.

Friendship Renewed

And then I started traveling. Lo and behold, who was living in the Mission Viejo area of southern California? Sterling. He'd married, had two children, and he was the advertising executive for the Tuttle-Click Automotive Group. And he was available to go to lunch whenever I stopped by.

He'd always give me a bad time whenever I stepped into his office.

"Workin' hard today, are ya?"

"I just flew into John Wayne Airport, Sterling."

"And I bet your arms are damn tired, too. Damn tired." He'd

---

29 I mentioned earlier that my nickname while growing up was "Red." I was a blue-eyed, red-haired Irishman.

30 To this day, I have no idea how Sterling avoided being drafted. I never asked, and he never explained.

smile—no, *grin* is a better word—and ask, "How much work do you actually do? Do your kids know you hardly ever work? Do they know you just fly around and then take friends to lunch? Or do you tell them you're going out to lunch with someone important? Which you are, by the way."

Non-stop, good-natured razzing was Sterling's forte. We both loved it.

For more than a decade, I saw Sterling every year because I was traveling. Typically we'd have lunch or dinner, but on occasion, we'd break free and do something outrageously fun. On December 7, 2002, we went to the Rose Bowl, and I watched with delight as Washington State University demolished UCLA 48-27. In 2004, we drove to Las Vegas to meet a mutual, East Coast friend—John Markowski, my former college roommate—who was attending a convention for accountants. We spent a three-day weekend together—a guys' weekend—watching shows and gambling.

That all changed when John Markowski called me early Friday morning, June 23, 2006, while I was attending my company's regional meeting at Lake Tahoe.

"Hey, Red, I'm glad I finally tracked you down. I don't know how to say this, so I'll just say it. Brenda called to tell me Sterling's dying. He's at a hospital in Mission Viejo, and Brenda says that he only has a few days to live."

Talk about "knock me over with a feather."

"What are you saying, John? Dying? What do you mean dying?"

"He's had lymphoma for ten years. Brenda said the chemo always got him back on his feet, but nothing is working now."

It took me a moment to collect my thoughts.

"Okay," I said. "I'll be at the hospital tomorrow morning. First thing."

"Good, I'll see you there. I'm flying out from Baltimore," John said. "I'll be there by noon."

I called Brenda and she confirmed all that John had explained to me.

"Oh, Brenda, I am so sorry."

"I know," she said. "He would love to see you. Please hurry."

I explained the situation to Vicky Bush, my regional vice-president, and she said, "You better get a move on. I'm sorry about your friend."

I flew home, and took the first flight to Orange County the next morning. Twenty-five minutes after landing, I was at his bedside. Markowski joined us just after noon.

Sterling had been my best friend during the twelve years we attended Catholic school. Our friendship continued through our college years. He was a groomsman in my wedding in 1969 before he moved to southern California. Serendipity struck when we both realized we could renew our friendship when I began traveling. I saw Sterling every year.

He died late on a beautiful summer afternoon, June 24, 2006. A Saturday. He was exactly 58½ years old. Exactly. Remembering his age is easy because he was one day younger than me; Sterling was born on December 24, 1947, a Christmas Eve baby. Sterling—all his contemporary California friends called him Jimmy—died of lymphoma in Mission Viejo, with his family and friends gathered around his hospital bed. I was glad to be there.

I spoke at his funeral, and told all his California friends the story I related earlier—about him quitting his job in a heartbeat to take a vacation. It's always good to hear laughter at a funeral.

Sterling died too soon, way too soon. If he taught me anything, it was to stop thinking about doing it...and do it. His death in the summer of 2006 helped me stop marking time. Even now I hear his voice, *Hey, Red, it's time to carpe diem.*[31]

Influential Phantoms

At some point, every road warrior walking through yet another crowded airport concourse or checking into the next unremarkable

---

31 Let me simply say this: Sterling's death forced me to confront the problems of my first marriage—and consider how I wanted to spend the time I had left.

hotel asks, "How did I get here?" Let me recast that not-so-simple question: "How did a former English/Social Studies teacher, who fell in love with acting and theatre in college, and who always had an unfulfilled *wanderlust*, end up traveling every week and talking to English and Social Studies teachers about textbooks in school districts large and small in virtually every corner of the United States...and sometimes overseas?"

Just lucky, I guess. But I could never have arrived "here" without the help of others.

Two women—my ninth grade English teacher and my collegiate drama mentor—need to be acknowledged. These are the two women whose efforts put my feet on the career path that I ultimately pursued. These women both fit a category I like to call "influential phantoms"—people whose influence is recognized years after all contact with them has ceased. I never realized what influenced me to be an English teacher, until I recognized the voice of my former ninth-grade teacher speaking to me as I addressed my own classes.

Her name was Miss Manzolillo. Throughout twelve years of Catholic school, my English teachers were all nuns—except for Miss Manzolillo. Her energy, and love of language, proved infectious. A voracious reader, she did all she could to encourage her students to read.

"Step into a book," she'd urge, "and you'll find worlds you cannot find anywhere else." Looking back, I'll venture her style was unorthodox, but she forsook orthodoxy for effectiveness.

Like all other classes in Catholic school, we began with a prayer. But after that, she'd seize an open text, step around her desk and say "I read this last night. You're going to love it."

And then she'd read to us. Sometimes it would take a minute or two, sometimes it would take the entire class, like the time she read Flannery O'Connor's *A Good Man Is Hard to Find*, a short story that ends with the murder of an entire family. We were horrified.

"Who's this guy Flannery O'Connor?" we asked. "What kind of guy would write a story like that?"

"Flannery O'Connor is a woman," she informed us, and that realization horrified us even more than when we thought the author was a man.

Whenever she read to us—whether short story, newspaper article, or poem—Miss Manzolillo always pressed us to understand the author's purpose and meaning—urging us to "find out what was on the author's mind," or to "experience the experience." We could tell she loved everything she read to us.

It was years later when I realized she understood that teaching is as much the transfer of positive energy as it is the acquisition of knowledge. She taught me that teachers have an obligation to be interested and to be interesting. Miss Manzolillo was interesting because she understood her audience. For instance, she understood the psychological needs of teenage boys—the most reluctant of all readers. She knew that the students she taught felt the hormonal urges every teenager feels, and she knew how to channel those urges, so teenage boys could be interested in things those boys thought dull and uninteresting.

"We're going to begin reading Shakespeare's *Romeo and Juliet* today," she said. "And you're going to love it."

Most of the boys in class, including me, were betting she was wrong. But it didn't take long for us to realize it was unwise for us to bet against Miss Manzolillo.

"It's a love story, but you probably know that already. It's also a love story that ends badly." She paused and peered across the sea of young faces. "I'm sure some of you already know that sad story personally."

Laughter and groans from the class.

"And Act I, scene I, will really get your attention when you realize Shakespeare opens his five-act love story with two horny teenagers standing on a street corner talking dirty."

Nervous laughter from the class, and from somewhere in the room someone asked, "Really?"

"Yes, really," Miss Manzolillo assured us. "Horny boys, talking dirty. Some things never change," she said.

And we laughed…and then the entire class…boys and girls…willingly dove headfirst into *Romeo and Juliet*. It took a while to find the dirty parts, but the search did not go unrewarded. Just read:

Sampson: *'Tis true; and therefore women, being the weaker vessels, are ever thrust to the wall: therefore I will push Montague's men from the wall, and thrust his maids to the wall.*

Gregory: *The quarrel is between our masters and us their men.*

Sampson: *'Tis all one, I will show myself a tyrant: when I have fought with the men, I will be cruel with the maids, and cut off their heads.*

Gregory: *The heads of the maids?*

Sampson: *Ay, the heads of the maids, or their maidenheads; Take it in what sense thou wilt.*

There's more, but methinks 'tis sufficient. Who knew that Shakespeare could successfully be part of sex education? And this was just the first scene. We all signed up for the journey into Elizabethan drama.

I'm guessing it was decades later when I realized I'd become an English teacher because of Miss Manzolillo. I never told her that; I wish I had. All teachers need to know that they've shaped a life in an important way.

Speak the Speech, I Pray

I was a college sophomore when Dr. E. Annette Monroe drove me into the arms of theatre and all that it entails—acting, directing, lighting, staging, rehearsal, etc. Nothing in my life would ever be the same. She taught me that everything in life is pregnant with dramatic potential, and that the best way to live is to embrace the drama. Under her careful tutelage, I tried out for the first of sixteen productions that would occupy the last three years of my waking life at Kutztown State College. My first show was a production called *Barabbas*,[32] directed by Dr. Monroe, and I had the lead.

Theatre helped me become a confident public speaker, a necessary skill for any English teacher. In fact, during my junior and senior years, I was the stadium announcer at our home football games. That's a seat on the fifty-yard line with all the hot dogs and hot chocolate I wanted.

Whenever I asked myself the question we all ask ourselves at one time or another, "How did I get here?" Miss Monroe's name sprang instantly to mind. Without her encouragement and guidance, I never would have gone to my first audition. I would never have fallen in love with theatre. I would never have realized that so much of life *is* theatre—like teaching and selling. I truly believe that. When you're teaching and selling, you are creating a whole world for the listener, a world filled with what you already believe, what you already know, and what you want them to believe.

I might have spent my entire career as an English teacher—selling poetry to high school students—but now I wanted to sell books to English teachers. Teaching for fifteen years had helped me expand my knowledge and hone my performance skills, as well as intimately understand the lives of English teachers. While both positions were different aspects of theatre, selling books was in some ways more difficult. After all, I saw my students for 180 days—and they were a captive audience. On the other hand, my customers might see me for

---

32 The production was a script adapted from the novel *Barabbas* by Pär Lagerkvist.

only an hour—and they could choose to ignore me.

Sometime after the death of my friend Sterling, I began feeling the urge to say thank you to everyone who had prepared me for the life I was leading—a life successful because of the gifts they'd given me. I needed to say thank you for the counsel, knowledge, and encouragement they provided.

In the late spring of 2008, I seized the chance to thank Dr. Monroe—later Mazzaferri, and now Robertson. During one of my trips to Pennsylvania, I found her phone number and called. When she answered, I recognized her voice immediately.

"Dr. Mazzaferri?" I asked.

"Yes. Well, it's Dr. Robertson, now, but I still answer to that name," she said in a teasing tone.

"Dr. Robertson…this is John Scannell."

"Oh, my word, John. A voice from the past. How are you?

"I am well."

The conversation was like all conversations after 37 years, filled with the well-ingrained niceties.

"Good to hear your voice." "How's the family?" "Are you still teaching?"

Finally, I asked her if she might have some time over the next two days to get together.

"Sure. Would you like to come here tomorrow evening? I'd love you to meet my husband. I tell him about my former students and Reader's Theatre so much, and it would be wonderful if he could see that one of those people really exists."

The next evening, I arrived with flowers and a smile. She greeted me at the door, made a fuss over the flowers, and introduced me to her husband, the other Dr. Robertson, now a retired physician. We all settled comfortably in the kitchen.

For a quarter hour we navigated the bright waters of days past, and then I changed the subject.

"Dr. Robertson...Annette...I wanted to see you tonight for a very particular reason." From her reaction, it was clear my tone was more serious than I intended.

"You're not ill are you?" She looked concerned.

"Oh, no. No. Nothing like that," I said. "I came here to say something that has been on my mind for some time now." I paused, hoping the right words would find expression. "I taught for fifteen years. English and Social Studies. I've spent the last twenty years as a national textbook consultant. And I've been very successful...because of you. I want to tell you how grateful I am to have been your student. I came here specifically to say thank you...to you. Everything I've done in my classroom, and all my success as a national consultant, all that is directly attributable to you. You filled my life with theatre, and all its possibilities."

I paused.

"You always saw something in me—something I didn't see until later. And I'm glad you did. You gave me the lead in *Barabbas*. You allowed me to be president of the Reader's Theatre. When I fell on my face in *Rhinocéros*—God, those reviews were devastating"—I paused again, the memories of an awful performance stopping my words.

I realized her husband probably had no idea what I was talking about. I turned to Mr. Dr. Robertson. "I was in Ionesco's *Rhinocéros*. It's Theatre of the Absurd. Initially, I had just a small role, but I was also the understudy for the lead, Berenger. Two weeks before we opened, our lead quit...and I...I bombed. Badly. Very badly. It was awful." I shook my head at the memory. "No hole was deep enough for me to crawl into. I craved invisibility."

I looked directly at Mrs. Dr. Robertson. "Do you remember what you did for me when that happened?"

"Yes," she said, "I wrote you a note."

"Yes, you did. And it was the nicest note. You told me to be brave, to persevere. You told me I had the talent to continue." I began tearing up. "You said, 'Don't let this discourage you, John. I've seen what you can do.'" I smiled at my mentor. "I still have your note."

Her face radiated a quiet joy.

"So that's why I'm here. To offer you my deepest thanks, face to face, thirty seven years later. You need to know my life would probably have been entirely different, if not for you. You gave me direction—and the ability to pursue that direction. And you encouraged me. You always encouraged me."

I pondered how many people have the skills and ability to be successful, but never go ahead because they don't trust themselves. They don't have someone who believes in them—someone who encourages them as Dr. Robertson had encouraged me.

"You know, I taught for fifteen years, and there were times when I wondered if I had touched anyone's life. Then a former student came to see me, and she told me she'd become a teacher because of me." I laughed remembering that moment. "I carry her words in my heart."

"Oh, John," she said in a quiet whisper. "Thank you. Thank you."

When I departed that evening, I felt a kind of elation.

Dr. E. Annette Monroe Mazzaferri Robertson died on February 16, 2011, but not before I'd had the chance to tell her that her thoughtfulness, kindness, and gentle encouragement influenced my life in so many positive ways.

Postscript

Family and friends made my road warrior life possible, but I would be horribly remiss if I failed to include my pets—my wonderful dogs and whimsical cats—the canine and feline side of the family I embraced when I met Wendy. Eight years from retirement, I met Wendy and I also met her three dogs and three cats.

The dog closest to her heart was an eternally enthusiastic flat-coated retriever named *Miss Aria*. She also had a chow/golden mix named *King*. The youngest dog was a chow/shepherd mix named *Baloo*, named after the bear in Kipling's *The Jungle Book*. *Baloo* was a massive 85-pound mound of red-haired fluff. Over the years, this trio offered me an abundance of love, their tails wagging hello whenever I returned home. I can say without hesitation that nothing matches the excitement and enthusiasm—and love—of a dog. *Aria, King* and *Baloo* have gone to Dog HQ, but I know their love always made me want to come home as quickly as possible.

Wendy also filled my life with cats. There was the sleek, black, domestic long-hair cat named *Almond Joy*......aka *Kitty Boy*...aka *Almondo Suave'*; a silver Persian named *Mercedes*, famous for her silent meow; and a Manx named *Nicky*. *Nicky* would headbutt my hand and arm, telling me he was glad I was home and that he needed a chin-scratch.

These dogs and cats were members of my family that I happily returned to each week. A new generation of pups now greets me at the door, and only one remains from the days when I flew hither and thither. His name is *Luigi di'Ogee l'Amour*, and I'm happy that he and I are now full-time companions. All these wonderful pets were part of my lifeline—invaluable tethers—like the many humans in my life.

Family, friends, and pets are tethers for us all, keeping us all centered. They know us and accept us, warts and all. They tell us "Safe journey," and "Welcome home." They are as necessary to a road warrior—or to any human being—as air and water.

Their love, counsel, and encouragement always kept me grounded...even when my head was literally in the clouds.

G is for Guns

*Speaking personally, you can have my gun, but you'll take
my book when you pry my cold, dead fingers off of the binding.*
—Stephen King

*I'll carry on, carry over, carry forward, Cary Grant, cash and carry,
carry me back to Old Virginia, I'll even 'harakiri' if you show me
how, but I will not carry a gun!*
—Cpt. Hawkeye Pierce (Alan Alda), M*A*S*H (TV series)

GUNS ARE AS American as apple pie and baseball, although admittedly I'll always prefer apple pie and baseball to guns. When my demise comes, I hope it's from arteriosclerosis or an errant foul ball, rather than a bullet. Fortunately for me, the two places where I spent most of my professional time—airports and schools—generally banned guns.

Guns are anathema at airports and on airplanes—unless you happen to be part of the airport's security team, or an air marshal, or an active-duty soldier aboard one of the United States giant military cargo planes like a C-5A Galaxy. Then guns are allowed. Tanks, too.

Since the 9/11 attacks, every passenger desiring to fly the friendly skies has had to deal with the often gruff groundlings that work for the Transportation Security Administration. The infamous TSA. I've occasionally wondered if the TSA employee manual begins with the simple sentence, "Prepare to be unpopular."

After all, TSA folk treat all passengers as if they're "packin' heavy heat." Everyone must remove jackets and bulky outerwear; remove hats; empty ALL contents of ALL pockets; remove belts with buckles—yes, pants have fallen down[33]—and shuffle shoeless through the security checkpoint. Everything goes in a bin on a conveyer belt that moves through an x-ray machine—Madame Curie would be proud—and passengers and belongings are lovingly reunited on the far side of security.

As one of my road warrior colleagues described it, "Airport security checkpoints have become strip clubs without the drinks." That's probably because drinks—all liquids, with the possible exception of breast milk—are also *verboten*.

All this to ensure American passengers' safety. Theoretically. Despite all of TSA's efforts, it's more likely that your bottle of water will be confiscated than your .38 caliber pistol. In June of 2015, the acting head of TSA was fired "because in 95 percent of test cases, real guns or fake bombs made it past the TSA."[34]

That's not very comforting.

Most aggravating, the search for guns, bombs, and exploding water bottles has more than doubled the amount of time required for a passenger to get through security. Security checkpoint lines often stretch for hundreds of yards—and holiday traveling requires a special fortitude that would have been unthinkable before 9/11.

Without wishing to diminish the danger posed by knives, children's scissors, and grandma's knitting needles, the weapon that most passengers fear the most would be guns. That's the reason I named this chapter *G is for Guns*, rather than *K is for Knitting Needles*.

---

33 When one travels as much as the typical road warrior, witnessing a pair of fallen pants is likely to become part of the TSA experience. I actually considered writing a chapter *E is for Exposure* or *O is for Ooops!,* but decency prevented me—and the fact is, I have no salacious pictures.
34 June 3, 2015, *Washington Post*, Ashley Halsey III

I was always glad that guns were anathema in schools. My work as a textbook consultant took me into schools every day, so I was happy that schools posted signs: *This school is a gun-free zone.*[35] Whenever I saw that sign, I took heart that it was unlikely I'd be shot by a crazed ninth grader unhappy with the grade he'd received on his bungled five-paragraph essay.

Even though I make light of it, I have seen that "gun-free zone" sign in many schools—but never once have I seen it posted in an airport.[36] Perhaps that very sign should be posted in every airport and on every airplane. Schools are proud to state the obvious. Where guns are concerned, nothing should be taken for granted.

Nevertheless, I've often marveled at various school districts' paranoia with ALL guns, even small, plastic, key-ring guns. When I read about students suspended or expelled for possessing an obviously-harmless piece of plastic, I wonder about the intelligence and judgement of the administrators. School administrators call it "zero-tolerance," but it sure feels like "zero-thinking." No school policy should ever absolve an administrator of being thoughtful and sensible. Unhappily, I sometimes feel that "zero-thinking" is a trait shared equally by the TSA and school districts.

While I appreciate that all schools have always had qualms about loaded guns, I also recall one particular worthwhile gun experience when I was in the eighth grade. My class was studying American History, and one of my classmates brought a German luger to class—a pistol his father had taken from a dead German soldier. It wasn't loaded, and no one ran screaming from the classroom. Instead, everyone gathered around to look at it.

All of our fathers had been in World War II. My father had flown a B-24 Liberator on thirty-five missions over Nazi-occupied Europe. My classmate Mike Flynn's dad had been PFC Flynn with the Marines

---

35 If only those signs came equipped with magical anti-gun force fields. Students still die in their schools from gun fire every year. The problem has gotten worse, not better.

36 As for "gun-free zone" signs at airports, that may have changed. But if not, why not?

in the Pacific Theatre, who'd fought on Iwo Jima and been poised for the invasion of Japan. Then the atomic bomb brought the war to an abrupt halt.

All of us had been born because our fathers had returned safely from the war—whether in Europe or the Pacific. Guns had figured mightily in their lives, and by extension, our lives as well. Growing up, my friends and I played "Army" for hours on end with plastic pistols and rifles. We supplied our own sound effects—a kind of guttural, throaty sound—and arguments often erupted over whether one player or another had actually been "killed" after being shot by a plastic gun and a sound effect. Like many kids' games, the rules were all *ad hoc*.

For my parents and my peers, World War II—and the stories our fathers told us—were knit into the fabric of our memory. Perhaps that's why guns didn't seem so threatening. But times change.

I can say with virtual certainty that, for decades, no one ever expected to be shot to death in a school.

I can hear my older brother Bill saying, "Bored to death, maybe, but not shot to death."

School shootings were unheard of when I was a student in the 1950s and 1960s, as well as during the fifteen years I taught middle school and high school English.

Unfortunately, school shootings have become a staple of the American news cycle. And while they don't all make the nightly news reports, these shootings occur where I spent almost all of my consulting time: school buildings. None of this escaped my attention as a road warrior, nor the attention of my colleagues in the book business.

The first school shooting to capture America's attention was probably the Columbine High School massacre on April 20, 1999. Twelve students and one teacher died, as well as the two students who had brought their guns to school on that fateful day.

But Columbine was hardly the first shooting. Three years earlier, there had been a shooting at Frontier Middle School in Moses Lake, a small town of barely 20,000 people in central Washington, and probably the last place one would expect gun violence.

My very first textbook sale—a middle school literature sale in 1985—had been in Moses Lake, and the person who'd been chairman of the selection committee was an English teacher named Carol Smith. She was teaching on the second floor of Frontier Middle School when 14-year-old Barry Loukaitis killed his algebra teacher and two fellow students that day in February 1996, just a few doors away from Carol's English class.

Carol knew everyone whose lives had been stolen by Loukaitis' bullets, and that shooting changed her life. Carol and I were good friends, and the killings changed my life as well.

The shooting had shaken her to the core: "How can one keep working when one's sense of safety and security have been fatally compromised?" she asked.[37]

Carol left classroom teaching shortly after the shooting, and when I've recounted the event to many of my friends—the story Carol told me firsthand—I find myself referring to Carol's leaving as collateral damage. Her departure from the classroom was a terrible shame because she was a good person and an excellent teacher.

When the Frontier Middle School shooting occurred, everyone took comfort in the knowledge that such incidents were "rare," "quite unusual," "virtually unheard of." Remember, that was 1996.

From an article published on *EverytownResearch.org*,[38] between the years 2013 and 2017, school shootings are happening at the rate of one per week. If that's the case, how much collateral damage do schools suffer when staff decide to leave, or when certain students, tempted to drop out, wonder if it's wise to stay?

Today's students, savvy consumers of social media reportage, must wonder if they have more to fear than bad grades.

---

37   That's the same question I asked myself when I climbed aboard an airplane after the 9/11 attacks.

38   https://everytownresearch.org/school-shootings. The site also offers current data.

Knowing that guns—real, toy, or fake—were forbidden in all schools throughout the land actually made my job psychologically easier. But after 9/11, school security tightened considerably, which made my job physically more difficult. I was locked out of one California high school because the entire grounds were protected by an eight-foot high cast iron fence with foreboding pikes. I had to ring a buzzer to get in. In one New Jersey high school, I had to pass through a metal detector, the same kind I passed through at the airport.

Perhaps most daunting was the California high school surrounded by a ten-foot high cyclone fence topped with razor wire. I parked my car two blocks from the school because I couldn't find a way to access the student or faculty parking lots. As I walked with my computer bag to the school, I felt as if I had a bulls-eye strapped onto my back. I was honestly scared. Certain parts of the world have dangerous reputations—deserved or not.

To gain entrance, I had to present myself to a security guard—a man as big as a Buick who could have played defensive tackle on any NFL team—who sat behind a locked gate.

"Do you have an appointment?" he asked. He scrutinized me carefully, granting no lenience for my very nice suit. If it was his job to make me feel uncomfortable, he was good at his job.

"Yes," I said, feeling my pulse race. I told him the name of the teacher I hoped to see, and he picked up a phone and confirmed my appointment with someone on the other end.

When he was satisfied I wasn't a threat, he unlocked the gate and I stepped through. NFL-guy pointed me toward the office and resumed his seat, ready to intimidate whoever came next. I proceeded along a walkway hemmed in on every side by metal fencing, all of it topped with razor wire. [See: I is for Incarceration]

I am only here to visit a teacher, I thought. *I don't think I could teach here.*

The teacher I met explained that the safest place in the world was inside the school. "The neighborhood may be dangerous," he explained, "but, in here, we are perfectly safe." What I didn't tell that teacher was that my car was parked outside the fence—a truly unsettling feeling. After my meeting, I hurriedly returned to my car without incident—comforted by the notion that either nobody fired a gun at me or they missed. I wondered if business men wearing suits got a pass.

So, guns—weapons of all kinds, but mostly guns—were much on the minds of schools and school administrators. As the school-shooting statistics mounted, guns were much on my mind, too, working as I did in the schools every day.

The universal gun ban, everywhere and in all schools, made my work in Alaska's Yukon-Koyukuk School District that much more curious. First, some amazing facts about this district and this part of Alaska. The Yukon-Koyukuk Census Area is the largest census area of any county or county-equivalent in the United States at 147,805 square miles. Depending on what source you review, the current population is between 5,525 and 6,150—approximately 1% of Alaska's population. By comparison: the entire state of Montana is smaller than the Yukon-Koyukuk Census area, and New York City occupies only 302.6 square miles of land where 8,623,000 (2017 estimate) people live atop one another. Put another way, 47 of the 50 states are smaller than the Yukon-Koyukuk Census Area.

The Yukon-Koyukuk School District—an area within the Census area—serves 1,400 full-time students in ten village schools located along the Yukon, Koyukuk, and Tanana river systems, a geographic area larger than the state of Washington, encompassing about 71,000 square miles of territory. Another 1,500 students are enrolled in the correspondence program named Raven Homeschool. Travel to seven of the ten village-school communities is by small aircraft. Local travel within the communities is by boat during the summer months and snow machine or dog sled in the winter.[39]

On this trip, I was heading to a village school on the Yukon River with three Yukon-Koyukuk teachers. The village was named Nulato, one of the stops along the famous Iditarod Trail. Nulato could only be reached by small aircraft or boat. Since I wasn't taking the boat, I would fly west out of Fairbanks and reach Nulato 306 air miles later. The trip was unique from beginning to end.

My trip's beginning was at the Fairbanks airport.

It was mid-January, and at this time of year, the land of the midnight sun is best characterized as the land that's mostly midnight, because the sun shone each day for only a few short hours. I would be flying in the daytime twilight to Nulato with four other passengers—three teachers and Yukon-Koyukuk's superintendent. The scheduled Nulato meeting was to approve the purchase of our textbooks, and my job was to answer any questions about the programs they were about to approve.

I don't recall the name of the airline, but I remember vividly that we would be flying in a small, six-passenger, twin-engine plane. The gentleman in charge of boarding the plane made it abundantly clear that strict weight restrictions would apply.

"This is not your Boeing 737," he said as he pointed to a large industrial scale adjacent to the check-in counter. "I would like everyone flying today to get on this scale. Please have all the baggage or equipment you plan to take with you today and place it on the scale, too."

All five of us—four women and me—obediently climbed up on the scale together.

The airline representative looked at the weight total and remarked, "I think we're going to have to lose about 30 pounds."

---

39 Information posted on the site for the Yukon-Koyukuk School District at https://www.yksd.com/Domain/3.

"Yeah, I know," I said. "I've been meaning to do that for years."

Everyone laughed, but the airline rep was not joking. Some piece of luggage would have to be left behind, but none of my fellow passengers seemed inclined to part with their belongings.

"Well," I said, "we aren't staying overnight, so my suitcase can stay here." That left us only three pounds shy of our goal when one of the teachers decided to leave a small cosmetic case behind. We were all set to go.

We boarded the plane, strapped in, and flew to Nulato. I doubt we ever got above 1,500 feet because I found myself watching a snowy, barren, uninhabited landscape race beneath us.

Ninety minutes later, we touched down on a Nulato airstrip carved out of the wilderness. I don't know why I was expecting an airport. When we deplaned, the temperature was -17°F. Although I was wearing a woolen overcoat and gloves, my head was unprotected. It was damn cold.

After a few words with the pilot about when we'd be ready to return to Fairbanks, the superintendent motioned the rest of us toward a vehicle parked off to one side of the landing strip. We all walked toward a dark blue pick-up truck, a plume of hot exhaust rising from its tailpipe.

Clearly, the people in Nulato and in the Yukon-Koyukuk School District believe in "making do with what you've got," because not everyone could ride in the cab with the driver. With nary a word, two teachers and I climbed into the truck bed while the superintendent and the third teacher crowded into the cab.

"It's only a mile to the school," one of my companions said as she reached deep into what appeared to be a pillow case. "Here," she said, "put this on your head. You shouldn't be bare-headed in this kind of weather."

She handed me a lush, warm, beaver hat that I quickly pulled low over my ears. I've never forgotten her kindness.

"Before I came here," she said, "I taught in Illinois. Back then I was a huge animal rights advocate." She shrugged. "After a few months living here in Alaska, I finally figured out why God created the beaver." She pointed toward me. "To keep your ears from freezing off."

As we drove slowly toward the school, I asked her what else she had in her pillow case.

"A few items, in case we get stuck out here," she said nonchalantly. "Some candy bars, a change of clothes, my toothbrush. Nothing much."

"In case we get stuck?" I asked.

"Doesn't happen very often," she admitted, "but it happens. Just wanted to be ready." She paused for a moment and said, "Didn't anyone explain this to you?"

I just shook my delightfully warm head. No one had explained anything about this trip.

We drove into the snow-filled school parking lot and stopped next to the school's front entrance. A few cars and a dozen snowmobiles sat randomly here and there. I asked my companion where all the cars might be? "There aren't many cars," she said. "There are no roads into or out of Nulato. When you're here, you're here. Otherwise you have to rely on snowmobiles, boats, or planes."

Coming to Nulato was a genuine education. I felt as if I had entered an entirely different world. When I walked into the school, my feelings were reinforced. There, in the school office right behind the principal's desk, was a gun rack with several rifles resting on pegs.

I stopped and pulled off my beaver hat.

"Wow," I said quietly. "Look at those rifles. You don't see that very often in the lower forty-eight."

My companion explained that most of Nulato's students walk to school.

"This is the wilderness, for miles all around," she explained. "The older students carry rifles to protect themselves and the younger students as they go. Occasionally, they encounter wolves or bear... even a stubborn moose can be a threat." She paused for a moment. "This isn't like the city."

No, it wasn't.

Nowhere did I see a sign declaring this school to be a "Gun-Free Zone." Clearly, it was quite the opposite. Still, I have to admit, as I looked at those rifles hanging on the wall, I felt safe.

H is for Hooky and Horse Racing

It may be that the race is not always to the swift,
nor the battle to the strong—but that's the way to bet.
—Damon Runyon

Horse sense is the thing a horse has which keeps it
from betting on people.
—W. C. Fields

LIKE MILLIONS OF Americans, I follow horse racing three times a year-
-the Kentucky Derby, the Preakness, and the Belmont Stakes—racing's
Triple Crown. I watch from the comfort of my living room, and I never
bet. I'm one of those people who likes to spend my money rather than
lose it. The truth is, I'm not a betting man because I seldom win—
which means I generally lose. While I've never been a lucky gambler,
horse racing and racetracks have always held a certain fascination.

Triple Crown Groupies

I spent one lovely spring week in May 1997 working in Baltimore.
I loved coming to Baltimore. Yes, it's touristy, but wherever I go, I
love being a tourist. By midday Friday, I was lunching at one of the
restaurants at Baltimore's bustling Inner Harbor before leaving for the
airport.

At some point during lunch, I mentioned to the waitress how
much I was enjoying Baltimore's beautiful weather—Seattle had been

unseasonably chilly—when someone asked me if I was on my way to Pimlico.

The voice, coming from behind me, belonged to a young woman sitting at the counter. She was twentyish, tanned, and dressed in worn blue jeans with a bright blue tank top stamped with the Purdue University logo. Her sunglasses sat atop her very blonde hair. She dipped one of her french-fries in some ketchup.

"Pimlico?" I asked turning slightly in my chair. "You mean the Preakness?"

"Everyone's going," she said with a broad smile.

I think I raised my eyebrows. I know I looked over my glasses. My own children call that the "Dad's-not-sure-if-he-believes-you" look.

"Okay, maybe not everyone."

"Did you ladies fly down from Lafayette, Indiana, for the Preakness?"

"Nope, we drove. We drove through the night to get here," she said with pride.

"That must be…what?…six hundred miles?" I said.

"Six hundred and sixty—or thereabouts," said her equally-tanned friend swiveling toward me on her counter stool. She wore a bright yellow Purdue t-shirt, and her sunglasses hung on a chain giving her a slightly librarian look.

"This can't be spring break," I said addressing myself to the co-eds. "Ah, I see. You guys are playing hooky, aren't you?" I asked, wagging a parental finger at them. We all smiled and laughed at my light-hearted accusation.

"Well, we could be graduate students doing research," said Ms. Blue Tank Top.

I returned to my "I'm-not-sure-I-believe-you" look.

"Okay, we skipped one class. Yesterday." She hesitated. "But we don't have any classes today. So technically, I suppose, we played hooky yesterday."

"But not today," Ms. Yellow Shirt chimed in. "Not today."

"So, you're going to the Preakness tomorrow?" I asked.

"Yep," they said in unison. They could barely contain themselves. "We went to the Kentucky Derby last year—that drive was less than two hundred miles—and next year we're planning a trip to Belmont Park."

"Belmont Park? Wow. That's a least 800 miles from Lafayette... one way. You guys are serious horse racing lovers," I said.

"Not really. We're only interested in the Triple Crown. We decided last year that we wanted to go where each of those races is held. We really can't afford to fly, so we decided we could drive to each of the racetracks."

"Everyone's entitled to their own brand of insanity," I said smiling. Understand, I didn't make that comment as an insult. Where people travel, how people travel, and why people travel is truly idiosyncratic. Perhaps the Triple Crown was on their bucket list. It's not on mine, but then neither is climbing Mt. Everest or camping on the side of Mount Rainier, two things I see as another form of insanity. I've always felt that way about people who love to go hiking and camping. To me, hiking and camping can be reduced to one word: Bugs. They love me, and I hate them. I have the psychic scars to prove it. Let me quote a colleague who shares my loathing: "My idea of camping," she once told me, "is Motel 6."

"So who are you hoping wins the Preakness?" I asked.

"Well, Silver Charm won the Derby, and we think it would be really exciting if we could see a horse that wins the Triple Crown. So we're pulling for Silver Charm."

"Silver Charm." I'd watched the Kentucky Derby earlier in May, but I didn't recall the winner. "Okay. How much are you betting on Silver Charm?" I asked.

"We don't bet," they said, again in unison, as if they were singing the lyrics of a song they'd practiced forever.

"Really? You don't gamble? Even after driving six hundred and sixty miles one way to see Silver Charm? Did you bet last year?"

They shook their heads. They hadn't bet the Derby either. I didn't say it out loud, but I suspect they were on a budget, and they felt that betting—like airfare—was just a waste of money.

"Tell you what," I said. "I'm not going to the Preakness. I fly home to Seattle later today. But…" I opened my wallet and pulled out two five-dollar bills. "Here's two fives. I want each of you to put a five-dollar bet on Silver Charm. To win. Will you do that for me?"

I held out the money. They looked at one another and then at me. I could tell they weren't quite sure.

I pushed back from the table and placed the money between them on the counter. "Here, I want you to get the full Preakness experience. Just imagine you're standing at the rail tomorrow, screaming for your horse as he comes down the home stretch. Betting makes the experience more vivid. If you win, keep your winnings."

"And if we lose?"

"You can't lose. You're playing with my money."

"You're serious, aren't you?"

"Absolutely. Place your bets—five dollars to win—and root for Silver Charm. And don't worry about the ten dollars. I'm a national consultant and I've got an expense account. That means I'm traveling on company money. I'll expense this under 'Lunch with Purdue University students.' I just won't tell them that Purdue is six-hundred miles away."

"Six hundred and sixty," Ms. Yellow Shirt reminded me as she folded up her fiver and put it in her purse.

I wished them luck, and they both thanked me as we all headed out into the Maryland sunshine.

In case you're wondering, Silver Charm won the Preakness that year. And two hooky-playing, young, female Boilermakers bet the winning pony. At least I hope they did. I never knew these two young ladies by name. Most encounters on the road are anonymous—conversations that begin and end spontaneously—a pleasant but momentary intersection of lives.

I hope they bet Silver Charm.[40] I can't remember what the return

---

40 *Silver Charm* lost the third jewel of the Triple Crown. He placed second in the Belmont Stakes to *Touch Gold*. Once again, gold trumps silver.

might have been on a five-dollar bet, but winning is always better than losing.

Working While Playing Hooky

What I hadn't told these two hooky-playing co-eds was that I myself had once played hooky at Churchill Downs five years earlier. I had flown to Louisville, Kentucky, for the 1992 National Council for the Teachers of English (NCTE) annual convention. It's always held in November, and typically the meeting is scheduled for the weekend before Thanksgiving. As McGraw-Hill's national language arts textbook consultant for secondary schools (grades 6-12), I attended all the NCTE conferences because my company purchased exhibit space and set up booths stocked with textbooks for teacher visitation. Between scheduled meetings, when they had some free time, thousands of teacher attendees had a chance to drop by and peruse the educational materials we hoped they'd consider using in their classrooms.

My role at the NCTE was simple: Sell books.

For reasons I no longer recall, the NCTE in Louisville hadn't been on my assignment list. Ask yourself: How bad can that be? When one spends 180 nights each year sleeping in hotels—sleeping in a bed not one's own—being told that I didn't have to make it 183 nights was not a disappointment. It made no difference to me that I wouldn't be staying in the famous Galt House, a hotel whose name is more historic than the building—the original 1837 antebellum structure was demolished in 1921. The Galt House may be the only Louisville hotel overlooking the Ohio River, but when traveling on business, a room is a room is a room is a room.

But plans changed, and about a week before the NCTE conference was to begin, my boss re-assigned me. That necessitated making last-minute flight and hotel reservations. One can always find an airline seat, especially if one is willing to pay for first class, and I was.

While never profligate with company money, I seldom balked

at spending the company's money when they changed the circumstances. As for hotel accommodations, all the downtown hotel rooms nearest the conference center had been snapped up months earlier. After a brief conversation with my travel agent, I'd be resting my head in a room at the Holiday Inn near the Louisville Airport.

That was serendipity.

As I checked into my hotel late Thursday afternoon, I asked the hotel desk clerk if it might be possible for me to tour Churchill Downs, probably America's most storied horse racing park. I hadn't rented a car, and I wondered if the Holiday Inn shuttle could take me there.

"Certainly, Mr. Scannell. We can shuttle you to Churchill Downs. It's only a mile from here. But they're not offering tours this time of year."

"Oh," I said. I'm sure I looked disappointed. "I was hoping to get a peek at something I've seen on television since I was a kid."

"I'm sorry. I didn't make myself clear, Mr. Scannell. The horses run in November, so Churchill Downs is open. There will be ten races tomorrow. The doors open at 10:30."

"Oh…that's good news." I felt elated. "That is good news. Thank you. I'll probably go tomorrow."

The hotel clerk—her name plate told me she was Jill, Hotel Manager—smiled at me, the happy tourist standing in front of her. "If you are definitely going tomorrow, Mr. Scannell, would you like to use our box?"

"You have a box at Churchill Downs?" Elation became amazement.

"Sure do. The box accommodates six people. Would you like the six tickets for tomorrow?"

Sometimes you're asked a question that you automatically know the answer to. Without knowing the cost of the tickets, I immediately said, "Why, yes, I would. How much are they?"

"Just a minute," Jill said as she reached beneath the counter. She placed a shoebox on the counter, lifted the top, and found a five-inch thick stack of tickets held by a fat rubber band. She whittled down the pile and discarded all the now out-of-date tickets.

"Here are the six for tomorrow," she said handing them to me. "As you can see, no one ever uses them. No one ever asks. Just take them and enjoy yourself. There's no charge."

I could have kissed her. I didn't, but I could have. If I ever make a movie of this moment in my life, I'll write a demure kiss into the script.

"How can I thank you? This is exceedingly generous."

"No need, Mr. Scannell. I'm glad you can use the tickets. If there is anything else I can do, please let me know."

As I took the elevator to my room, my mind was plotting the best use of six tickets to a box at Churchill Downs. The horses were running! I sat on the edge of my bed and placed the tickets on the end table. Night was falling.

Even now, I clearly remember four of the five people I took the next day. I invited a teacher friend from eastern Washington who had helped me win my first big literature adoption, and the curriculum director from Baton Rouge, Louisiana. Two nuns—one from Pennsylvania and one from North Carolina—were also invited because they were the curriculum directors of two large dioceses. After all these years, I cannot say why the fifth person has vanished from memory. All I can say for certain is the unremembered fifth person was also a woman—most curriculum directors were women. Most English teachers were women, too. I was the anomaly.

I already knew—and liked—each of these five women. We'd spent hours together at their offices and with their selection committees discussing the value that our textbook programs could bring to their students. Their business was pending, and it was very important to me. And to McGraw-Hill. Normally, I would have invited them to dinner, but now something better than dinner had presented itself. These invitations would prove much more fun.

"Hello, Carol? This is John Scannell."

"Hi, John. How are things with McGraw-Hill these days?"

"I'm glad you asked. They are wonderful. That's why I'm calling." I paused. "How would you like to play hooky tomorrow?"

"That depends. What did you have in mind?"

"I have tickets to a box at Churchill Downs," I said. "Home to the Kentucky Derby. The first race is at noon, and I'm hoping to ask five English teachers—or curriculum directors—to play hooky with me. We'll be munching lunch, drinking wine, and betting on the ponies. Are you interested?"

Everyone said yes. Immediately, in most cases. Churchill Downs possessed some mystical charm. I didn't get a single no. A hesitation, maybe, but not a single no. Clearly watching horses race is far more entertaining than sitting in lectures on misplaced modifiers, grammatical *faux pas*, or Existentialism in the modern novel.

We all arrived at Churchill Downs about 10:45 on Friday morning on the Holiday Inn shuttle. The only item of note was that the two nuns arrived in civilian garb. I asked them why.

"No point in giving scandal," said Sister Philomena. "If I came in my habit, someone would be sure to call the bishop and complain."

"Absolutely," said Sister Charlotte. "If we came in our habits, somebody here would be certain that the eleventh commandment was 'Thou shalt not bet the horses'."

Everyone laughed. We were six awestruck, giddy, horse-racing novices, playing hooky. And in a playful mood.

As we passed through the turnstile, a sign announced that classes were available every half hour on deciphering the racing form so one could decide which horse to bet. The temptation was too great. How could a group of six English teachers decline the opportunity to go to class—even at Churchill Downs? Instead of going directly to our box, we detoured to the classroom.

We learned about odds, about reviewing a horse's racing history—over various distances and on various turfs—and we learned about pari-mutuel betting. We were a very attentive audience, and we asked quite a few questions. As we left our Churchill Downs' classroom to find our box, I tried to imagine the difference between a literate bettor and a truly educated one. It's one thing to read; another to understand.

We arrived at our Holiday Inn box about a half-hour before the first race, and everything impressed us. Perhaps it was the Churchill Downs mystique, but I suspect it was more than that. Our box was situated along the home stretch—about twenty yards shy of the racing finish line and directly above the entrance from the paddock. Directly beneath our feet, beneath the railing where we sat, the horses walked through a tunnel from the paddock and emerged directly below us on their way to the track. How marvelous! As the horses for each race entered, we hovered a scant ten feet above horse and rider.

Moments after we settled in, the wait staff came by to take our drink and food orders. Another bonus. Naturally, my company paid for everything. Over the years, I can say with conviction that the part of my job that I loved best was showing teachers just how much I appreciated them. Whatever impression people have of the teaching profession, teaching is often a thankless task, with little pay and fewer perks. As a textbook consultant, I made it my mission to diminish that inequity whenever possible—even if was only a day at the races.

It was a remarkable thing. That day, six relative strangers engaged in nonstop conversation and laughter because we all shared a love of reading. We laughed about e.e.cummings' allergy to capital letters, and Ogden Nash's playful rhymes:

> *When called by a panther,*
> *Don't anther.*

We traded silly stories about our lives as English teachers, and I recited poetic parodies like the one of Joyce Kilmer's *Trees*. The editors claimed that the author of the following poem is Joyce Kilmore.

> *I think that I shall never see*
> *A sight more sickening than a tree*
> *A tree that takes up so much space*
> *Where cheese box homes could stand in place.*
> *A tree that houses only birds,*
> *On land I'd like for human herds.*

I'd memorized that ages ago after reading an edition of *Mad* magazine as a kid. They roared with laughter. English teachers are like that.

We talked of novels we were reading. We each lobbied for our favorite novel—*To Kill a Mockingbird* got my vote; *Pride and Prejudice* led the list with two votes. We talked of teachers we loved—especially the teachers whose vitality and fervor for the language destined us for the English classroom.

I told them about Miss Manzolillo, my freshman English teacher at Notre Dame High School. To this day, I'm fairly certain her first name was Miss, but it doesn't make any difference. I became an English teacher because of her. A diminutive woman—maybe 4'11" on a good day—Miss Manzolillo swept into class each day, said the perfunctory Our Father—Notre Dame is a Catholic high school—and then began each class by saying, "I read this last night. You're going to love it."

Then she'd open a book and begin reading. Most of the time, we loved it; occasionally we didn't. But none of us ever had the heart to tell her we didn't like something that she so joyfully embraced. To her, literature was something to be devoured…and savored…and loved.

Miss Manzolillo was a sorceress, the teacher who enticed every reluctant boy in class to open *Romeo and Juliet* by telling them that Act I, scene I, had two teenage boys talking dirty on the streets of Verona. None of us could resist.

So our day at the races was one of shared stories, shared preferences, reveling in the things that made us English teachers.

And yes, we placed our bets on each of the races—including the trifecta and the daily double. Despite the earlier class, Sister Charlotte decided she only wanted to bet the grays, and Carol insisted that she liked jockeys wearing red silks.

"I think gray horses are beautiful," Sister Charlotte said unapologetically. "They should win. Even when they don't, they should."

Carol's feelings about jockeys wearing red were similar.

One of my guests asked me why I wanted to come to Churchill

Downs. I told them of my experience as a youngster when my dad would sit at the dining room table the morning of the Kentucky Derby. He'd open the local newspaper, the *Easton Express,* and carefully study the racing statistics for each horse entered in the Derby. He'd make notations on a yellow note pad before ultimately choosing the horse he believed would win.

"This is the one," he'd declare. "This is the horse I'm betting my hundred dollars on."

And he'd take his fictional hundred dollars and make a fictional bet on a real horse. As race-time approached, we'd all sit in our living room and watch the race on television—always rooting for Dad's horse.

"Until today," I said, "Churchill Downs was little more than a flickering television image to me. Just another place, far away, that I'd see once a year. But today it's real. And the next time I watch the Kentucky Derby on television, I'll be sitting right here with my friends. I'll be right here, even though I'm in Seattle." Vicarious experiences are endemic among academics.

I told them about my Dad and Mom going to the races when I was a child. They'd go to Monmouth, New Jersey, once every two or three years. Although trips to the track were infrequent, my Dad would spend hours poring over racing forms on the weekend, and then he'd place fictional wagers on the horses he hoped would win… or place…or show. The day after the races, he'd consult the list of winners, calculate the pay-outs, and tally up his winnings. Then, he'd show the results to Mom and declare, "We're rich, Vera, rich! I won twelve hundred dollars yesterday."

"That's wonderful, Jack. Be sure you put it in the bank," she'd say. My mother loved my father's fictional betting life as much as he did.

So the six of us spent our day talking and wining and dining and betting. We laughed, and we traded favorite recipes, stories of students, and tales of teachers past and present. We explored our hopes for the coming year.

The sunshine and cool sixty-two degree temperature proved to be perfect weather.

Only one of us won any money. I think Carol ended up five dollars in the black. I wondered aloud if nuns liked betting on the horses even better than playing bingo, when Sister Philomena reminded me that "Thou shalt play bingo" was the unofficial eleventh commandment in the Catholic Church.

Language and laughter flooded our day like Kentucky sunshine.

Here's the ironic thing. I don't know that anyone ever said a single word about buying books. In truth, they weren't there to buy, and I wasn't there to sell. We were there to bond, to be sure that we knew the other person well enough to trust. We were there as people genuinely interested in the education of children, and in having fun together—but in a way that is unique to people who professionally teach others to read and write—and to understand what they read and write. Never an easy task.

As one of my invitees said as we drove home, "We spent the day in a lovely outdoor restaurant, with good wine, great company, wonderful conversation, and horse racing for dessert."

Another pointed out that the theme of this year's NCTE was *Celebrating Ourselves as Teachers*. "I can't think of a better way to celebrate ourselves than by spending time with colleagues gathering new experiences and knowledge. Today at the racetrack, of course, I also learned how to place a bet."

"What we really needed to learn is how to win the bet," I said, speaking the obvious.

"We already did," she explained. "I think we all won today, didn't we?" It wasn't a question. "Author Tim Cahill says that 'A journey is best measured in friends, rather than miles.'"

When I reflect on my career in publishing, I remember that the camaraderie and laughter that day was special, probably because the whole event was totally impromptu. For all of us. All any of us had to do was say "Yes." During my twenty-six years as a publishing consultant, I can't remember a more enjoyable day with teachers. I think we all won in so many unexpected ways that day, something my wife

Wendy calls "the magic of ordinary days."

When I returned to the hotel, my message light was blinking fre-netically. I had four new messages. All of them from Chuck McIlvaine, a fellow language arts consultant.

The universal theme was: "Scannell, where the hell are you? You missed your shift at the booth. Please call." Or words to that effect. Each call voiced increasing concern.

I called Chuck McIlvaine, left a message, and he returned my call within the hour.

"Where have you been, Scannell?" Chuck asked. I couldn't tell if he was angry or concerned.

"I've been at Churchill Downs, Chuck."

"You're kidding?" I heard amazement tinged with curiosity.

"Nope. I'm very, very serious." I told him who I'd invited, and I talked at length about the delightful day we'd shared. There was no need to explain why I hadn't shown up at the booth during the day. He understood. I told him how I'd unexpectedly gotten the tickets from the hotel manager, and it seemed like an ideal situation if I could just take advantage of it.

When the truth dawned on him, he laughed. "So you were at the races all day?"

"Yep, me and my girls. And guess what?"

I could tell he was mulling over the "what."

"Okay, what?"

"I have six tickets for tomorrow as well. Nothing better than Saturday at the races—especially if it's Churchill Downs. I'm not go-ing to the races because I have to be at the booth. I was thinking maybe you could use them…?" I let my voice trail off. All I could hear was Chuck laughing even louder and collecting himself.

"I don't know how you do it, John."

"I gotta tell ya, Chuck, neither do I. Today was sheer, unadulter-ated luck. I was hoping to take a tour of Churchill Downs, and I end up spending the day with five of my biggest customers. So…you want those tickets for tomorrow?"

Of course, he wanted them. Of course, he went. And of course, he took several of *his* most important customers.

Would it be too bold to say that Chuck and I probably closed about $8-$10 million in business from our trips to the track? Far more than we would have sold if we'd both manned the McGraw-Hill booth each day.

Chuck and I, both old-school types, believed in relationship selling, understanding that people don't just buy from people, they buy from friends. People who teach English don't just buy books from people they know, they buy books from people they trust. From people they would be proud to call friends. From people they can read like a book.

That Friday in Louisville, five friends and I played the horses and hooky at Churchill Downs.

And we all won.

I is for Incarceration

We are all sentenced to solitary confinement
inside our own skins, for life.
—Tennessee Williams

He who opens a school door, closes a prison.
—Victor Hugo

WHEN I TOOK a job in publishing I never imagined I'd end up in prison. But I did. Eleven times.

Don't worry. I'm not a repeat offender. I went to prison to provide training for English teachers who were implementing our literature and writing programs as part of the prison's educational offerings. Well-behaved prisoners could earn the right to attend school, and like schools everywhere, prison schools needed textbooks.

The California Office of Correctional Education puts it like this.

The GED assessment or the HiSET exam is provided to incarcerated students who possess neither a High School Diploma (HSD) nor a High School Equivalency (HSE) certificate. Students receive instruction inEnglish/Language Arts, Mathematical Reasoning, Science, and SocialStudies in preparation to take an HSE exam.

Our texts were purchased by the California Department of Corrections to help inmates achieve a High School Diploma (HSD) or a High School Equivalency (HSE).[41] So, I reported to prison.

Although I'd worked in schools in each of the fifty states—as well as in several foreign countries—working in the prison schools was a stark revelation. If you ever feel the rules are too stringent in the outside world, try a day inside penitentiary walls—even as a visitor—and you'll quickly change your mind. Before I worked inside a prison, I thought I had some sense of what prisons were like. I was entirely wrong.

Let me take a moment to describe the process of actually entering the prison—as a visitor, of course—and perhaps you'll feel just some of the discomfort that I felt.

Like everything else in government, acquiring permission to enter a prison begins with the paperwork parade. Weeks before I visited the prison, a letter arrived from the principal of the particular California prison where I would be working. Attached was a waiver, which absolved the prison, all governmental authorities, all governmental employees, and pretty much anybody else favored by the prison system, of any responsibility if things went south while I was working there.

California's approach was very simple. I was expected to sign the waiver. No waiver, no admittance. In a nutshell, the waiver stipulated that if I were taken hostage, the State of California would not bargain for me and would not place my safety or interests above, or even on par with, whatever they decided was their best course of action. All the prerequisite particulars were sobering. As my wife, Wendy, put it, "If anything bad happens while you are inside the prison walls, you're royally screwed."

She may have used a slightly more vivid synonym for "screwed", but it was clear what the state would NOT do if the prisoners decided to play "Capture the Consultant" with me. The waiver also included permission for the State of California to run a background check on me so they could be certain I wasn't a murderer, a rapist, a bank robber, a drug dealer, or any of a wide variety of possible felons.

I'm a bit embarrassed to admit that I'd already worked in two

---

41   Many states call this the General Equivalency Diploma (GED).

prisons before Wendy, an accountant whose life revolves around noticing and understanding worlds of details, asked me if I'd ever read the waiver. When I said I hadn't, Wendy quickly picked up the waiver and dove into the deep end.

"You haven't read this?" she asked, studying the unsigned waiver. "You realize you're signing your life away."

"I can't work inside the prison if I don't sign," I offered.

"You really haven't read this?" She flashed me a dubious look. "You really need to read this." She emphasized *read.*

"It's just a formality, Wendy." I repeated my lame excuse for not reading the waiver. "I can't go inside if I don't sign."

"So don't work inside. Have the teachers come to a local hotel near the prison. Your company can afford that."

"It doesn't work that way."

She paused, shook her head, and asked with a wry smile, "How's your life insurance?"

Moments after I assured her she would be a comfortable widow, I signed the waiver.

When I received subsequent waivers to work in the next eight prisons, Wendy and I reprised the same conversation. So did my consultant colleague, Bernice, who worked the Mathematics side of the textbook aisle. She was expected to sign the same waiver, and she'd had the same "Are-You-Really-Going-Inside-the-Prison?" conversation with her husband that I had with my wife.

"Maybe our spouses are the sane ones," I said to Bernice. "Are you sure about this?"

"Not really. I'm a California girl born and raised, and I'm about to see parts of California I've never seen before. My husband thinks I'm crazy."

"Really? He thinks you're crazy?" I asked Bernice. "He said that?"

"Those were his exact words."

"I guess our spouses are the sane ones."

We both felt misgivings.

"Have you computed the odds of us being taken hostage?" I asked as we pulled our technology from the backseat.

"Nope. I'm big on algebra not probability."

Working in a prison meant I'd dress as I usually did—jacket and tie—except I wouldn't be wearing my customary blue shirt. Prison regulations explicitly stated: *NO blue shirts*. Inmates wore blue. Bernice and I did our best to look like outsiders, not insiders.

We performed the same ritual when arriving at the prison parking lot.

1. We locked our cellphones in the trunk of our car. Cellphones were *verboten*.
2. We took a moment to collect ourselves.
3. We looked at the prison entrance, turned to look at one another, took a deep breath, and said in unison, "Time to go to work."

Going to work meant the outside world would disappear for the next several hours. *Going to work* also meant filling out additional paperwork at the prison Visitor Center, listing the model and serial numbers of our computers and LCD projectors. After the paperwork, the prison staff inspected our technology for possible contraband, and then they inspected Bernice and me for possible contraband. Only after being declared contraband-free, and surrendering our dignity and our driver's licenses, only then were we given an ID to be prominently worn while inside the prison.

This was all preamble—because we weren't even inside the prison, yet.

To enter the prison we were escorted by someone from the prison school—usually the principal. He met us at the entrance, and from that point we were in his hands.

Walking into the prison's Visitor Center was easy enough. Walking into the prison was daunting. Think of it as "walking through the wire," because as we exited the prison side of the Visitor Center, we were confronted by a tall, chain-link fence topped with razor wire. Beyond that first fence—perhaps fifty-feet further—was another chain-link fence, also topped with razor wire. The principal mentioned that the scoured, beige dirt between the fences was no-man's-land, and always under surveillance. For us to get past both the first and second fences, there was a passage way—think of it as a chain-link tunnel—and yes, it was topped with razor wire, too. At each end of the chain-link tunnel were chain-link gates that could only be opened electronically by a guard in one of the watchtowers.

The principal accompanying us signaled the tower guard who then opened the gate immediately in front of us. As soon as we entered the chain-link tunnel, the tower guard closed that gate behind us. It was only a fifty foot walk to the next gate, but during that walk, we were acutely aware of being caged inside an inescapable prison, completely surrounded by fencing and razor wire. Once we arrived at the other end, the tower guard opened that gate, and as soon as we stepped through, the gate closed behind with an ominous metallic clang. That noise announced our arrival.

We were now inside the prison.

Our sense of isolation and vulnerability may have been psychological, but it was as real as the razor wire at every exit. The prison's physical environment only exacerbated those feelings. Prisons are drab, foreboding places, visually bland, devoid of color. All gray and beige. There was no real greenery to speak of. No trees. No bushes. No view. Nothing said "Home." Everything screamed "Prison."

My primitive brain screamed, *How soon can we get out of here?* My English teacher sensibility kicked into high gear: *Austere and prison are synonyms.*

Bernice and I conducted our first prison workshop at the High Desert State Prison in Susanville, about 90 miles north-northwest of Reno, Nevada. High Desert redefined austere. I mentioned that impression to one of the prison's English teachers, adding that the prison seemed to be in the middle of nowhere.

"Well, it's not exactly the middle of nowhere," he said, "but pretty close. It's all desert for miles around. Escape might be possible, but anybody on foot can easily be seen."

As the work day progressed, the sense of being incarcerated was cumulative. With the day's work completed, Bernice and I both wanted to escape, too. The principal helped us retrace our steps to the Visitor Center as quickly as possible, but the word "quickly" doesn't always apply when razor-topped fences and guard-activated gates stand in the way. After we traded our prison IDs for our own driver's licenses, we stepped into the high desert sunshine and experienced an unanticipated sense of exhilaration. Bernice and I both looked at each other and laughed.

"We survived," Bernice said triumphantly.

"Yes we did," I said. "And no one was taken hostage." Then I began reciting a few lines from Richard Lovelace's famous poem, *To Althea, from Prison.*

> *Stone walls do not a prison make,*
> *Nor iron bars a cage...*

"You can stop right there. I don't know who said that," Bernice said as we walked to our car, "but he's about as wrong as he can be."

"That poem's in our British Literature book," I said proudly. "It's a classic. Written in the seventeenth century by Richard Lovelace while he was in prison."

"Well, all I can say is, Richard Lovelace was never a guest of the California Department of Corrections. If he had been, he'd revise that poem."

I had to agree.

Bernice and I experienced that same unsettling sense of isolation and vulnerability about a month later when we walked into Centinela State Prison in the southernmost part of southern California. It, too, sits in the middle of a desert about 15 miles north of the Mexican border.

Perhaps the only time we felt that a prisoner might actually have "a room with a view" was during our last prison visit when we worked at San Quentin. San Quentin pushes out into the beautiful blue waters of San Francisco Bay. We wondered: Would a view of the bay be comforting and uplifting? Or only a daily reminder of what one had lost?

Probably the most unnerving aspect of working in a prison—besides signing my life away if I were taken hostage, or being completely incommunicado, or being thoroughly searched at the entrance, or knowing that fences and razor wire blocked any escape, or not being able to wear a blue shirt that matched my eyes—was the walk across the prison grounds to the school. Even though we were accompanied by a prison school official, we walked past areas where the general prison population was milling about. It was during our trek to the school at the Solano State Prison near Vacaville, that we came to appreciate the importance of observing prison rules.

The rule was simple. *Don't cross the line.*

I'm not talking about a figurative line. This line was very real. As we walked along one of the cellblocks, we noticed that the sidewalk had a wide blue stripe painted right down the middle. The half of the sidewalk closest to the cellblock wall belonged to prison personnel and civilians—like Bernice and me. The half of the sidewalk furthest from the wall was for the inmates. As we walked, the principal told us to carefully observe that stripe because the other side of that line was the inmate half, and beyond that stretched a large field filled with hundreds of inmates standing, sitting, kneeling—even lying down. Some were exercising. Some were throwing footballs or basketballs. They stood alone or gathered in groups on the dry, brown, well-worn grass. Along the edge of the grass, every twenty yards or so, stood a prison guard weighted down with armor and weaponry. The guards made me feel safer, but I wondered how they coped on hot days.

"The inmates are not permitted to cross that line," the principal said, pointing at the wide blue stripe bisecting the sidewalk. "Stay on the wall-side of the blue line, and you'll be fine."

My brain whispered, *May the stripe be with you.* I was tempted to hum Johnny Cash's *I Walk the Line*. I resisted the temptation, but the tune played in my head along with *Folsom Prison Blues*.

Was I foolish for believing that a foot-wide stripe could actually protect me? Perhaps. My daydreams had me walking on the wall side of the blue stripe even as the gathered inmates looked at Bernice and me like lions observing gazelles on the African savannah. (Don't ask me why I ever thought of myself as a gazelle. I'm probably more of a wildebeest.) Anyway, in my daydream, whenever they charged to devour us, the blue stripe acted like some kind of force field. All the inmates slammed heedlessly into the invisible barrier and knocked themselves unconscious.

The stripe always saved us. At least in my daydreams.

Nothing awful ever happened to us while we walked to and from the prison schools, and I suppose we can thank striped sidewalks for affording us some protection. Nonetheless, I'm happy the stripe's invulnerability was never tested.

When Bernice and I arrived at San Quentin, we were both struck by the irony of the setting, certain the surrounding beauty of San Francisco Bay teased and mocked the inmates. *All this beauty*, it said, *and you can't enjoy any of it.*

In my own imagination, few prison names resonate more ominously than San Quentin. Reinforcing that perception, San Quentin's front door reminded me of a medieval castle's portcullis. It was visually intimidating.

Perhaps Alcatraz conjures greater uneasiness, but Alcatraz closed in March 1963 when I was only a sophomore in high school. San Quentin's imposing, castle-like entrance, and the knowledge that death-row inmates are housed there, all contributed to the sense that San Quentin is the quintessential *Big House*.

Bernice and I had been invited to help train the teachers who worked within San Quentin's walls.

After the usual paperwork and pat-down routine, the principal escorted us out into a courtyard. We hadn't been walking more than ten seconds when a siren shrieked out a warning. Clearly, there was a problem.

"Let's step over here," the principal said, directing us to stand along the fence on the far side of the courtyard. "There's probably some disturbance in one of the wings. That siren is a non-movement alert."

"A non-movement alert?" I asked.

He was about to explain when a cadre of prison guards, clearly responding to the siren, rhythmically trooped across the courtyard. I counted at least twenty guards, double-timing two-by-two, all wearing black riot gear including hard hats with faceplates, brandishing black truncheons in their right hands and shields in the other.

I was about to say, *That's not something you see every day*, when I realized that prison guards in riot regalia may well have been something the principal did see every day. *This is prison, John,* I reminded myself, *not the Hilton.*

When the riot troops had moved out of sight, we resumed our walk to the school. It was then I noticed that everyone we saw was sitting down. Everyone.

"Why is everyone sitting on the ground?" I asked.

"As I said, that siren is a non-movement alert. All prisoners, wherever they are, are expected to sit down and stay down until the all-clear."

"But we're still moving," Bernice said.

"Are either of you wearing blue or orange jumpsuits?" asked the principal with a broad smile.

"Nope. No blue or orange here," she said.

"Me neither," I quickly agreed.

"The prisoners know there are consequences for not complying with the non-movement order," the principal explained, "so they

127

simply sit where they are."

It felt very strange. Inmates sitting against fences and on steps. Some had plunked themselves down in the middle of open areas. They sat quite still, like statues, as if someone had played Freeze Tag with the inmates.

"You mentioned consequences?" I asked the principal.

He pointed to the guard towers and the unmistakable glint of rifles in the sunshine.

"What do the inmates do if it's pouring rain when that siren goes off?" I wanted to know.

The principal said, "They get wet."

This definitely isn't the Hilton, John.

San Quentin proved to be my last prison workshop. Although I never stayed longer than a few hours in any one prison, I found going into prisons frightening and unnerving. It only took signing eleven "We-ain't-gonna-rescue-you" waivers before their true import finally hit home. I must be a slow learner. After my eleventh educational stint—the one in San Quentin—I decided I'd never go back.

As we climbed into our rental car in the San Quentin parking lot, I informed Bernice of my decision.

"So what if they want you to do another prison workshop?" Bernice asked.

"If they want me back," I told her, "they'll have to extradite me."

J is for Jumping Ship

We shall never cease from exploration
And the end of all our exploring
Will be to arrive where we started
And know the place for the first time.
—T. S. Eliot

THE DIFFERENCE BETWEEN going where you want to go, and going where you have to go, is the difference between a leisurely, sumptuous dinner with a bottle of Barolo, and a fast-food burger with a coke. One is a joy; the other is sometimes a necessity.

Because traveling for work is more necessity than joy, coming home is usually a relief. Anything that obstructs that return home, especially at the end of a grueling sales campaign, is aggravating.

During the fall of 1988, Texas proved to be a grueling sales campaign. For a dozen weeks,[42] I worked in every corner of Texas, and that's when I discovered just how many corners a state can have. From the Rio Grande Valley in the south to the Llano Estacado[43] in the northwest, from the Sabine River along the Louisiana border to the Mountains of El Paso in the west, I traveled the vastness of the Lone Star State. Texas is, indeed, "a whole 'nuther country."

Now it was Friday, December 23rd. Christmas loomed large, and

---

42 That fall I described myself as a Texas commuter. Seattle to Dallas. Seattle to San Antonio. Seattle to Houston.

43 Llano Estacado means "Staked Plain." This part of Texas is flat. F-L-A-T. The local joke is that this geographic region is so flat, no one robs banks here. It takes you three days to get out of sight.

it was time—probably past time—to go home for the holidays. My children, Mandy, Becky, and Ben—ages 8, 6, & 4—were waiting for me and Santa. My eighteen-year-old college freshman, Michelle, was also waiting for me, but I can't say for sure if she was waiting for Santa or not…being a college freshman and all.

I always looked forward to getting home, primarily because of the enthusiastic greeting I received when I walked in the front door. I confess, I never tired of the squeals, giggles, and hugs of the boisterous homecoming hubbub. Complete with all the catching-up.

It was particularly important to get home on this December 23rd. Yes, it was my birthday, but I also anticipated a raucous Friday night birthday party around the Christmas tree with family and friends.

My late morning Dallas flight departed right on time, and we would have landed on time in Seattle except for the stubborn, impenetrable, low-dwelling Puget Sound fog. It settled close to the water and hugged the foot of the Cascade Mountain range even as we passengers could view the proud peak of Mt. Rainier glistening in the sunlight. We were actually circling above the puffy, sun-lit fogbank blanketing the Puget Sound region, when the captain explained that low visibility made landing at Sea-Tac impossible. I think his exact words were, "We do not have the FAA minimums to land safely. Therefore, we've been redirected to Portland. I apologize for the delay."

So we landed in Portland, Oregon, one hundred and sixty-eight miles south of our destination. Everyone deplaned, and Delta personnel announced we should remain close to the gate because our flight could be called at any time. Airplane passengers tend to be an obedient lot.

I fretted about getting home for my party—but there was still plenty of time. The agents manning the Delta gate seemed confident that we'd get going in short order.

They were right. About ninety minutes later, we re-boarded our Boeing 727, and pushed back. Those of us who flew the Seattle-Portland route regularly knew that our trip would be a forty-five minute hop.

But hopping can't happen if you never take off...and we never took off.

Never.

I watched as our plane taxied and then parked beside a whole line of other parked passenger jets, herringboned along the tarmac. Apparently we were one of many Seattle-bound jets who were not actually bound for Seattle. Not yet, anyway.

The PA system crackled to life. In a tone both comforting and frustrating, the captain apologized for the delay and announced that the fog in Seattle had shown no willingness to dissipate. He promised to provide regular updates.

That meant we'd be parked here until a) the Seattle fog decided to lift or b) the cows came home. I know about Seattle fog, and I know about cows, too, having worked on my mother-in-law's Pennsylvania farm for two summers. Our departure odds were zero. We were airline captives.

Airline captives seldom rejoice unless they're flying first class, and coach captives pretty much never rejoice. With all seats filled, and the plane carefully parked for an indeterminate duration, I realized that my birthday revelers might be celebrating without me. That thought bothered me.

What bothered me more, however, was that the airline had re-boarded us on a flight to nowhere. They had taken all possible traveling alternatives away from us because we were aboard a non-moving airplane. Imagine what might have happened if the announcement at the gate had sounded like this:

"Ladies and gentlemen, we are about to re-board your flight to Seattle. However, we have no plan to take off because Sea-Tac International is thoroughly and completely fog-bound, and the visibility ceiling is well below the required FAA minimums for a safe landing. That means you'll probably be seated on our fairly snug Boeing 727 for several hours unless we get

clearance to proceed to Seattle—an event that the lovely lo-cal weatherperson tells us is unlikely. After parking for several hours, we'll recall the plane to the gate, after which you and your luggage will board a charter bus for the Emerald City. In summary, you will have wasted three or more hours on this plane, and possibly a few more hours waiting for the bus, when you might have been finding an alternative means of transportation to a destination that is less than a three-hour drive away. Thank you for flying Delta."

I knew two things for certain. First, if I'd known we'd be pushing back just to park, I would not have re-boarded the plane. Second, I would have gone directly to the rental car desks and driven myself home.

The gentleman across the aisle from me was also a road warrior. This was my first year of weekly flying, but he'd been persevering for more than a decade. We commiserated with one another, both wishing that the airlines would just have told us, "Hey, no one's flying into Seattle today." That's what we'd call the friendly skies.

"You know," I said to him, "I could easily have rented a car and driven home."

"I know what you mean. I live in Olympia, and my wife could have driven down here in under two hours."

We agreed that waiting, and wondering when the wait would end, was not our forte.

"It's silly, but I don't want to miss my birthday party."

"That's not silly. Birthdays only happen once a year. Birthdays are important."

That's when the thought hit me. I looked across the aisle and said, "Maybe we can still jump ship." I gave him a *Who-Knows?* shrug. "Doesn't hurt to ask." Reaching up, I pushed the flight-attendant call button.

A moment later, a flight attendant arrived from the rear of the plane. She reached over my head and turned off the call light.

"Yes, sir, what can I do for you?"

"Miss, I need to speak with the captain," I said smiling at her over my right shoulder.

She responded very politely. "I'm afraid the captain is busy, sir. Is there something I can do?"

"Nope," I said as I pushed up from my seat and began walking toward the cockpit. "I just need to ask the captain a question. He can't be any busier than we are."

I walked up the aisle toward the cockpit, the flight attendant pursuing me and issuing a flurry of quiet but intense "Please, sir" entreaties. I was composing what I wanted to say if the cockpit door actually opened.

Just for the record, this happened in 1988. Post 9/11, none of this could ever happen. Anyone walking toward the cockpit would be seen as a threat and possibly shot. Since 9/11, two things have disappeared: easy, informal security and Boeing 727s. In 1988, the travel world still had both.

I knocked on the cockpit door. Not a pounding, menacing knock. Not a mousy scratch. A regular knock. And the cockpit door swung open revealing three flight officers: pilot, co-pilot, and engineer. The engineer sat closest to the door and swiveled toward me. The pilot turned in his seat.

"I'm sorry, captain..." the flight attendant began speaking from behind me.

I interrupted her. "Hello, captain. I'm sorry for the interruption. My name is John Scannell, I'm in seat 27C, today is my birthday, and I have a favor to ask."

The captain seemed more curious than upset. He motioned to the flight attendant that it was alright. "Happy Birthday," he said. "What's on your mind, Mr. Scannell?"

"Thank you, sir," I said smiling at his greeting. I took a brief moment. "What are the chances we'll actually take off for Seattle?"

His brow furrowed. "Not good. Wish I could tell you otherwise."

"Well, in that case, captain, I'd like to get off the plane. Is that possible? If I can't, I'm afraid I'm going to miss my own birthday party."

The captain studied me for a moment, then switched his attention to the flight engineer. "Could we get a van out to the plane?" he asked.

"I don't know," said the engineer. "Let's find out."

While the engineer was talking with someone in the terminal, I talked to the captain about all the friends who'd be singing "Happy Birthday" to me tonight. If I drove home, I could get there.

The engineer broke into our conversation. "They say they can send a van."

"Good," the captain said. "Tell them to drive to the rear door," he added.

The engineer gave the van people the okay. "They'll be here in about ten minutes," he said.

The captain signaled for the flight attendant lingering behind me to come closer. Then he looked directly at me and began speaking in quiet, measured tones. "Now, you need to do something for me. Everyone on this plane wants us to take off—just like you." He shook his head. "Just like me. No one can know that you're getting off, okay?"

I understood. "Yes, sir."

"So you'll need to collect your things and leave as quietly and unobtrusively as possible. Two minutes after you leave the cockpit, we're going to lower the rear door of the aircraft. Go down the stairs and wait for the van. Can you do that for me? I don't want an insurrection on my hands."

"Thank you, captain. I'll be very, very quiet." I turned to leave.

"Happy Birthday, Mr. Scannell...from all of us at Delta." His smile was all the permission I needed.

I walked back to my seat and nonchalantly took down my carry-on. My checked luggage would have to wait. My fellow road warrior mouthed the question, "Are you getting off?"

I grinned and mouthed the word, "Yes."

He reached under his seat and pulled out a small carry-on, and the two of us walked to the rear of the Boeing 727. We would be departing via the exit known famously as the D.B. Cooper door. Once lowered, we stepped down to the tarmac and waited for the van. As the van took us back to the airport concourse, I offered my fellow-departing passenger a ride north with me. He declined and went to find a payphone[44] to call his wife. I went to rent a car.

I was almost out of luck. All the rental venues had posted signs: "No Cars Available." Only Hertz had cars. Correction: Hertz had only one car—a Lincoln Town Car requiring a $150.00 drop charge for anyone bound for Seattle. That was almost a dollar per mile, so it's easy to see why no one had rented it. Seattle natives had already concluded that the fog would prevent airliner landings, so driving was the only realistic option. They'd be happy to drive if cars were available… or affordable…which they weren't.

Noticing other disconsolate, stranded passengers scattered around the rental area, I decided to rent the Town Car. I would have a six passenger vehicle with five empty and available seats. I stood up on one of the molded, plastic benches, and shouted at the top of my voice. "I'm going to Seattle and I can take five people. I'll be leaving in ten minutes. First come, first served."

In less than a minute, five people gathered round, volunteering to be my passengers. One well-tanned couple had just returned from Hawaii and were clearly dressed for warmer weather. Three others, an older gentleman and two women—I'm guessing, late thirties—joined the couple as I explained that we'd split the costs six ways: cash or check. Payable now.

I'd need thirty-four dollars from each to cover the rental cost and the drop charge of $150.00. I'd take care of the gas and do all the driving.

The young couple wondered if I could treat them as one person—they were newlyweds—and I reminded them that we pay by the seat,

---

44 Another sign of different times. In 1988, there were NO cellphones in my world of travel.

just like the airplanes we were no longer aboard. As for luggage, the Hawaiian couple had none—it was still on their plane—and all the other bags fit easily into the spacious trunk. We left Portland under sunny skies at about 2:00 p.m., but daylight dimmed to twilight once we hit the Puget Sound basin around Olympia. We'd driven into the same fog that had denied us landing at Sea-Tac. It slowed us a bit, but I dropped everyone at Sea-Tac around 5:30 p.m.

I refueled and dropped off the rental, picked up my company car which was parked at the airport, and arrived in time for a typical joyous homecoming…and my birthday party.

As for my fellow passengers who had stayed aboard the plane, they arrived in Seattle just after midnight on a charter bus. When I went to retrieve my luggage the next morning, I discovered a madhouse of stranded passengers and unclaimed luggage. Christmas Eve or not, the unrelenting fog kept airplanes grounded and passengers waiting. I was glad to be home.

When I told my colleague this story, she asked me how much of the rental cost I had declared on my Travel and Expense report for December 23rd. I didn't answer.

"You didn't expense the whole $200.00, did you?"

"That's an impertinent question," I said.

"Well…?" she asked, her tone both inveigling and curious.

"Silence is golden," I said.

And so it is.

K is for Karma and Kansas City

*I'm a true believer in karma. You get what you give,
whether it's bad or good.*
—Sandra Bullock

*But life inevitably throws us curve balls,
unexpected circumstances that remind us
to expect the unexpected. I've come to
understand these curve balls are
the beautiful unfolding of...karma...*
—Carré Otis

I CONFESS, I possess no sophisticated understanding of karma. None. For me, karma can be summarized in my mother's words: "Nice gets nice," or the inverse—something my Mom assured me was equally true—"Nasty gets nasty." I can't say how that squares with the Christian concept of turning the other cheek. After all, if "Nasty gets nice," that turns my mother's edicts upside down.

When I was a youngster, if someone took a swing at me, I'd seldom swing back. In truth, my brother Bill did most of the swinging. "Someone takes a poke at you," he advised me—his younger brother—"hit him back. Hard. Then run like hell." That never sounded terribly Christian to me, but it made sense.

Fortunately, I seldom needed Bill's advice because I seldom found myself in a fight. Whenever the guys I was with decided to have a "pissing contest," I trusted in flight, not might. Being an instinctual coward, I'd end up climbing a tree, hurdling fences, or dashing across someone's backyard, never stopping until I burst through my front door, safe and untouched.

As I grew older and assumed the various roles of parent, teacher, and textbook consultant—which are simply different branches of sales[45]—I recognized the futility of fighting. I mean all kinds of fighting: physical, mental, and verbal. Few people, perhaps no people, listen, learn, or make sales decisions while you argue with them and tell them they are wrong.[46] As a parent, teacher, and sales consultant, I learned the value of a "meeting of the minds," or sometimes a negotiated surrender that ratified the adage, "The customer is always right." Curiously, that adage is frequently invoked when the customer is wrong.

Simply put, being nice helps to raise good kids. Being nice helps to teach students. Being nice helps to sell books.

Before I took the job with McGraw-Hill as a national language arts consultant, the man who would soon be my boss, Steve McClung, interviewed me as we ate lunch at the SeaTac Hilton.

"What makes you think you can sell language arts books?" he asked.

It was a reasonable question. Steve was looking to hire a person who could sell literature and writing textbooks, so it struck me as precisely the right question. I succumbed to my basic instinct to mine the moment for a bit of comedy. "Mr. McClung," I said, "I've been selling poetry to high school students for more than a dozen years."

Steve smiled at my response, and then looked up from his sandwich. "Fair enough, John," Steve said, "fair enough. But I should ask if those students have been *buying* poetry for more than a dozen years?"

---

45 All teachers are salesmen. Successful teachers always understand that; unsuccessful teachers seldom do.

46 Harry Truman once said, "I have found the best way to give advice to your children is to find out what they want and then advise them to do it."

I didn't expect Steve's question, but I liked it a great deal. It showed he actually listened to my answer. One of Steve's strengths was his serve and volley interview style. Listen...and ask the next question based on what you've just heard.

I knew I needed to consider my next answer carefully. "Are they buying what I'm selling? Yes, I believe they are."

"Tell me why you believe that."

He wasn't going to let me simply assert success.

While I was teaching, no one ever asked me that question—*Are you successfully teaching poetry? Or the novel? Or writing?* The curriculum required poetry, prose, and writing—and I taught the curriculum.

I could have said: *Steve, I teach poetry because it's part of the required curriculum. It really doesn't matter if the students like it. It's part of the curriculum. I have to teach it. Their liking it is beside the point.*

But I didn't say that, because I didn't believe that. I learned early on that students' enjoyment of poetry or prose or writing was not beside the point. In fact, their enjoyment of language was the entire point. A teaching colleague once told me that the best teachers "teach what they love," or "they find out how to love it" if it was something they didn't particularly care for.

"My job was to help my students fall in love with literature," I said. "My job was to help them open doors that they'd never been able to open before. I frequently began with the poems they knew from childhood or the songs they heard every day on the radio..." and suddenly I was off and running, back in my classroom, selling Steve McClung on the joys of poetry.

Half an hour later, Steve reached across the table and placed his hand on my arm. "I'm sorry to see that it's so difficult to draw you out," he said with a broad smile.

It took me a moment to realize that, in the middle of my consultant interview, I'd become Mr. Scannell, Poetry Teacher. I began to apologize.

"Don't apologize, John," Steve assured me. "You were doing great. I can see you love poetry...and I bet you love commas, too." He laughed as he said that.

"It shows that much?" I asked.

"You bet it does. And that's the kind of enthusiasm we need when we talk to teachers. A lot of people are selling books, but we need someone with the passion to make potential buyers say, 'Yes.'" Steve leaned forward. "I can teach you everything you need to know about our books, but I can't teach you to be passionate about poetry, the five-paragraph essay...or commas. That's what you bring to the table."

Steve's comments were reinforced a few months later when the Texas regional manager drawled approvingly. "Well, sir, an ounce of enthusiasm is worth a pound of information...and boy...you've got a whole ton of enthusiasm." Words to live by—especially if you are in a sales career.

Perhaps my whole point is that the best teachers love what they do. Teaching is an altruistic profession, and its practitioners realize that they'll rarely be compensated properly, so their satisfaction must come from something other than money. Their silver lining is this: they love what they teach, and they do their very best to infect their students with that very same love.

My job was to sell these English teachers the tools we published—textbooks to help their students fall in love with the subject their teachers already loved.

Teachers are lovers. Some may love English. Some may love science or math. But they are all lovers. That's why I always enjoyed working with teachers.

So, during my entire consultant career—selling textbooks from sea to shining sea—I did my best to bring a genuine enthusiasm for what I was selling. Loving what I was selling as much as I did, it was easy being nice. And 99.9% of the time, "Nice got nice" in return. What my mother would define as good karma.

—⚭—

The story that follows is about the one-tenth of one percent—when nice didn't get nice—when the positive energy I hoped I radiated found nothing reciprocal, but instead sank into a psychological black hole. It was rare, but it did happen on occasion, and when it did, my patience and my humanity were tested.

On this occasion, my consultant job landed me in the presence of an unhappy teacher—actually, an unhappy person who also happened to be a middle school social studies teacher. As a member of the Kansas City School District textbook selection committee, her job was to evaluate the quality of McGraw-Hill's middle school textbooks. My job was to help her and her middle school colleagues—ten women and one man—see how our books could transform the lives of their Kansas City students.

We were all gathered in the school district's central office—eleven committee members, the curriculum director, and me. The curriculum director had taken a moment to introduce me, and then I stood before the committee, the screen behind me displaying a power point slide of the three programs they would be evaluating. I would be presenting our World Studies program for grades six and seven, and our US History text, *The American Journey*, for grade eight.

Part of my job would be to walk them through the books and enthusiastically show them why all three programs would be the best choice for their students. The teachers were all seated in student desks arranged in a large semi-circle, a configuration I liked because I stood equidistant from all the committee members. It also allowed me to approach any teacher at any time.

"Thank you for inviting me here today," I began. "You're going to find a lot to love about our middle school social studies programs."

Suddenly, a hand shot up on the left side of the room. One of the committee members—a well-dressed black woman—had a question. It turned out to be more accusation than question.

"You're trying to sell us the dumbed-down version of your US History book, aren't you?" she asked in an unfriendly tone.

After more than a decade of textbook consulting, I'd faced hostility for a variety of reasons, but this question was new. *Dumbed-down books?* Alarm bells clanged a warning in my head—*Be nice and find out what she's talking about.* I decided to see if I could quell whatever misgivings this woman was having.

"I don't know what you mean," I said. That was true. I had absolutely no idea. "*The American Journey* you have on your desk is the same eighth grade book that we offer in every school district in the United States."

"That's your story," she said, folding her arms.

This teacher, whose name I did not know, made no attempt to disguise her antipathy. I looked around to see if I could find an ally elsewhere on the committee, hoping someone would speak up and help me disabuse Ms. Grumpy of her belief that we were trying to sell a less rigorous book to Kansas City.

"It's not a story, I can assure you," I said. "We sell the same books everywhere. Every textbook—including *The American Journey*—is written for a specific grade level. We can show you published and reliable readability scores for all our books. *The American Journey* has several readabilities, all suitable for eighth grade. Dale-Chall and Fry readabilities…[47]"

"Yeah, yeah, yeah," she said waving her hand dismissively. "That all sounds impressive, but everyone here knows that you don't sell the same books to the inner city. Kids in Kansas City always get the dumbed-down versions."

Wow! I thought. I could feel my *nice* slipping away.

An unwelcome thought popped into my head. *Maybe she's the committee's attack dog. Isn't it curious she's decided to make her colleagues complicit by saying, "Everyone here knows…?"*

I scanned all the members of the committee. *Did they all think that our books are dumbed-down?* As I caught the eye of each, they looked away. I'd seen this behavior before. Ms. Grumpy was a loose

---

47   There are established readability indices that publishers are expected to use so that school districts and teachers can be assured that the textbooks they purchase are appropriate to a specific grade level.

cannon, and no one knew how to deal with her. Worse, no one wanted to deal with her. She was my problem.

"Well," I said, in as bright a tone as I could, "I don't think I'll be able to convince you that we sell the same textbook wherever we go." I began walking the length of the semi-circle. "But I want to assure everyone here that there are no dumbed-down versions of any of our books. I wish I knew where your colleague"—I pointed back at Ms. Grumpy—"got that idea, but it's just not true. I've sold this book all over the US, and it's always the same text—whether I'm in Miami or Seattle...or Kansas City."

"You're right," the woman said defiantly, "you won't be able to convince me."

"Alright," I agreed. "I won't try."

A voice in my head snarled: *Be nice, John. The customer's always right.* "So let's talk about something that you have right in front of you. Okay? Let's dive into *The American Journey* and you'll all be able to reach your own conclusions..."

She interrupted me. Apparently the "dumbed-down books" accusation was only her opening gambit. "I also found that there are certain ethnic groups that you have largely ignored," she said.

Her criticism about ethnic groups surprised me, because publishers are paranoid about creating books that are inclusive—making certain that all ethnic groups are fairly represented. School districts have refused to purchase certain textbooks when publishers have foolishly dismissed one ethnic group or another. America's melting pot was no longer predominantly white—particularly not in history textbooks.

A voice in my head told me to ignore her, but a more insistent voice said that ignoring her would cause even bigger problems. I turned and addressed her directly, but my *nice* had evaporated. "Really? I think we've dealt with the various ethnic groups very well. Which groups do you feel haven't been fairly treated?"

"Which groups? How about the Chinese, for starters?"

I looked around the room for help. Everyone sitting on the committee was a social studies teacher. How could it be lost on them that the reason the Chinese were scantily represented in our text was because the book's narrative ended just after the Civil War as Reconstruction began? We didn't ignore the Chinese. They weren't here, not in large numbers, anyway.

Just because the Chinese weren't prominently featured in our book didn't mean they weren't there. The Chinese helped with the famous California Gold Rush and the building of the transcontinental railroad, and *The American Journey* mentioned those contributions. But large-scale Chinese immigration was still decades away.

I felt a snide comment well up inside me and made no effort to unsnidify it.

"Well," I said, "the reason the Chinese are only briefly mentioned in our textbook is that they weren't here. Not in substantial numbers, anyway. America's population was about 31,000,000 at the beginning of the Civil War, and the Chinese population wasn't even close to one-half of one percent." I paused, and began again with undisguised sarcasm. "You'll be pleased to know we only discuss ethnic groups in our book *after* they've arrived here in America." I emphasized *after*. "That's the way these things work."

She did not respond well to my tone.

"What about the way you treat blacks in your textbook?"

"Blacks?" *The American Journey* dealt extensively and honestly with the slave trade and with the slavery issue as it pushed the United States inexorably toward Civil War.

"Yes, blacks," she seethed. Then she went on the attack. "The people *you* kidnapped from their homeland. The people *you* sold into slavery. The people whose children *you* shamefully tore from the arms of their parents and sold to other slave owners." Her attack felt viciously personal.

"Whoa!" I said. "Hold on!" I felt my face redden and tried to suppress a growing anger. "I may be white, but neither I nor my ancestors did any of those things."

"*Your* people did," she said accusingly. She squinted at me and growled, "*Your* people did."

It's probably never a good idea to let anger shape the argument. But I was angry as I moved directly in front of her. "No. You're wrong. *My* people didn't." The entire committee could feel the heat in my words. "*My* people were still in Ireland until 1886. All *my* Irish relatives emigrated more than twenty years *after* the Civil War. They came through Ellis Island twenty years *after* slavery. None of them ever caught slaves. None of them ever owned slaves. They had nothing to do with slavery. Nothing." I was shouting.

Shouting is never a good sales strategy, so I did my best to calm down. I lowered my volume, but not my threatening tone. "And your accusations about *my people* and about *me* are frankly...offensive. Even racist. So let me suggest you simply keep quiet until you know the facts. I didn't expect you to know my relatives came after the Civil War, but I did expect that you'd understand why the Chinese weren't here and that we've treated the issues revolving around blacks with thought and sensitivity. But you didn't. Now, please, be quiet and let me get back to the job I was sent here to do."

I'd just suggested she didn't understand her subject matter, and she glared at me, sullenly refusing to open any books during the remainder of the presentation. Her ten colleagues and the curriculum director, however, toured all three books with me during the rest of the scheduled hour. When I asked if there were any questions, Ms. I-Will-Completely-Ignore-You pushed out of her desk and strode ostentatiously toward the door. She stopped at the entrance, turned toward her colleagues, and declared, "I would never vote for this man's books. He's the racist, not me." And then she was gone.

The room was dead silent. I felt awful—knowing I'd broken the cardinal rule of selling: Thou shalt not get angry. I turned to the curriculum director and said, "I'm sorry. I should not have lost my temper. I owe you an apology." I looked at all the committee members. "I owe all of you an apology."

"No," came a lone voice. "No, you don't."

I turned to see who had defended me, and it was another black woman who had been seated next to Ms. Grumpy.

"She was wrong to attack you like that." Her voice was tinged with regret. "She does things like that all the time…and she shouldn't." She looked at her colleagues. "And we shouldn't let her." Several nodded their heads in agreement. "Mr. Scannell, you acquitted yourself and your books very well." She looked at the curriculum director. "Didn't he?"

The curriculum director meekly smiled and said, "We should all thank Mr. Scannell for coming here today to present his books." Quiet applause.

Then the unexpected happened.

"Mr. Scannell," said my quiet defender, "I believe it's we who owe you an apology. Thank you for your patience and perseverance." A murmur of assent briefly filled the room.

Perseverance, perhaps, but patience? I mused. This kind teacher's comment was appreciated, but I had crossed some line, violated some unwritten rule. Nevertheless, I allowed myself a smile and said, "Thank you," even as the committee members began gathering their things to depart.

As I packed up my projector and computer, several committee members stopped to tell me some variation of "I'm voting for your books. They look wonderful." I wondered if they meant it, or if it was just the guilt talking.

We got the vote. I doubt that it was unanimous, but we won the vote and got the business.

Was it karma?

I'd lost my temper, raised my voice, and allowed myself to be snarky and sarcastic—to a customer, no less—but a customer who I believe was completely wrong. Still, my intemperate outburst could hardly be called nice.

Then I remembered a comment that always accompanied my mother's "Nice gets nice" counsel. "Don't be afraid to apologize,"

Mom would say. "Apologies can take you a long, long way." She was right. I had apologized and discovered that I did, indeed, have several allies on the committee.

As things turned out, Ms. Grumpy probably didn't vote for my books. I wondered to myself if a woman as angry as she appeared to be—at my book, at me, at the world in general—should even be in the classroom. Her colleagues may have wondered the same. Anger can be toxic.

Sometime after I learned that we'd won the business, it occurred to me that Ms. Grumpy would have to use *The American Journey* in her US History classes this coming September—whether she voted for my book or not.

A quiet voice in my head whispered, *That's karma.*

L is for Luck

I am a greater believer in luck,
and I find the harder I work the more I have of it.
–Thomas Jefferson

Success is simply a matter of luck. Ask any failure.
— Earl Wilson

SOMETIMES MY TRAVELS were so fraught with problems—bad weather, faulty equipment, or impossible traffic—that my good friend Rick would grin and say, "Sounds like if it weren't for bad luck, you wouldn't have any luck at all." Those weeks were rare, but I understood that traveling weekly demanded that all the stars align—frequently. When they did, my sister called it "God's watchful eye." My wife called it "good karma." I called it good luck.

When I'd tell Rick I had my share of good luck, he'd grin even wider and say, "My friend, you've had more than your share."

That may well be, so I've decided to talk only about good luck.

There I was. I'd boarded my Alaska Airlines flight—Seattle to San Diego—and I was seated comfortably in first class in seat 4A. My carry-on was stowed and I was ready for push back when the flight attendant at the front door announced, "Ladies and gentlemen, welcome aboard. This is Alaska Airlines flight 238 bound for Los Angeles.

Anyone not intending to go to Los Angeles this morning should de-plane now."

How many times had I heard similar announcements? *How could anyone get on the wrong flight?* I'd always wondered. Normally I don't listen to these announcements, but for some reason I heard the words "Los Angeles," and I panicked. I turned to the gentleman next to me. "Isn't this flight going to San Diego?"

He looked at me and reiterated what the flight attendant had just said: "I hope not. I'm going to LA."

"Oh my god, I'm not," I said. "I'm going to San Diego."

"I'm sure you are," he said without a hint of sarcasm. "But this plane is going to LA."

In a panic, I excused myself and slipped past my seatmate, re-trieved my carry-on from the overhead bin, and went directly to the flight attendant who had made the announcement. "I'm supposed to be going to San Diego," I said.

She asked to see my boarding pass, and then she walked with me down the jetway to the concourse. My San Diego flight had already boarded at the adjacent gate. She handed that gate agent my board-ing pass.

"This gentleman got on the LA flight by mistake. Not sure how." Then with a big smile she patted her colleague on the back. "He's your guy."

The agent smiled. Without hesitation, he ushered me through the jetway door. "We've been paging you for the past five minutes."

We practically galloped down the jetway.

"I'm guessing you couldn't hear us if you were already aboard the LA flight."

As we arrived planeside, he handed my boarding pass to the flight attendant framed in the doorway. "Mr. Scannell is in 4A."

"Thanks," she said. "Welcome aboard, Mr. Scannell."

For a brief moment I wondered if she could be thinking something unkind—*Next time try to be on time!*—but I sat down and buckled up, happy to be where I was supposed to be.

Was it luck? Maybe. In twenty-six years of flying, that was the only plane I'd mistakenly boarded. It wouldn't have been fatal if I hadn't discovered my error, but it would have been really inconvenient. After all, my luggage was headed for San Diego, and that was also where my rental car waited.

Traveling requires planning, a dose of good luck…or God's watchful eye…or karma. A close reading of all documents and all signs also helps.

The truth is I never took off on the wrong plane, nor did I ever lose a piece of luggage. Never. In light of the stories one hears about destroyed luggage or luggage never located, that strikes me as incredibly lucky.

Whenever I traveled, I always checked a bag. Only when I was on a day trip that required no overnights—a commuting "down-and-back" trip—did I rely exclusively on the overhead bin or the space beneath my seat. Otherwise, "always" applies.

Many of my colleagues seemed genuinely fearful of checking baggage. "They'll lose my luggage for sure," one of my fellow consultants told me with conviction. "I can't risk that." I'd explain that I'd been traveling almost every week for more than a decade—checking a bag whenever I stayed overnight—and I'd never lost any luggage. True, on several occasions my baggage was not immediately available at my destination, but my bag and I were happily reunited within twenty-four hours. On one of my trips from Seattle to Pittsburgh, my bag stayed aboard when I deplaned. As I understand it, my bag enjoyed a brief vacation in the Miami sunshine while I endured the Pittsburgh winter. By the next day, my bag returned to assist me with Pennsylvania's frigid weather.

My experience with checked luggage has been very positive. The horror stories about bags being destroyed or lost forever are rare, and I have none to tell. In twenty-six years of checking luggage, no airline ever lost any of my luggage. Misdirected, yes; lost, no.

Only once did my checked luggage cause me problems by showing up just as expected. The following story should clarify that problem.

My flight to Philadelphia had been a long one—or so it seemed. Some transcontinental flights pass in the blink of an eye, others drag on as if you were flying through Hell's vestibule. This was not one of those a blink-of-an-eye flights, and it was nice to be on the ground.

Many of my colleagues did all carry-on because they hated "the waiting game," even more than the prospect of lost luggage. The waiting game is the period of time between deplaning and the arrival of the first piece of luggage on the baggage carousel. Their issue was simple: where luggage retrieval was concerned, too many airports were, in my mother's words, "Slower than molasses in January." I understood that, but I still checked luggage. What I wanted to avoid were the hassle and anxiety of "The Lamentable Search for Space in the Overhead Bins." [See: D is for Don't] I never had to worry.

Then, in Philadelphia, I encountered an entirely new problem. It is one predicated on the ubiquitous signs populating the baggage area warning passengers: "Many bags look alike." *Well, duh. Of course, they do,* I thought. *That's why I love my hard-sided, burgundy-colored, Samsonite two-suiter.* Few people chose hard-sided luggage, and even fewer chose burgundy. Additionally, my unique bag was easy to spot the moment it appeared on the conveyer belt.

As soon as I spotted my burgundy bag coming down the carousel chute in Philadelphia, I stepped closer to the revolving belt. I swiftly grabbed my luggage handle and was on my way, leaving the soft-sided, black-bag folk to search for their own nondescript "Why-do-all-these-bags-look-alike?" luggage. In no time at all, I'd gotten my rental car and driven to my hotel just a mile or so away. I checked in, walked into my room, and complimented myself on an unusually swift airport exit. The only remaining task was my arrival ritual: hang up my suits; put toiletries in the bathroom; wash my hands and face; turn on the news.

I unlatched my suitcase.

It was not my suitcase.

I have never worn high heels, black slips, or sexy black silk underwear. Honest. And the lovely perfumed air that wafted into my room was something that I could only enjoy on someone who was not me. From the outside, this could have been my bag, but...from the inside...it clearly belonged to someone else—and that someone was of the female persuasion.

I'd picked up someone else's bag, and no one could have been more surprised than I was. Worse, some woman would be at the baggage carousel waiting for her already purloined luggage, or entering her hotel room and discovering black loafers—size 10½—and mundane, unimaginative, white Hanes briefs and wondering, *How did this happen?* Moreover, my suitcase lacked her seductive, perfumed aroma.

I searched for her name. There was no name tag on the bag. However, monogrammed on a beautiful silk blouse were the initials ELF. *So where was my elf?* I wondered. Her burgundy bag also bore the same monogram above the handle on the outside—ELF. My bag bore a JRS, monogrammed in the same place. My bag also lacked an ID tag.

I mused, *Had she ignored my monogram as clearly as I had ignored hers?*

I called the American Airlines 800 number and asked if they could give me the phone number to baggage claim at Philadelphia International Airport. They could, and I called.

"Baggage claim. American Airlines," a woman said.

I actually felt stupid, and I wondered how often this happens.

"Hi. My name is John Scannell, and I came in today on your flight from Seattle—probably an hour ago." *Just say it,* the voice in my head insisted. *Just tell the woman what happened.* "And I'm in my hotel room right now with someone else's luggage." Yep, I felt stupid.

"Is it a burgundy Samsonite hard side?" she asked.

"As a matter of fact, it is," I said. I felt a rising sense of confusion. "Yes." I also felt the need to explain. "When I picked it up…"

I was interrupted when the American Airlines baggage claim person shouted on her end. "George. Hey, George. We found the bag. Yeah, he's on the phone. You need to talk to him."

All I could do was wait on my end while someone named George came to the phone.

"Hi," said the man. The man named George, I'm supposing. "You picked up the wrong burgundy Samsonite?"

"Yeah. I'm sure it belongs to a woman…"

He interrupted me. "Where are you? Are you close to the airport?"

"Yeah, real close. I'm at a hotel in Essington."

"How quickly can you get here?"

"If I leave for the airport right now, I can be there in ten minutes. Maybe less."

"Great. Miss Fidalgo is still here. You have her bag. And she has yours. Tell you what. I'll be curbside outside American Airlines baggage claim. You won't even have to park or come in. Just drive up, Miss Fidalgo and I will be right there, standing at the curb. I'm sure you'll see your burgundy Samsonite hard-side that looks just like the one you mistakenly picked up."

I did just as he suggested, and there they were, the American agent, Miss Fidalgo, and my burgundy bag snuggled between them. I thought an opening line like *I've seen your underwear without you in it* would probably be too much for a simple baggage exchange. I settled on a much more apologetic line as I pulled her bag from my back seat.

"Miss Fidalgo, I'm so sorry. I just saw your bag, and I was certain it was mine." We both looked at our two bags sitting side-by-side at the curb and marveled at their sameness.

"They're twins," I said.

"Carbon copies," she said.

"Except for the monograms."

"Well, I never looked for that," she said. "I never have to. Who else has a burgundy hard-side Samsonite these days?"

"Me?" I said in a questioning tone.

"Yes," she said. "You and me. We're probably the only two people in the world with Samsonite burgundy hard-side luggage, and we end up on the same flight. I never noticed the monogram until I was putting the bag in my trunk." She turned to me and thanked me for coming back so quickly.

"Forgive me, Miss Fidalgo. I failed to notice the difference until I saw your lovely clothes. None of them would fit me very well. And vice versa."

"So...you opened my bag?"

I think I blushed. It's one of my curses. "Yes, and I must say, it smells divine. I'm glad you didn't open mine. Your bag clearly smells like a lovely woman."

She gave me a quick laugh.

"Thank you." She shook my hand and gave both the American Airlines agent and me a satisfied look. "Well, it's time to get home."

I returned to my hotel and vowed that I would never ignore the Many-Bags-Look-Alike signs ever again. As an extra precaution, after returning home, I immediately plastered my suitcase with decals from Washington State University and the University of Washington. As time went on, the number of collegiate decals decorating my bag proliferated to a point that caused my daughters to ask, "Why would you have such an ugly bag, Dad?"

"Because no one would ever mistake it for theirs."

So, I've been lucky. I've always ended up on the correct plane, and my luggage and I were seldom separated—except for brief periods of time. My friend Rick used to say that it's up to all of us "to spread the luck around," and there was one time when that admonition was truer than ever.

After concluding my work in Charleston, West Virginia, I was driving north to Pittsburgh on I-79.

I found long drives far more appealing on sunny, early summer days like this one. This trip would take about four hours—more if I stopped for a bite.

One of the advantages of my consultant job was seeing the United States from above the clouds; another was enjoying America's varied landscape through the driver's window. Today, I was enjoying green countryside with the occasional rocky bluff rising above the highway. In the shadows of one of these bluffs, I saw a faded, old Ford Fairlane station wagon pulled far right onto the highway shoulder. Just beyond lay a field that ended at the foot of a solid granite wall. Three adults gathered near the right rear wheel of the car, clearly distressed.

I don't know how I saw or knew any of this while speeding north at 70 mph. But as I saw them disappearing in my rearview mirror, something prompted me to return to see if I could help. In a few moments I was making an illegal u-turn across the median of I-79—the ones where the state police cars cross when they need a quick turn-around to give some unsuspecting driver a ticket.

I passed the parked Ford from the other side of the highway, and even from that distance I could see a man whose posture spoke of despair. I broke the law a second time, re-crossing the highway so I could again drive north. My own Ford Taurus pulled in behind their decaying, unwashed Fairlane, its paint cracked and peeled, its rear window cracked, and the interior stuffed with...well, with stuff. I stepped out of my car. As I got closer, I could see a flattened passenger-side rear tire.

Two young children were playing in the grass away from the highway, and an old woman sat in the passenger-side back seat, her legs on the gravel, mopping her brow with a dirty cloth. The day was very warm. A woman stood with her back against the front door, and the man sat on the ground, staring at the flat tire as if he could alter its flattened state by sheer will.

"Hi," I said. "I drove by earlier, and something told me you could use some help."

The man stood up as quickly as he could. It occurred to me that I represented a threat, although I was still wearing the suit I'd been wearing in Charleston.

The woman leaning against the front door—I'm guessing it was his wife—said, "Praise Jesus."

The man looked at me. "Got a flat tire."

He pronounced tire like 'tar.' "Do you have a spare?" I asked.

"Nope. No spare."

"Do you have a jack?"

"Don't make no difference. Ain't got no spare."

With all the "stuff" jammed into the back of their ancient station wagon, I suspected they'd been living in the car. If that were true, they probably didn't have money for a spare. I realized they needed help.

"If you had a spare, would you have a jack and a lug wrench to replace that tire?" I asked as gently as I could.

"Sure. But I ain't got no spare, and the other tire is shot, sure." He walked to the left side of the car and pointed to another threadbare tire that had "FUTURE FLAT" written in capital letters.

The eyes of all the adults watched me as if I could somehow provide a solution to their problem. I realized there was only one solution as we walked back to the flat.

"I have a suggestion," I said. "Morgantown is ten, maybe fifteen miles, up the road. I bet they have a tire store there. If we take this tire off, I bet we can get a new one."

"Mister, I just told ya," he began.

I held up my hand. "I know. I know." I felt a huge wave of sympathy surge over me. "Look, I can help, if you'll let me. We'll drive up to Morgantown and buy you a new tire…it's on me."

Then I said something that surprised even me. "If you have your spare tire…"

"It's flat," he said.

"I figured that out," I said. "If you bring that flat tire, too, I'll get you a second new tire."

His wife looked at him intently, shaking her head "Yes."

"Jesus sent him, Isaac. He's an angel. You go on up to Morgantown with him. I'm sure it's God's will."

Until that moment, I didn't know Isaac's name. I don't think I ever knew his wife's name.

"Hi, Isaac. I'm John. Let's get that jack and lug wrench and we'll get going up the road."

It took some doing, but we emptied the back of the station wagon enough to get the jack and pull the already-flat spare out. The older woman who everyone called Grandma kept telling us to be careful. "It's really hot out," she said as we jacked up the car while she sat in the backseat. We removed the flat, loaded both flat tires in my trunk, and took our leave.

"Don't know when we'll be back," Isaac said. "Take care of Grandma and the kids. We'll come soon as we can."

Two hours, two tires, and many dollars later, we returned to the car.

And that's when it happened. I had a panic attack. Or at least that's the way I've described it ever since. As Isaac and I were replacing the tire on the passenger side, I imagined Isaac standing over my lifeless body with a bloodied lug wrench. How that image infiltrated my imagination, I have no idea. But it seized me and animated my every move as we jacked up the left side of the car to remove the other terribly worn tire. Fear made my pulse race. Unreasonable fear perhaps, but I wasn't in a position to question the source of my fear.

I suddenly stood up, looked at my watch, and said I had to go.

"At's alright, John. I got this, now," Isaac said.

Sweat dripped from my face.

"Can I send you some money when I get it?" Isaac asked.

"No need, Isaac. No need. I'm glad I could help. You just take care of your family." My sense of peril, as irrational as it was, hadn't abated. I just wanted to get away.

"You're an angel, John," his wife drawled as she walked over and took my hand. "You know that don't you?" She peered into my face. "God sent you." Then she quoted scripture. Twelve years of Catholic school had made various scriptural passages very familiar. "Matthew says, 'Come unto me, all you who are weary and burdened, and I will give you rest.' We were weary and burdened, and you gave us rest, John. God bless you." Then she kissed my hand.

All I could muster was, "You're very welcome," before I climbed back into my car and continued my interrupted drive to Pittsburgh.

As I drove away, I began crying almost immediately. I was sobbing so hard I had to pull over.

Years later, as I write this, I often wonder what happened to those five people. Husband, wife, two children, and Grandma, living in an old Ford Fairlane station wagon with bad tires, while I had a company that paid for my airfare, my cars, my hotels, and my dinners. A family of five, living by their wits, who had no one looking after them and certainly no expense account.

To this day, I still don't know what possessed me to return to them to help, or what made me suddenly fearful when Isaac and I returned from Morgantown with their new tires. They'd been nothing but kind, and they had treated me like a saint.

There is one thing I know for sure: I liked being someone else's good luck.

I liked being their angel.

M is for Math

Life is a math equation. In order to gain the most,
you have to know how to convert the negatives into positives.
—Anonymous

Five hundred twenty-five thousand, six hundred minutes,
Five hundred twenty-five thousand moments so dear.
Five hundred twenty-five thousand, six hundred minutes.
How do you measure,
Measure a year?
—Rent (the musical by Jonathan Larson)

I REMEMBER WATCHING the 2009 George Clooney movie, *Up in the Air,* and being fascinated. That was me. Well, not the hatchet man part that Clooney was playing, but the travel part…that was me. Clooney's character was poised to become the seventh person to earn ten million frequent flyer air miles, when suddenly he's pulled off the road. He'd worked all his life and he was so close—so close. Budget problems, his company tells him. Even more aggravating, he would have been the youngest to reach that milestone.

Ten million miles. That's incredible. Putting ten million miles in context, consider that the average distance between the moon and the earth is a paltry 239,000 miles. That means George Clooney's character, Ryan Bingham, would have flown a distance greater than twenty round-trips to the moon. That's roundtrips…not one way. Or if you prefer a comparison closer to home, Ryan Bingham flew the equivalent of four hundred complete revolutions around the earth—at the equator. Just how much seat time that is boggles the imagination. In a Boeing jet—whether a smaller 737 or the jumbo 747 or the latest 787 Dreamliner—the average speed is 500 mph, allowing for some slowing down during final approach. That totals a minimum of 20,000 hours in his airline seat. Twenty thousand hours equals five hundred 40-hour work weeks—which is ten years of work weeks if you consider a work year as fifty weeks of work with two weeks for vacation. Ryan Bingham can only be described as crazy, or as a road warrior *extraordinaire*.

I've deliberately not yet included the time spent commuting to and from the airport, or the minimum preflight arrival time recommended by the TSA since 2001. They suggest two hours. Someone who has flown 10,000,000 miles has flown at least 5,000 times. Now that's pure statistical guesswork, but it allows for an average trip of 2,000 miles. 5,000 trips equals a minimum of 10,000 hours even if we lump the trip to the airport with the pre-flight waiting time. So now we are up to 30,000 hours either in the plane or getting to the plane. That adds another five years of work weeks.

This is what is meant by the expression "life on the road."

Each of those 5,000 trips probably entailed renting an automobile and at least a one night stay in a hotel, and on average at least two or three days. If we use two days as the average, that's 10,000 nights in a hotel—or twenty-seven years spent far away from home. That's twenty-seven complete, 365-day years without regard for weekends or holidays spent far away from home in strange beds.

This is the sort of mathematic meandering that can happen when you have time on your hands and time in your seat.

I was a "road warrior" for more than a quarter century (1988-2014), and I have known many strange beds. While I'm not in the same league as Ryan Bingham, I am entirely familiar with the road warrior life. I lived it for twenty-six years and 4.7 million air miles. Granted, that's only forty-seven per cent of the 10,000,000 miles that the fictional Ryan Bingham accumulated, but it's substantial never-theless. And it's factual.

For twenty-six years, I averaged 180,000 air miles annually.[48] That's a monthly average of 15,000 miles. Knowing I seldom trav-eled in July and hardly at all between Thanksgiving and New Year's Day, I could revise that monthly average. But why bother? It wouldn't change the total number of miles. I cannot say if my busiest year for mileage was 2004, but that's the year I spent 184 nights in hotels. A quick review of my Travel and Expense reports over the years reveals that I spent an average of 150+ nights a year in a hotel bed.[49]

What exactly do those figures mean? Let's do the Math, beginning with 365 days, and whittling the work year down from there to see how many days I can actually call "work days." There are 52 week-ends each year, so I can subtract 104 Saturdays and Sundays from the work year. Now 261 days remain. When I began my publishing career, I had two weeks' vacation, and by career's end, I had four weeks. If I use three weeks—15 days—as the average number of va-cation days, I have 246 work days left. Now I factor in eight holidays and the phantom vacation days like Black Friday or Christmas Eve or the week following Christmas. My company may have counted these as work days, but road warriors everywhere knew they were *de facto* vacation days. They total about 16 days. Now I am sitting on a 230-day work year—forty-six weeks.

I won't account for illness or sick days because I always managed to get sick when I actually had time off. That's sick, isn't it? I'm certain something psychological accounted for my interior monologue—*You can't get sick right now, John. Wait until Thanksgiving.* I will also leave

---

48 I've plugged in my accumulated 4.7 million air miles to do this math. Admittedly, some of that mileage was achieved during 1985 – 1987 before I was a national sales consultant, but I expect I flew less than 40,000 miles during that entire period.

49 On a handful of occasions—fewer than ten—I actually stayed at Bed & Breakfasts, particularly in Pennsylvania, Virginia, and North Carolina.

out personal days. So the baseline number for my working days per year is 230.

Spending 184 nights in hotels represents approximately 80% of my work year. On average I spent two-thirds of my work year in hotels. A quick computation reveals I spent approximately eleven full years –a full year being 365 days—sleeping in hotels.

Totals tell one story, but a daily schedule frequently provides a better understanding of the math that shapes a road warrior's day-to-day life. Let me abandon the interesting but abstract generalities and talk in specifics.

As a textbook publishing consultant, my travel varied every year based on where the business opportunities were. Certain states— which publishers called "adoption states"—selected new books on a cycle decided years earlier. For instance, during one school year, they might be selecting science books. The next year might be social studies. Then a different discipline the following year. Publishers knew in advance when certain subjects would be up for review and purchase. For instance, in 1990-1991, publishers knew that North Carolina planned to review language arts educational materials—textbooks, workbooks, videos, etc.—in their state for all grades, kindergarten through twelfth grade.[50] They would purchase them at the end of the 1990-1991 school year, and teachers would begin using them in the fall of 1991.

Simply, they planned to spend a lot of money on books for reading, literature, and writing instruction. As one of several national consultants for Glencoe/McGraw-Hill publishing, my responsibility was to persuade middle school and high school teachers—individually and collectively—to select a Glencoe/McGraw-Hill program using a combination of enthusiasm, pedagogy, and theatre. Consultants for

---

50   The following year it might be Math or Science or Social Studies. Each discipline came round every six years or so.

my competitors—who worked to move teachers in a different direction—would do the same for their company.

I realize I'm talking about the educational setting before the digital world changed everything. Twenty-five years ago, each middle school/high school English teacher[51] met with 125 to 150 students each day—sometimes more than that, but that's a story for an entirely different book. Since the central theme back then was "individualizing instruction," it's easy to see that teachers were tasked with the educational version of *Mission Impossible*—without the fun theme music playing in the background. A reliable, pedagogically-sound textbook program could offer teachers a useful tool for carrying out an already difficult task.

Successful selling is all about solving problems. If my books could solve more problems more easily than the "the other guy's books," then my company would get the business. My job was to diagnose which problems teachers found most pressing, and demonstrate how our textbook programs best solved those problems. A good program, everyone hoped, could make life easier for the English teacher.

As a former English teacher, I was never sure that one "could make life easier for the English teacher." English teachers consciously choose the discipline that every other teacher relies on—the one that teaches the use of the English language. Every other subject area—Math, Science, Social Studies, even Foreign Language—expects students to possess a clear grasp of English. And every other subject area expects English teachers to send them students with the capacity to read with understanding and write with clarity.

Every English teacher I've ever known understands that to mean there could never be "an easier life for English teachers." Rewarding perhaps, but never easy.

No one would ever purchase a textbook that would make life more difficult.

---

51 Synonyms are reading teacher, writing teacher, language arts teacher. They're all the same person.

The Logistics of "Getting There"

On this North Carolina trip, I had four consecutive days of presentations to various textbook committees scheduled Monday through Thursday, January 14-17. We were scheduled for a different North Carolinian city each day. Our Monday began in Raleigh, North Carolina, and then the publishing caravan moved to Greensboro on Tuesday, Winston-Salem on Wednesday, and ended the week in Charlotte.

Because I live on the West Coast, a Monday presentation meant Sunday travel. No NFL football for me. I'd pack the night before—two suits, three shirts, two ties, underwear, socks, toiletries, and my novel. The truth is, my bag was almost always packed and ready to go—and typically my alarm woke me at 3:15 a.m. After a quick shower and a cup of coffee, I backed out of my driveway for Sea-Tac International Airport on Sunday morning at 4:00 a.m. I always gave myself at least an hour to drive to the airport, but the thirty-mile drive took me less than 45 minutes. I loved the 4:00 a.m. Sunday morning traffic I never encountered.

I parked my car at the Jet Motel, and its shuttle whisked me to the Delta Concourse in less than five minutes. I checked my luggage at the Delta counter and made my way to the departure gate in the B concourse. Soon after I began weekly travel, I joined Delta's Crown Room. On this day, I settled down with my novel, Pat Conroy's *The Prince of Tides*, and read until they called my flight.

The first leg of my Delta flight was from Seattle to Atlanta, where I'd have a brief layover. Then on to Raleigh, North Carolina, for a total distance of 2,536 air miles.

Depart Seattle	6:15 a.m. [PST]
Arrive Atlanta	2:35 p.m. [EST]
Depart Atlanta	3:30 p.m. [EST]
Arrive Raleigh	4:25 p.m. [EST]

Departure and arrival times were subject to change without notice because weather, equipment, and personnel—i.e. flight crews—didn't always cooperate. That day, the weather, equipment, and personnel cooperated and the anticipated schedule proved fairly accurate.

Sometime around 4:35 p.m. [EST], I stood at the baggage carousel at the Raleigh-Durham International Airport to collect the bag I'd checked through. On average, I could expect my suitcase to appear on the merry-go-round thirty minutes after my flight landed. Twenty minutes, if I was lucky. After that, I'd pick up my rental—this week I'd be renting a Hertz van because we'd be leaving behind all the textbooks after every presentation. We figured we'd need between 240 and 300 textbooks. Without exaggeration, that's literally a ton of books.

I figured I'd be behind the wheel of the van and driving toward the hotel by 5:15 p.m. [EST] I keep referring to EST—Eastern Standard Time—because I began my day in the Pacific Time Zone. My body told me that it was actually 2:15 p.m. because whenever I flew east from Seattle, I had a twenty-one hour day. Somewhere I lost three hours—three hours I would recoup on the return flight. Flying west, I'd have a twenty-seven hour day.

On this day, transit from my own bed to my next bed was just forty-five minutes shy of twelve hours. Half a day. And that's just one-way, and it doesn't include my daily commute wherever I happened to be. Compare that with the typical work-commute time in the United States—25.5 minutes one way, or 51 minutes roundtrip. That means the average worker spends 4 hours and 15 minutes every week traveling to and from work. My commute that day was almost three weeks' worth of the average daily commute. You can do the math.

Just imagine what happens when the weather turns foul, or the plane needs de-icing, or the equipment suffers problems, or the new crew hasn't arrived. The hours pile up. On five occasions over my twenty-six years of traveling, the plane never left.

But this trip to Raleigh was a typical *good* day. The only thing that would have made any of my good days better would be to have a trip cancelled—or have my employer find a Star Trek transporter unit so I could instantaneously beam myself to my destination. Imagine Seattle to Raleigh at the speed of light.

Unlike good days, there is no typical bad day. All bad days are unique, and uniquely maddening…and always memorable.

I once drove thirteen hours from Nashville, Tennessee, to Martinsburg, West Virginia, to deliver a keynote address at a big conference. Bad weather had aborted my plans to fly to Dulles and driving was my only option. [See: W is for Weather] That was a bad day… and a bad night.

I once waited at Atlanta's Hartsfield International Airport for hours because of thunderstorms in the Roanoke, Virginia, area. We took off hours late only to fly into the teeth of the raging thunderstorm that had stubbornly refused to leave Roanoke. [See: P is for Prayer] That rock-and-roll flight was a bad day.

Without question, traveling is very much a question of time. But the element that creates the greatest interest when traveling is "where." When people asked me where I've traveled in the United States, I tell them it's easier to tell them where I haven't traveled, because my travels have taken me to all fifty states. I've also traveled to six foreign countries, calling on Department of Defense teachers overseas.

Focusing only on my domestic work, I have worked in almost every city larger than 100,000. As of 2016, there were 307 cities that had a population exceeding 100,000. Of those 307, I'd worked in 299 of them. Ten American cities are larger than one million—New York, Los Angeles, Chicago, Houston, Phoenix, Philadelphia, San Antonio, San Diego, Dallas, and San Jose, and I spent quantum amounts of time in each of these. Another 105 cities fall into the 200,000 – 1,000,000 range. Remarkably, the only city in this category that I hadn't worked was Chesapeake, Virginia. I don't know how I missed it. That leaves

192 cities whose population is between 100,000 and 200,000, and there are only seven cities on this list where I hadn't worked: Port St. Lucie and Pembroke Pines, Florida; McKinney, Lewisville, and Frisco, Texas; Clarksville, Tennessee, Sterling Heights, Michigan; and Surprise, Arizona. That last one came as...well...as a surprise.

I realize the list I consulted only named cities exceeding 100,000, but I've also worked in many, many towns that are much, much smaller. I've pondered which might be the smallest. Perhaps Nulato, Alaska. [See: G is for Guns] Nulato's really a village of about 260 souls whose claim to fame is that it's a checkpoint on the Iditarod Trail, a few hundred miles west of Fairbanks and nestled along the Yukon River. If you travel several hundred miles further southwest on the Yukon River as it makes its way to Norton Sound, you'll find the small town of St. Mary's with its 550 denizens in the Yukon River delta. I overnighted there once, despite the fact that St. Mary's lacks both hotels and restaurants. The school principal accommodated me with a bunk bed in the back of the high school, and he was kind enough to stop at the local grocery so I could purchase frozen enchiladas that I heated in the school's microwave. That's a small town.

I've also presented to teachers in schools in places like John Day, Oregon—population 1,674—and Warsaw, North Carolina—population 3,151. I chuckle to myself when I realize that the major league baseball stadiums I've visited [See: B is for Baseball] could each accommodate about 40,000 fans—give or take. That means the average major league stadium could seat 155 Nulatos, 72 St. Mary's, 24 John Days, or slightly more than a dozen Warsaws.

I am always amazed when I consider the mathematics of my life. I have traveled to hundreds of cities, towns, and villages—places large and small—places both well-known and obscure. I have flown 4.7 million miles and driven at least 1,250,000 miles. I have slept in thousands of different beds and spent years of my life far from home.

Traveling invariably rewards all road warriors with a variety of mathematical curiosities. Let me offer one: the distance across Texas on I-10 is 880 miles from the New Mexico border to the Louisiana border. I've driven every mile, and the city of Orange is the last Texas town before crossing into Louisiana. However, the distance on I-10 to the Atlantic Ocean from Orange is only 784 miles—almost one hundred fewer miles than the trip across the Lone Star State. I always knew that Texas was big, but this I-10 statistic provided a curious exclamation point to Texas' size—something I realized when I did the math.

Here is the image one teacher used to explain this fact to me. "Imagine a hinge running north and south along the eastern edge of Texas—that's the border Texas shares with Louisiana. Now, using that hinge, flip Texas over on its back. El Paso will be almost 100 miles out in the Atlantic." That image has stayed with me.

Math, as it applies in terms of time and distance—flying in an airplane or driving behind the wheel of a car—has played a mighty role in my work life. When I finally retired and cleared out my storage locker, I was astonished to find more than 375 maps tucked away. Most of them were roadmaps—you know the ones I mean, the ones that are impossible to refold. As my Dad always said, "The only way to refold a roadmap is incorrectly." I continually proved him right.

I'd forgotten I had these maps because I hadn't used a fold-out paper map for almost a decade. Roadmaps fell victim to the march of technology, just like typewriters and rotary phones. When I retired in 2014, I was accustomed to using a portable GPS. Wendy had purchased it for me several years earlier, and by the time I finally stopped traveling, most rental cars came with GPS installed. Who needed maps?

All the maps I had begun collecting in 1988 were resting comfortably in a plastic bin in my storage area. In 1988, I never traveled without a road map. Never. The reason was simple. Either I had a map, or I was lost, and lost was never a good thing. Additionally, the best maps flagged the schools I intended to visit with a small icon and provided other important information.

I sorted through the stacks of roadmaps—held in regional categories by fat rubber bands. No one would ever use them again. Not even me. I once pulled a roadmap out of my glove box, and my grown son laughed.

"Oh my God," Ben said unfolding the map. "An antique."

"Yeah," I said. "This is the map I used when I came west in my Conestoga wagon," I told him. It's a strange feeling realizing that the paper world has dissolved into the digital universe. In every way.

I was fascinated as I randomly reviewed one map or another, tracing my fingers over marks made decades earlier while plotting my course to different destinations—mostly schools and hotels. The best maps always indicated shopping centers, hospitals, prominent buildings, places of historical interest, and sports venues like Fenway Park. I shudder to think how many hours I spent studying my various unfolded maps, spread atop my hotel bed.

I had maps of cities, large and small, maps of states, maps of regions. Stacked among all the domestic maps, I found maps of Saipan (Northern Mariana Islands), Heidelberg (Germany), and British Columbia (Canada). I also had a wine map of the Napa Valley, a map of North Carolina's Outer Banks, and several maps of Civil War battlefields—like Shiloh, Vicksburg, and Gettysburg. I also found maps of various national parks—like Yosemite, Death Valley, the Grand Canyon, and the Everglades. I'd been to all of these places—and each of these maps guided me around a real city or to an historical location or through a national park.

Now these places live only in memory—memories evoked by badly refolded maps, stored amidst their fellow roadmaps, and safely tucked away in a plastic storage bin. I may live to regret it, but all those maps found their way into the recycling bin.

Only two survived. I kept an old map of Seattle—a 1972 map that I think was the first map I acquired when I arrived in September of that year. And I kept a map of New Orleans—autographed by then Governor Edwin Edwards—who later went to prison in 2001 on charges of racketeering. I approached him in New Orleans legendary *Café du Monde*, where we were both enjoying *café au lait* and *beignet*. I complimented New Orleans vibrancy, and asked him if he would be kind enough to sign my New Orleans roadmap. He responded graciously, and, as he signed, he asked me where I made my home. When I said Seattle, he proved he was every inch the politician that made him a minor legend in the state of Louisiana. He complimented Seattle to a fare-thee-well, and insisted I should return more often and enjoy New Orleans' "unique brand of hospitality."

I still have that map. And that memory.

I never really counted the number of miles[52], the number of hotel rooms, and the number of cities, towns, and burgs I encountered. I never counted the number of beers drunk or brats consumed at each of the thirty major league stadiums—and many minor league ballparks. [See: B is for Baseball] I lost count of the many musicals I saw. Some, like *Les Misérables*, *Phantom of the Opera*, *Hairspray*, *Showboat*, and *Wicked*, I attended multiple times, going whenever I could. Each year on the road, I attended four or more musicals and probably twice as many baseball games. I cannot recall how often I was lured into more than two dozen national parks—from Florida's Everglades to South Dakota's Mt. Rushmore to California's Yosemite—but when my work and the nation's spectacular geography aligned, I went.

More than anything else, traveling taught me to live in the moment, wherever I was. I always realized I might never pass that way again.

The voice in my head insisted, *Enjoy it, now.* I obeyed.

So when my wife tells people, "John's been everywhere," she ain't exactly lyin'.

I haven't been everywhere in the USA, but pretty close.

---

52 The airlines and hotel chains were happy to do that for me.

N is for Nine-Eleven

*So many names, there
is barely room on
the walls of the heart.*
— *Billy Collins, American poet laureate*

*If we learn nothing else from this tragedy,
we learn that life is short and there is no time for hate.*
— *Sandy Dahl, wife of Flight 93 pilot Jason Dahl*

MY PARENTS ALWAYS appreciated the importance of telling the story of where they were when the news of the Japanese attack on Pearl Harbor bowled them over. It was Sunday, December 7, 1941, and my mother, a single, twenty-two-year-old telephone operator, was working a switchboard when "all the phones lines lit up like a Christmas tree."

That's how she always described it—"The phones lines lit up like a Christmas tree."

Everyone was calling everyone. The war raging in Europe, until that moment a distant war, suddenly perched on the doorstep of the United States like a hungry vulture. Unlike Mom, my dad, a bachelor with a manufacturing job in Brooklyn, was relaxing at home, sharing the Sunday comics with his older brother Ed in the living room of their mother's Hoboken apartment and listening to Glenn Miller's *Chattanooga Choo Choo* on the radio. Suddenly, the delightful Sunday music was interrupted with a special announcement.

"Everyone just got quiet," Dad said. "The Japanese had attacked us. A sneak attack. The details were sketchy, but we knew this meant war. What else could it mean? I was twenty-five and your Uncle Ed was twenty-seven. No one said it that day, but we both knew we'd be heading off to war. All day long we just sat and listened to the news. No one knew what to say. The news only got worse later in the day."

There are historical moments that are also extremely personal moments—moments that change lives. For my parents' generation, the personal moment that history labeled "Pearl Harbor" is indelibly etched in their memories. For the Baby-Boomer generation—those of us born after 1946 when millions of GI's returned home from WWII to resume their lives—the assassination of President John F Kennedy on November 22, 1963, in Dallas became our Pearl Harbor. Like my parents, I've plied my own children with the stories of "where I was when I heard the news of JFK's assassination."

"I was sitting in Chemistry class when I heard the announcement," I'd tell them. "It was just before noon on Friday. I was a junior at Notre Dame High School, and my lab partner and I were comparing notes from an experiment we had just completed, when we heard the voice of Sister Joachim come over the public address system. That was rare. Mid-day announcements were unusual."

"We've just received word that President Kennedy has been shot in Dallas," Sister said. "That's all we know at the moment. Let us all say a prayer for our president." The public address speaker fell silent. Stunned, we said an Our Father, a Hail Mary, and a Glory Be, and then the room fell eerily silent.

The room would have been completely silent except for the quiet sobs of one of the girls in the back of the room. Over the next few hours, the news went from bad to worst: President Kennedy was dead. No longer were the tears reserved to one person. I watched as my teachers openly wept, as if their hearts were breaking. Words like "How?" and "Why?" tortured all of us. In some ways, they torture us still.

Virtually every American of my generation has a similar, detailed story that begins with, "I remember exactly where I was and what I was doing when JFK was shot." I've often wondered if someone might have written a book, *Where I Was When JFK Died.*[53]

My mother said she was watching television in the living room while ironing the collars of our white shirts. Dad's assistant burst into his office at J.T. Baker with the news. "Jack, turn on your radio. The president's been shot."

Certain days have been imprinted like a white-hot branding iron on our memories. Though the memory dims, the scars remain. So, we pray for ordinary days. Days that don't need to be remembered.

And then nine-eleven happened, and once again our memories were branded by tragedy.

Do you remember where you were when New York City's premier skyline feature—the Twin Towers—were under attack? Do you remember where you were when a plane exploded into the Pentagon?

I remember where I was.

I was in my Sacramento hotel room.

I'd flown into Sacramento Sunday evening, so I could work a bit to the south—in Modesto—on Monday, and then on Tuesday, I'd be working in the Sacramento City high schools. On Wednesday, I'd drive over to San Francisco and work the Bay Area.

As a morning person, I never minded beginning my day at 4:30 or 5:00. I've always loved early mornings—some of my colleagues thought this strange—and I frequently began my day with a brisk walk. On Tuesday, September 11, 2001, I'd gotten up about 5:00 a.m. because I had several before-class appointments with teachers. That meant showing up around 6:30 for my first appointment, so today's walk would have to wait. I showered, dressed, turned on the television to a news channel, and opened my laptop.

---

53 The answer is "yes." *Where Were You? America Remembers the JFK Assassination,*
© 2013 Compiled and Edited by Gus Russo and Harry Moses.

The television was my daily companion. After thirteen-and-a-half-years of traveling, and after almost 2,200 nights in hotel rooms, I used the televised morning news to fill the auditory void left vacant by a lack of conversation. Yes, I'd talk to myself—out loud—just to make sure I hadn't gone deaf overnight. Turning on the news was my strategy for overcoming the silence. Occasionally I'd talk to the television.

This morning, however, proved different. Uniquely, horribly different.

It was probably 5:50 a.m. when I turned on the television. The image that immediately caught my attention was the black smoke pouring from a burning high-rise which appeared to be one of the towers of New York's World Trade Center. Was I watching a film clip from some still-to-be-released movie? I wasn't sure. Special effects had evolved so incredibly over the past two decades that filmmakers could achieve virtually any special effect they wished, and make it seem real—like a burning World Trade Center tower.

The news anchors interrupted my brief imagining, their voices betraying the horrible reality of what I was watching. This was no movie. I closed my laptop and sat transfixed in front of my television.

"An airliner crashed into the North Tower at 8:46 a.m.," the broadcaster said. That simple fact was all anyone knew for certain. No answers presented themselves. Almost every word hung out as an unanswered question.

The plane had collided with the North Tower just moments before I'd turned on my television—sometime just after 5:46 a.m. Pacific. I turned up the volume on the TV and made myself a cup of coffee as the awful, inexplicable drama unfolded in real time on television screens across America—and very likely across the world.

Viewers everywhere were thirsting for answers, but none were coming, not even at 6:03 a.m. when we witnessed the fireball bursting from the north side of the South Tower. A Boeing 767 smashed into the south face of the building, and live television broadcast the crashing airliner in real time.

What is happening? My God, what is going on?

No one knew, but the speculation among the news folk began to fly. And now the televised images, filling the screen on all channels, were of both towers burning. I felt only a growing sense of confusion and sorrow. Rooted to the chair, unable to turn away, I realized that it was 6:20 a.m. and that I was supposed to meet a Social Studies department chair in ten minutes. I wasn't going to make that meeting. I called the high school office and told the secretary that I wouldn't be able to keep my appointment with Ms. Johnson.

"Have you been watching the television?" she asked.

"Yes," I said.

"It's awful," she said. "Those poor people, those poor people." Like me, she was clearly confused and upset. None of us had yet connected the dots. None of us yet knew that the world was changing before our eyes.

"Yes." I paused. What could I say that might make a difference? Nothing. "Please let Ms. Johnson know I won't be coming."

"I'll put a note in her mailbox," she said. She sounded as if she were beginning to cry. "What's this world coming to?"

Another question without an answer.

At 6:37 a.m., a plane crashed into the Pentagon.

Strike three, I thought.

The television news folks started using phrases like, "We're under attack," and no one was doubting them. Even after years of drawing daily comfort from the familiarity of the televised morning news—including bad news—I'd come to realize that hotel rooms are lonely places. And at this moment, I felt particularly lonely…and frightened.

It was time to go home. Sacramento and San Francisco would have to wait for another day.

I called the school where I was supposed to have my second appointment that morning and cancelled that as well. Fortunately I had direct access to the teacher's number and could leave a voicemail. I apologized profusely, but looking back, I doubt any apology was necessary. Under the circumstances.

My cellphone rang. Ms. Johnson was returning my call and

thanking me for the heads-up about our cancelled appointment. "I'm guessing no one will be keeping any appointments today," she commented. "Someone here just said they've closed the airports and grounded all aircraft flying in American airspace."

"Really?" was all I could muster.

"Where's home for you?" she asked.

Our voices were both filled with a sadness I hadn't heard before.

"Seattle. I live near Seattle."

"Well, John, it looks like you'll be driving home. Long drive." There was a noticeable pause. "Thanks for letting me know, John," she said. "Travel safely."

"Thanks."

Yep. I'm driving north, I said to myself. *I'm going home.* As I changed from my suit to my jeans, I watched the South Tower's spectacular collapse. *There were people inside that building,* I thought. I heard the secretary's voice: *Those poor people. Those poor people.* I sat on the edge of my bed and wept uncontrollably. I felt myself growing numb as I listened to the fear-fueled speculation from the television news folks, and through my tears I watched the North Tower fall in equally spectacular fashion. The New York skyline was obliterated in an all-enveloping cloud of dust and smoke. It was 7:30 a.m.

I tried calling home, but everyone had already gone off to work or off to school. My wife, Faye, would be in her high school getting her art materials ready for class. And my landscape architect daughter, Michelle, would be out and about beginning her day, too. My son Ben, a high school senior, was probably walking into his first period class. As for my daughter Becky, a sophomore at the University of Washington, and my daughter Amanda, a senior at Washington State University, I had no idea what their schedules might be.

Time to get going, I told myself. *Time to get home.* I opened my hotel room curtains and saw that it was a bit cloudy, but otherwise a nice ordinary Sacramento September day. But a voice cautioned me, *Nothing today is ordinary.*

I checked out of my hotel, climbed into my rented Ford Taurus, and pointed my car north on I-5—that interstate runs 770 uninterrupted miles from Sacramento to Seattle. As I pulled onto I-5, I began calling Hertz because I worried there would be a monstrous drop charge.[54] All I got was a busy signal. I guessed I wasn't alone in trying to call. I never got through to Hertz that day.

Sacramento International Airport is only a dozen miles north of the city, and just off I-5. As I approached the airport exit, I could see it was completely blocked off—state police vehicles, their lights flashing ominously, blocked any possible access to the airport from every direction. It looked as if the airport were on lockdown.

Nothing today is ordinary.

The prospect of a long drive ahead solidified into reality. That meant I'd better gas up at the next exit—Woodland, California. I pulled up to the gas pump, performed my credit card ritual, selected regular gas, put the nozzle in the car, and began filling my tank. When the pump clicked off, I waited for the receipt—expense reports demanded them—and climbed back into my car. As I drove off, there was a loud, metallic *thunk!* I'd driven away from the gas pump with the nozzle still in the car—something I'd never done before. Not in thirty-seven years of driving.

Nothing today is ordinary.

The noise stopped me immediately, and I knew at once what I'd done. I stepped out of the car and walked to the gas nozzle now lying on the pavement. I don't know what kind of look I had on my face as I picked it up, but the man gassing his car at the adjacent pump gave me an extraordinarily kind look and said, "It's that kind of day, isn't it?"

I shook my head as I fitted the nozzle into its gas pump saddle.

Nothing today is ordinary.

My long drive north began about 8:30 a.m., and I listened to the radio every mile of that trip. That took some doing as stations faded as I drove further and further north, moving from one reception area to

---

54 The amount a rental car assesses when the car is rented at one venue—Sacramento—and dropped off at another venue—Seattle.

the next. The World Trade Center attacks seemed to be the only story on any radio station.

Along the way each of my children found some time—and some way—to call my cell phone. Their first question was always, "Where are you?" I could easily have been in New York City as far as they knew. I remember once calling home from the observation deck of the World Trade Center and singing a few bars from the musical *On a Clear Day*. What a view! I could see forever up there…once upon a time. I'd never again be able to view the New York metropolitan area from that vantage point. It was gone.

My reply to my children's worried question was always, "Don't worry. I'm safe. I'm on I-5 near Red Bluff…or Redding…or Yreka. I'm heading home in my rental car since flying's not an option." Then I'd ask them how they were doing, but the conversation always came back to the World Trade Center attack.

"I'm just glad you're safe, Dad. Really, glad."

I was glad, too. Their calls meant the world to me

As I drove into Oregon, I called my friend and colleague, Gene Bindreiff. He suggested I stop near Corvallis where we could share a pizza. When we met around 5:00 p.m., I'd been driving 8½ hours, stopping only for gas and junk food. We commiserated over pizza and beer on the state of the world.

On that day, there was only one topic of conversation—unless you had a son in the military. Gene's son was a commercial pilot, but he also served in the Air Force reserve flying KC-46 Aerial Refueling jets—gas stations in the sky. He might be called to active duty.

The idea that planes could be turned into weapons gave us both reason to be concerned. "It's terrible, John," Gene said. "You realize that nothing will ever be the same?"

"I know," I said. "I called Sac City High this morning, right after the second plane hit, and all the secretary could say was, 'Those poor people, those poor people.' Her voice keeps playing in my head."

We could both feel a heavy, unshakable sadness sinking in.

"You need to get up the road, John. We all need to be home tonight."

"Thanks, Gene. See you soon."

After pizza, I knew I was more than halfway to Seattle. I felt I was in the home stretch. Despite what I'd seen at Sacramento, I wondered if I could return my Hertz rental at Sea-Tac International Airport that night. I'd parked my company car in a nearby lot when I'd departed on Sunday. I couldn't drive two cars home.

Access to Sea-Tac International reflected the access to Sacramento International. There was none, police cars blocking all roads. So I continued home, arriving at about 10:30 p.m. My trip had taken fourteen hours. Driving, gassing up, and pizza. The news on the radio was bleak and getting bleaker. It was good to be home.

The next morning, I called the Hertz venue at Sea-Tac at 8:00 a.m., and I was surprised by how quickly the phone was answered.

"Hertz rentals," the voice on the other end said with authority.

I hadn't expected anyone to answer. "Wow. You're open."

"Yes, we are."

"Well, I've got a rental I just drove up from Sacramento…"

"When can you get it here?" the authoritative voice asked.

"I understand Sea-Tac is closed…" I began.

"They are. But we're open. You say you have a car?"

"Yes. A Ford Taurus that I drove from Sacramento…"

"Great," the man said. "When can you get it here?" I could feel his urgency even over the phone.

"Well, it's rush hour, but I can be there by ten. Is that alright?"

"Ten's great. What's your name?"

I gave him my name and I suppose he was looking me up on their reservation system when I asked, "I need to know if there's going to be a drop charge." It could be horrendous.

He didn't miss a beat. "Nope. No drop charge. See you at ten."

I don't know who hung up, but I hopped into my car and got to the airport in less time than I imagined possible. And what happened when I dropped the car off was something I'd never experienced before or since—and I've rented thousands of cars. Let me call it an automobile "exchange" rather than a drop off. It went like this:

I stepped out of my car.

The Hertz gentleman asked me where I'd picked up my car initially. I said Sacramento.

The Hertz gentleman consulted his clipboard flipping through several pages, and then said, "Send Mr. Jackson over. Tell him his Sacramento car is ready to go."

Mr. Jackson showed up in a matter of moments even as the Hertz employee checked the fuel level—it was full—and gave my rental one last walk-around.

Mr. Jackson slid into the car and off he went.

I bet the whole exchange had taken less than three minutes.

Nothing yesterday—or today—was ordinary. Nothing about travel will ever be the same, either.

I must admit, I was proud of Prentice Hall's leadership after the terrible attacks on the World Trade Center. Marjorie Scardino, the CEO of Pearson—Prentice Hall's parent company—said that no consultant had to get on an airplane until they felt comfortable with the idea. *What an amazingly thoughtful response*, I thought.

Those of us who travel for a living know that nine-eleven changed not only the face of air travel, but its heart and soul as well. Perhaps we are safer, but safety comes at a cost—both monetary and psychological.

So, that's my nine-eleven story.

My traveling colleagues all tell similar tales. One friend, whose home is near Oklahoma City, was stranded in Philadelphia, and she and two colleagues took their rental car and decided they'd drive home—dropping each along the way. The first stop was Huntsville, Alabama, and the second stop was Nashville, Tennessee. After that, it was a straight drive west to Oklahoma City on I-40.

The day when 2,996 people died in a terrorist attack on the World Trade Center, the Pentagon, and in a lonely field in south central

Pennsylvania…the day we watched live and in color the attacks on the Twin Towers…that was the day when everything changed—in America, at least.

What kind of event sears a particular day into memory?

I'm not entirely sure, but I expect other cultures have their own stories of "The day when time stood still" or "The day when everything changed." Japan has Hiroshima (August 6, 1945) when more than 70,000 people died in the blink of an eye, followed by so many related deaths over the next months and years. Indonesia has the December 26, 2004 tsunami which swept more than 230,000 to their doom. Haiti has its horrifying earthquake in January 2010 when at least 100,000 perished.

I know where I was when Kennedy was assassinated. I know where I was when the Twin Towers fell. I sometimes wonder if people in those other countries ask one another, "Where were you when…?"

O is for Opportunity

*We often miss opportunity because it's dressed in
overalls and looks like work.*
—Thomas Edison

I will prepare and someday my chance will come.
—Abraham Lincoln

*NOTE: I briefly toyed with the idea of saying, "This is my Opportunity
to say nothing. Please proceed to the next chapter, P is for Prayer." But
I didn't. I hope I made the right choice.*

IN SO MANY ways, this whole book is about seizing opportunities. Equally true, one opportunity frequently leads to other opportunities. Taking the opportunity to become a national consultant for McGraw-Hill led to virtually all the other opportunities detailed in these pages.

Having spent fifteen years "cloistered in the classroom," I became enamored of the opportunities that the traveling life afforded. It's not so much that teaching didn't provide opportunities. It did. It's that traveling offered an entirely different set of opportunities—opportunities to see new places, to meet new people, to see the infinite variety of America's geography. The demands of my job compelled me to go where I probably would never have gone otherwise, to see things I would never have seen, and to experience things I would never have experienced. Very unlike the classroom.

For instance, while I was a teacher, I taught...and I also directed plays and musicals. During my tenure as a teacher, I became a certificated high school football referee, which meant I also refereed little league football—the kind with fanatical parents patrolling the sidelines, but that's a story for another day...and an entire book of its own.

Because my schedule was predictable and reliable, I became actively involved in my church, briefly teaching Confraternity of Christian Doctrine classes for a year. I became a lector[55] at Our Lady of the Lake parish in Seattle's north end, and I assumed the role of training and scheduling other lectors. For two years, I was President of the Parents Club for Our Lady of the Lake Elementary School.

My predictable schedule allowed me to spearhead fundraising efforts for my daughter's school. Using my directorial skills, I produced two dinner theatre fundraisers--the casts were members of the congregation. We performed the classic *Arsenic and Old Lace* the first year, and a year later, we shifted to something even sillier, the melodrama, *Deadwood Dick or The Game of Gold*. Dare I say I have never enjoyed fundraising more than when I worked with those two casts?

Being home also meant I had the time to take my oldest daughter to soccer practice, and time to attend her soccer matches. I took her to ballet lessons and watched her dance in Pacific Northwest Ballet's annual production of *The Nutcracker* at the Opera House at Seattle Center.

None of those things were possible once I began traveling.

I couldn't referee football any longer, because I was out of town most of the time. Even more problematic, I couldn't say that I'd definitely be home by a certain time because the airlines or Mother Nature or random mischance might decide to impede my progress at any moment. Nor could I schedule myself as a lector in my church, because whenever my work took me to the East Coast, I'd depart Seattle early Sunday morning so that I could be ready to begin work on Monday morning...in Miami...or Charlotte...or Philadelphia. Flying east swallows an entire day.

Several chapters in this book address how I seized opportunities—in

---

55 A lector is the person who reads the epistles at the Catholic Mass.

this case, opportunities for fun—that presented themselves. Just read *A is for Advice, B is for Baseball and Battlefields,* and *H is for Hooky and Horse Racing,* and you'll see what *carpe diem* really means. There's also a portion of *F is for Family and Friends* that focuses on seizing the opportunity.

Working throughout the United States, I did my very best to pursue both my favorite activities and seize unique opportunities wherever and whenever I found them But one needs time to *carpe diem.*

For instance, by 1996, I'd already worked twice in Hawaii. Whenever I mentioned those trips to friends, they assumed that I had somehow side-stepped the work part of the trip. Apparently, the name Hawaii was synonymous with cushy assignment.

"You went to Hawaii, did you?" they'd say. "Get any work done?"

Unfortunately, on my first two trips to Hawaii, my answer was, "Yes, I did nothing but work."

That bothered me. One wasn't supposed to arrive in paradise and just work. That's not the way it should be. Sadly, the words "surf and sand" and "hula girls" never appeared in my daily report, "What I Did in Hawaii Today." Not once. My two Hawaiian trips can be summarized in one dreary phrase: All work and no play.

Then, in 1996, Marguerite Smith, the rep for McGraw's International Division, called me, and said we were going to Guam and Saipan to work with some of the Department of Defense teachers. On my return flight, I would be stopping in Hawaii to work as well.

It was on this particular trip that I became familiar with the temporal peculiarities of international travel, particularly as they apply to the International Date Line (IDL).[56]

---

56 The International Date Line (IDL) is an imaginary line of demarcation on the surface of the Earth that runs from the North Pole to the South Pole and demarcates the change of one calendar day to the next. It passes through the middle of the Pacific Ocean, roughly following the 180 ° line of longitude but deviating to pass around some territories and island groups.

Marguerite would be flying to Guam from New York and I would be flying from Seattle. We wanted to dine together at the Hyatt on Sunday evening, February 11th, to plan our three days of work in greater detail. We would have our first appointment on Monday, February 12th.

That meant I'd have to depart Seattle on Saturday morning, February 10th, because I'd be crossing the International Date Line— where it was already February 11th. It takes a bit of mental gymnastics to wrestle with the IDL. When traveling west across the IDL, today instantaneously becomes tomorrow. When traveling east across the IDL, today instantaneously becomes yesterday. Understand?

When I landed at Guam International Airport, a sign prominently declared, "Where America's Day Begins." *No kidding,* I thought. *I lost a whole day—basically my whole weekend—to fly here. I left Saturday morning and arrived Sunday evening.*

On its face, the trip was actually quite simple. Seattle to Honolulu: six hours. One hour layover. Honolulu to Guam: eight hours. See? Simple.

I wish. Reality demands I pay attention to time zones and other time-related issues. My trip looked more like this:

1. Depart Seattle for Honolulu at 9:00 a.m. PST.
2. Fly for six hours and arrive in Honolulu. Honolulu Time is two hours earlier than West Coast Pacific Time, so the clock insists it only took me four hours to get to Honolulu. *It doesn't matter what your body is telling you,* says the clock, *it is 1:00 p.m. here in the Aloha State. So there.* When Seattle is on Daylight Time, the time difference is three hours.
3. Spend an hour waiting for the connecting flight to Guam. No beach time, I'm afraid.
4. Depart Honolulu for Guam at 2:00 p.m.
5. Fly for eight hours and arrive in Guam. The Guam clock is as perverse as the Honolulu clock. My body is arguing that it ought to be midnight, but the Guam clock disputes that. It

snidely informs me, *It's only 6:00 p.m. here where America's day begins. Guam's time is four hours earlier than Honolulu. So it only took you four hours to get to Guam.*

6. My body tells me I've been traveling for 15 hours. I left at 9:00 a.m. Add 15 hours and you end up at midnight. All the clocks are conspiring against me. *It's only nine hours since you left Seattle, not fifteen,* the clock says. There's that snide tone again. My imagination argues with the clock that this was the longest nine hours I'd ever spent. The clock ignores my imagination.

7. Even worse, the calendar is in cahoots with the clocks. *It's NOT 6:00 p.m. Saturday evening, as you'd hoped, but it is, in fact, 6:00 p.m. Sunday evening. Nyeh, nyeh, nyeh.* My entire weekend. Gone! Curse you, International Date Line!

Needless to say, I never had any of these problems when I was in the classroom. My clocks and calendars never leapt forward or backward. Time never stood still, but it never did somersaults either.

So I arrived in Guam at 6:00 p.m. ready for a soft bed and a pillow, but the clock said, *Not so fast.* Marguerite's plight was even greater than mine. Her flight had come even further—the first leg from New York to Honolulu took just under ten hours—and when we met for dinner that evening, it was with one eye shut.

Desperately jet-lagged—the medical name is *circadian dysrhythmia*—I found it ironic that I'd done nothing but sit on an airplane the entire weekend, and I was still exhausted. *Doing nothing is exhausting,* I thought. So the next day, when one of the social studies teachers with whom I was working told me that Magellan had landed on Guam on March 6, 1521, I instantly remarked, "I bet he didn't know what time it was when he stepped ashore, either." He gave me the strangest look.

My mental acuity improved as the week progressed and my jet lag abated. We flew north to Saipan and, while there, we visited one of those tragically unforgettable places—"Suicide Cliff." "Suicide Cliff," and nearby "Banzai Cliff," earned their names during the Battle of Saipan (June 15 to July 9, 1944). During the battle, more than 1,000 Japanese civilians and soldiers jumped to their deaths because they feared the "American devils raping and devouring Japanese women and children."[57]

All Marguerite or I could do was peer over the edge of the cliffs and watch the Pacific breakers crashing against the rocks far below... and imagine the horror half a century earlier. Apparently families intending suicide lined up youngest to oldest. The youngest was pushed over the edge by the next oldest until the mother pushed the oldest child. The father pushed the mother, and then the father ran backwards off the cliff, tumbling to his death and joining his family.

I wept as we stood there. Such tragedy amidst such beauty. It all felt surreal. As we looked beyond where we stood, all we could see were the peaceful waters of the blue Pacific stretching to the horizon.

We finished our work on Guam by mid-day Wednesday, and I was scheduled to fly to Hawaii via Japan's Kansai international Airport late that afternoon. I'd be spending 12½ hours in the air and slightly more than an hour waiting for my connecting flight in Japan. Traveling for that long a period requires mental preparation. However, the benefits of flying first class certainly decreased my need for mental preparation.

The most salient reason for getting mentally prepared was this: I would be departing Guam for Japan at 4:00 p.m. on Wednesday, February 14th. Valentine's Day. Fourteen hours later, I'd be arriving in Honolulu, Hawaii, at 10:00 a.m. on Wednesday, February 14th. A second Valentine's Day.

Mental preparation is always required when you arrive before you leave. It's a genuine H.G. Wells moment.[58]

---

57 Jennifer F. McKinnon; Toni L. Carrell (7 August 2015). Underwater Archeology of a Pacific Battlefield: The WWII Battle of Saipan.
58 My reference is to H.G. Well's book, *The Time Machine*.

It was morning in Hawaii, and my only scheduled appointment that day was a three o'clock visit with Honolulu's language arts curriculum director. I had lots of time.

Shortly after landing in Honolulu, I called my boss in Columbus, Ohio. It was late in the day there—approaching 5:00 p.m.—and I called to complain in a good-natured way.

"Hi, John," Steve said. "Where are you?"

"I'm in Hawaii, Steve, and I have a complaint." He probably didn't take me seriously because I was laughing as I spoke.

"Nobody ever has a complaint when they're in Hawaii," Steve assured me.

"Well, this is probably the strangest complaint I'll ever have," I said.

"Alright, what seems to be the problem?"

"Okay, Steve. Here it is. I lost my entire weekend when I flew to Guam. But that's not my complaint. I worked in Guam yesterday, and I'm working in Hawaii today. That means I'm working two Wednesdays this week. And I'm only getting paid for one."

"Two Wednesdays?"

"Yep. After working in Guam yesterday, I crossed the International Dateline last night in order to work in Hawaii today. So this week I'm working two Wednesdays."

"Amazing. Did you do better on the second Wednesday than you did on the first?" Clearly, he was pulling my leg.

"Shouldn't I get paid for two Wednesdays?"

"Didn't you say you're in Hawaii?"

"Yeah," I said, wondering where he was headed.

"When you're in Hawaii, Wednesdays don't count." I could hear him laughing. "Listen, John, you have my permission to take tomorrow off and go to the beach, okay?"

"But I'm scheduled to fly home tomorrow morning," I said with disappointment in my voice.

"Well, change your flight, John. Stay an extra day. I'll approve your expenses. How does that sound?" Steve asked.

He's the boss, I thought. "Sounds great, Steve. Really. That sounds wonderful. Thank you."

"See, I'm giving you your Wednesday back."

It did sound great. I traded my repatriated Wednesday for a Thursday, and stayed the extra day, taking the opportunity to go to the beach in Hawaii. Finally.

Opportunities—whether for fun or for sales success—often arise quite unexpectedly. Perhaps the strangest and most unusual sales opportunity I've ever had arose when I was working a literature campaign in Duval County—Jacksonville, Florida.

To make sense of what I'm about to relate, it's probably useful to know how schools are organized in Florida. Florida is one of those states that organizes all its schools by county, meaning all of Duval County is one school district. As a resident of Washington State, I'm far more accustomed to greater de-centralization. For instance, in King County, my home and the county that includes Seattle, there are at least nineteen school districts. Throughout Washington there are 294 school districts in 39 counties serving 1.06 million students. Contrast that with Florida's 67 county-wide school districts serving 2.63 million students.

Why is any of this important? In a nutshell, winning the business in almost any Florida county means a huge financial windfall. That's why all textbook publishers worked so diligently to win the business in Florida counties. Winning was very important, and the key to winning was knowing how to present one's books while selling against the competition. Selling against the competition was easiest if we knew what the competition was saying about us.

On this particular Tuesday, I was scheduled to present to the Duval County Literature Evaluation Committee just after lunch. We were the last of three publishers on the committee's presentation schedule—always a good thing—but we were scheduled just after lunch—probably not a good thing. The post-lunch malaise, some-thing all teachers have seen in their students, often makes concentra-tion difficult. Post-lunch presenters have to work extra hard to keep their listeners focused.

Knowing I wasn't presenting until after lunch meant I could spend a leisurely morning. Or so I thought. About 8:15 a.m., Steve Olsen, Prentice Hall's Florida manager, knocked on my hotel room door.

I could tell he was excited by the way he swept past me into my room. He walked directly to my television.

"Whatta ya watching?" he asked.

"The morning news. Why?"

Steve was looking everywhere. "Where's your remote?" he asked. He looked right at me and repeated himself. "Where's your remote?"

I found it next to my pillow and tossed it to him.

"What's going on?"

"Wait'll you see what's on TV," he said, pointing the remote and changing the channel. "You aren't going to believe this."

I was sitting on the edge of the bed. Steve sat down beside me.

"Watch," he said. "Just watch." He turned up the volume.

A dark-haired woman in a business suit was calmly talking, stand-ing in front of some tall bookshelves. *Perhaps it's a library,* I thought. She wasn't talking to the camera the way professional broadcasters do, instead she was holding an open book against her chest as she spoke—the pages facing outward as if she were showing them to some-body. Suddenly I recognized the woman, and I knew immediately what she was doing. She was a consultant for one of our competitors, and she was pointing out important features in her textbook. I was watching her literature presentation to the Duval County Evaluation Committee, broadcast live as a public service to the community.

"Is this what I think...?"

"Damn right it is. They're about fifteen minutes in, John, but we can see and hear exactly what the evaluators are seeing and hearing. I don't believe it. We've got to watch and take notes. We may never get another opportunity like this ever again."

He shoved several pieces of paper and a pen into my hands.

"Write. Take notes. This is unbelievable."

I can't ever remember seeing Steve so excited. Imagine. Both our principle competitors were presenting to the evaluation committee—back-to-back with a half-hour break—and we had a ringside seat.

I felt like a spy. For the next three hours I listened and took notes... and listened some more and took more notes. I kept circling those things our competitors said they did better than our program—and I knew they didn't. I kept circling assertions they made that I knew simply weren't so. I was enthralled by how they would promote their own program while selling against their competitors—including us. That bugged me because what they suggested was both false and smarmy. For instance, the first presenter said, "One program doesn't offer any leveled writing prompts. I think you'll be hearing from them after lunch. You may want to come back to listen to them."

That was us. And this presenter knew better.

As I said: False and smarmy. I became genuinely upset, and I started to say something to Steve. "Shush, John," said Steve. "Save it up and tell the committee the truth when we get our chance after lunch. Use all the ammunition they're giving you."

At one point, my notes were a litany of our competitors saying, "They don't do this" and "They don't do that." I kept yelling at the television, "Yes, we do, damn it. Yes, we do," and Steve kept calming me down.

"Don't worry, John, we'll get our chance."

Then we got our chance.

As the committee members gathered in the curriculum library after lunch for our presentation, I made sure I met each of them individually and thanked them for coming.

Steve Olsen, the Florida manager, thanked the committee for their dedication, and then turned the presentation over to me. As he walked toward me—his back to the committee—he winked, smiled, and whispered, "Go get'em."

Anyone who trains presenters always says a presenter's first words are critical. Before I begin, I always look at everyone, take a deep breath, smile, and then begin.

I looked. I breathed. I smiled.

"When you leave here an hour from now, you'll know why Prentice Hall's *Timeless Voices, Timeless Themes* is the best literature program you can select for the students of Duval County. Be advised, it's not the best program simply because I say so. I confess. I'm an extremely biased person. Of course, I'm going to say we are the best."

They laughed.

"I know *Timeless Voices, Timeless Themes* is the best program because our competitors seem to talk about us as much as they talk about their own program. So, today, I'm going to take a slightly different approach to our program."

That was true. This whole presentation was new—even improvisational.

"I'd like to ask all of you who took notes this morning to take out those notes and see if you wrote any of these things down. I herewith offer you a list of the things that our competitors are sure we don't do…or don't do very well."

I pulled out my summary compiled during my morning of television watching.

"Raise your hand if you heard any of these things."

I read my list of competitive attacks, and hands went up, again and again.

"Well, I beg to differ…regardless of being biased in these matters. I am here to say, it ain't so."

Again, laughter.

"Let me show you why I differ with the evaluations of our program by some very good folks—the folks you heard from this morning. They're tasked with selling some very good, but completely different programs. Fortunately for us, their programs are not as good as ours."

I could only hope my competitors weren't back at their hotels watching TV.

Our competitors had pummeled us all morning, and now it was

time to punch back—using our program. Point by point, I rebutted their insinuations that we were somehow inferior—and I could see the committee members rallying to our side as we looked at direct evidence in *Timeless Voices, Timeless Themes*.

"Keep in mind," I said, "when our competitors say negative things about us, they're not lying, they're selling." I looked at each member of the committee. "The programs you heard from this morning are not bad programs. In fact, there are no bad programs on the Florida adoption list. But since we are all English teachers who understand the comparative and superlative degrees, let us remember that there is good, there is better, and there is best. And there can only be one best. *Timeless Voices, Timeless Themes* is the best."

That day, I seized the opportunity to watch television, because apparently there's some really informative television on in the early morning, at least in Jacksonville, Florida.

Who knew?

P is for Prayer

Under certain circumstances,
profanity provides a relief denied even to prayer.
—Mark Twain

Dear Jesus, do something.
—Vladimir Nabokov, Pale Fire

I'VE NEVER BEEN afraid to fly.

When considering speed and distance, no form of travel is safer than air travel. When it comes to traveling safely, air travel is a statistical slam dunk. Consider: more than 8,000,000 people fly each day.[59] And virtually nobody dies.

In 2015, 136 people died in accidental airline crashes, down from the 641 who died the year before (2014). Using those figures, I computed the odds of being killed in an air disaster in any year are about one in fifteen million, but truthfully, that means the odds of dying approach zero.

True, one in fifteen million is not zero, but it is close. And reason enough to put fear of flying far down on my boogie-man list. Not everyone feels that way, however.

---

59 Statistics from 2015. If 8,000,000+ is the daily average that means almost three billion travel every year.

Nearer My God to Thee

In the summer of 2003, my daughter Amanda was getting married in Washington State. More than a dozen relatives lived on the East Coast, mostly Pennsylvania and New Jersey, and Amanda's July 12th wedding was here on the West Coast—3,000 miles away. For most of them, flying to Seattle would be more than an inconvenience. It would be a financial hardship as well, and I was the guy "with more frequent flyer miles than you can shake a stick at." Or so said my Mom. So I called each invitee and said I'd be happy to get them an airline ticket—using my frequent flyer miles—if they decided they'd like to attend Mandy's wedding. All fifteen invitees said, "You betcha!" including my Aunt Frances.

Toward the end of June, my 80-year-old Aunt Frances called me because her worries were outflanking her confidence about launching herself into the sky. During her entire lifetime, Aunt Frances had never ridden in an airplane. Not once.

Actually, it was her son, Dennis, who called me, and I could hear the urgency in his voice.

"John, Mom is having second thoughts about flying. She's talking about backing out. Do you think you could talk to her?"

"Sure, Dennis, sure. Put her on."

"John?" Aunt Frances began. Silence filled the next few moments as she composed her thoughts.

"John, I'm wonderin' if I shouldn't just not come to the weddin'."
I loved the way Aunt Frances could tie knots in the English language. Frances was everyone's favorite aunt—"the aunt with a heart of gold."

"Aunt Frances, Mandy is really looking forward to your coming."
I wondered if she could hear the hope in my voice.

"I know she is. That's the God's honest truth. And I've been hopin' to see Seattle and the Space Needle…" Her voice settled into silence. Then she quietly confessed, "I've never been west of Pittsburgh."

"So why are you having second thoughts?" I asked.

After a fairly lengthy silence, she spoke. "Do you think it's safe,

John? Aren't you ever frightened when you fly?"

I knew what she meant, but no, I've never been afraid to fly.[60] My father, a World War II bomber pilot, loved flying, and his enthusiasm had infected me. I once asked my father, "What makes airplanes fly?"

He looked up from the Horatio Hornblower novel[61] he was reading, looked me right in the eye, and offered me a quick, comic, and comforting reply. "Physics, son. Physics makes airplanes fly." He flashed me a quick smile and returned to his reading. He had a knack for cutting to the quick.

I'll admit to being a pragmatist. I throw the light switch without understanding anything about how electricity works or why, and I've spent a lifetime boarding airplanes confident in the knowledge that the laws of physics would keep me safely aloft. Unfortunately, I didn't think telling Frances that "physics" kept airplanes in the air would assuage her fears.

"Aunt Francis, how many times have I come to visit you over the past twenty-five years?"

"Gosh," she said, "I couldn't say for certain. I must see you a couple of times every year when you visit Emma." Emma was her older sister, my mother-in-law. "'Course you come in every summer, too."

"That's right, Frances. And every time I've come to visit, I arrive by plane. And do you know why?"

I think she was stumped.

"No...I don't believe I can say why."

"Because it's too far to walk," I said in a teasing tone. I waited for her reaction.

"You're making a joke aren't you," she said. "You think I'm being silly."

Note to self: don't tease Aunt Frances about her fear of flying.

---

60 There have been moments, while flying, when I've been afraid. But I'm not afraid to fly. See the last story in this chapter.

61 Horatio Hornblower was author C S Forester's famous seafaring hero. Forester wrote eleven books as part of the Hornblower Saga, the earliest one written in 1937 and the last volume written in 1967. My father loved them all.

"No, Frances, I don't think you're being silly. But let me tell you two things that I hope will help you get on that plane to come to Mandy's wedding."

Aunt Frances was a gentle soul, and a willing and attentive listener. I once said that she'd probably give the devil an audience if he asked for one. I could tell she was waiting for me to speak.

"First, every plane I have ever flown on has taken off and landed safely. No exceptions. Every one. And second, you'll see God's creation in such a different way when your plane is up in the air at 30,000 feet. Up to this moment, nothing in your life can prepare you for the wonders you'll see when you are flying higher than the birds, above the mountaintops, and above the clouds. That's why I got you a window seat. It's beautiful beyond words, and I want you to experience that firsthand."

I worried that I'd pushed too hard, but I knew playing the God card might influence her decision. I spent my life on the road selling books—and I knew instantly that I was using God to sell Frances—but I also knew I was selling her the truth. The world *is* a beautiful place from 30,000 feet.

"Okay, John." I could tell she'd actually made her decision. "Okay. Tell Mandy that I can't wait to see her in white. I know she'll be a beautiful bride. Tell her that."

Frances flew to Seattle for the wedding, and I picked her up at the airport. For the next week, her ecstatic exclamations—"I can't believe how beautiful the clouds are from the other side!" and "They gave me a soda, and I put it on the table, and nothing spilled!" –endeared her to everyone she met. When she returned home to Pennsylvania, she told her son that she believed that her trip west was the best trip she'd ever taken, and that she was looking forward to her next flight. Mandy's wedding trip not only cured her fear of flying, it opened up destinations she'd never dreamed of. Till now.

Madonna of the Skies

I can't say if Aunt Frances said a prayer as she boarded her plane, but over the years, I've watched my share of white-knuckle passengers who rely heavily on divine intervention. I remember once seeing a passenger with a dimpled bruise across the back of her hand. I found it curious, but later realized the bruise resulted from a rosary being wrapped too tightly. I've seen passengers with bibles in hand and solemn looks on their faces. For these folks, their fear is palpable and real. So they pray, hoping God will keep them aloft.

That thought—God will keep us aloft—occurred to me on one United Airlines flight between San Francisco and Chicago. After the usual boarding hubbub—the "hellos", the get-it-in-the-overhead-bin ballet, the "sorry about that's" and the "excuse me's"—I found myself sitting beside a very quiet, well-dressed woman. She wore a dark blue suit and a black pillbox hat that transported me back to the 1960s. I soon discovered I was sitting beside the wife of the Polish consul. Her husband occupied the aisle seat while I had my preferred window seat.

Shortly before we pushed back, her husband leaned forward, introduced himself and his wife Irena, and explained that Irena spoke very little English. Even as he told me this, Irena smiled that open but empty smile that says, "I don't understand a word you're saying...but I don't bite."

I smiled back at Irena and shook my head. We were a matched pair. She spoke no English, and I spoke no Polish.

As the plane pushed back from the gate and the flight attendant revealed the mysteries of the modern seat belt, Irena reached into her bag that she had stowed beneath the seat in front of her. A moment later, she sat back, clutching an eight-inch, carved wooden Madonna in her lap. There was no mistaking what it was. And I could also see that Irena was deep in silent prayer, head bowed, eyes closed, both hands wrapped tightly around Mother Mary. The term "white-knuckle" flyer suited her perfectly. Apparently, on this trip, God could relax because his mother would keep us aloft.

We taxied to our runway as the voice of the pilot on the intercom interrupted her prayer. "Good morning everyone. We are now number two for take-off. Will the flight attendants please be seated."

The plane turned, lined up for takeoff, and the roar of the engines filled the cabin. A quick sideways glance showed me Irena strangling her Madonna. Her prayers flew heavenward as we raced down the runway. Suddenly the jouncing of the ground-bound plane vanished as we took to the air. Moving heavenward above the San Francisco skyline, I watched Irena's tension dissolve. Just as quickly, Irena leaned forward and replaced her miraculous Madonna in her stowed bag. When she sat back, she wore a smile of pure relief.

Dare I say that the entire trip was routine? Nothing of consequence happened. Let me rephrase. The only thing of consequence is that we all arrived safely in Chicago. Ray, my son-in-law who pilots for Kenmore Air, a Seattle-based floatplane service, once said that being a pilot is hours and hours of tedium occasionally interrupted by a few seconds of sheer terror. That's doubtless true for passengers, too.

As we flew to Chicago, I read my book, or watched the world pass beneath us, just as I had countless times before. When the flight attendants performed their about-to-land ritual—"Please return your seats and tray tables to their full upright and locked positions"—Irena leaned forward and retrieved her Madonna. She reprised her take-off behavior until we were safely taxiing to the gate.

A colleague of mine once jokingly said that the reason I hadn't died in a fiery airplane wreck during my millions of miles circling the earth was because every plane had an Irena, clutching a Madonna, or a rosary, or a St. Christopher's medal, while frantically praying for divine intervention.

Maybe she was right.

I used to believe in the power of prayer.

When I began flying almost every week in 1988, I was a dyed-in-the-wool Catholic. Mass every week. The occasional confession. Prayer before meals—meals at home anyway. During the 1980s, I was an active parishioner at Our Lady of the Lake parish in Seattle.

The story of my Catholicism is hardly unique. I was born Catholic. Attended twelve years of Catholic school. Served as an altar boy. Had a "near seminary" experience at the end of eighth grade. Got married in the Catholic Church. Had all four of my children baptized in the Catholic Church.

Typical. That's what Catholics do.

Being Catholic disposed me to praying whenever a problem arose because prayer was the solution to everything. I mean everything. And traveling is a synonym for problems, as almost all road warriors will attest.

When planes are late…say a prayer.

When the weather won't cooperate…say a prayer.

When cars break down…say a prayer.

When hotel rooms have ants…or lizards…or roaches…or other guests who dislike you opening their door with another key when they are already occupying the room…say a prayer.

For Catholics, prayer is the automatic reflex. The universal solvent.

(In the interest of full disclosure, I am no longer a Catholic. I'm a dyed-in-the-wool atheist…if atheists are ever dyed-in-the-wool.)

As I said, problems and traveling are intimate companions. In the spring of 1993, when I was still Catholic and had some faith that prayer could solve problems, I experienced a "weather hold" as I waited at Atlanta's Hartsfield International Airport for the Delta Connection to fly me into Roanoke, Virginia. Beginning my day in Seattle, I'd slept through another routine flight to Atlanta, and now I was only 358 air miles short of my destination. These kinds of delays are unpredictable: some end with everyone boarding the flight and heading out; some end in cancellations. If Delta cancelled, I could drive, but I'd be adding another 85 miles and seven hours to my trip, clear proof that mountains, rivers, and forests have a way of multiplying the miles and the hours for the groundlings. Gate announcements about the weather hold hinted at a massive thunderstorm stalled over a large swath of western Virginia. Bad news. As any traveler knows, thunderstorms and airplanes don't play nicely together.

The silver lining in this thunderstorm was that I felt none of the normal pressure to get to Roanoke. I was headed to the wedding of my McGraw-Hill Publishing colleague, Melanie Leweke.[62] Melanie's nuptials were still two days off, so the pressure was off as well. Melanie had "retired" from consulting just a few months earlier because she decided that it would be next to impossible to start a family if she spent 180 nights out each year. Melanie was a science textbook consultant, and at her retirement luncheon, she correctly pointed out that the process of getting pregnant hadn't changed for quite some time, and she insisted that is was preferable to have the husband and wife in the same room at the same time if conception is the desired result.

She finished with a broad smile, "And that's why I'm now a *retired* science consultant." She emphasized "retired."

We all applauded her scientific judgment. The gracious offers from several irreverent consultants to help her with that pregnancy thing, if she decided to stay on the road, were gently and laughingly put aside.

First, however, she and Scott were going to be married, and I was now stuck in Atlanta with 90% of my trip complete—enduring the bane of all road warriors, *travelus interruptus*. No one knew if or when we might leave. Occasional announcements from Delta gate agents advised all passengers to remain close to the gate because the flight might be called at any time. I wasn't the only stranded passenger wearing a dubious look. What's the road warriors' favorite tune? *We've Heard That Song Before.*

Then they called our flight. Just like that. Everyone boarded the De Havilland Dash 8 without fanfare, and fifteen minutes later we

---

62 Melanie's last name is pronounced Le'-veh-key. I used to tease her that her name was actually pronounced [Lu-week'-ee] as if it rhymed with the word "squeaky." I've called her Squeaky Leweke ever since.

were airborne, on our way to Roanoke.

An hour later, as we descended through dense clouds to land in Roanoke, the massive thunderstorm that had stalled our trip in Atlanta announced that it hadn't left. Even the largest of planes avoid thunderstorms with their wicked updrafts and harrowing downdrafts. Experiencing turbulence can be frightening even when flying in the largest of commercial aircraft. Our De Havilland Dash 8 hardly qualified as large—and the bouncing and jouncing increased as we continued our descent.

The plane's PA system crackled to life. "This is your captain." The plane lurched hard to the left. "As you can see, it's still stormy here in the Roanoke area. So please remain seated with your seatbelts firmly fastened. We hope to be on the ground in a few minutes."

We hoped so, too. The erratic, unrelenting buffeting, up-down-and-sideways, reduced several passengers to tears. As we broke below the clouds, I glimpsed the runway landing lights off in the distance showing our pilots the way. My window streamed with the rain that still pelted the Roanoke area—and the airport. The turbulence never ceased, but just as it looked as if we were about to make our final approach, the pilot powered up the engines, trimmed the flaps, pulled up the wheels, and we ascended once again into the black clouds.

"This is your captain. We're going around to make another landing attempt. Please be sure you give your seatbelts an extra tug. I apologize for the turbulence."

As if it were his fault, I thought. I'd like to say that I wasn't frightened. But I can't. I cannot remember ever being as scared as I was that day when the thunderstorm threatened our aircraft. After 2,100 hours of fear-free flying, I was scared.

Being scared while flying was new for me. My Dad had been a World War II bomber pilot, and when air travel became part of my regular routine, I asked my Dad about its safety.

"Safest thing in the world," Dad said. "Pilots today have more training than pilots have ever had. They're ready for every possible contingency. Nobody's up there flying by the seat of their pants anymore. Don't ever forget that."

I was remembering my Dad's words when our plane lurched violently as we descended through the clouds. I hoped that our pilots were prepared for this thunderstorm contingency.

Again we broke below the clouds, and again, I caught sight of the runway lights. And again, our pilot aborted his approach, powering up and ascending into the ominous clouds. Our ascent only served to frighten us more, and one woman across the aisle wept openly. A passenger reached across the aisle and did her best to comfort her, but we all felt a rising wave of fear.

Two missed approaches. And the thunderstorm hadn't abated one bit.

"This is your captain. I know everyone's being knocked about back there, but please keep your seatbelts firmly buckled. We'll be landing on this approach."

As we broke below the black clouds for the third time, the fear was palpable. A passenger behind me offered a thought—perhaps a prayer?—that all of us were thinking. I'm sure everyone on board heard her voice, rising above the roar of the engines, above the sounds of the storm, and above our surging sense of panic.

"Oh Lord, let our pilot have thirty years' experience," she said.

From somewhere in the plane came an immediate reply. "After today."

Just two words—"after today"—and laughter filled the cabin. We all laughed because we all shared the same fear—and the same pilot.

Again I saw the runway lights outlining our path. We heard the loud *thunk!* as the landing gear locked into position. The noise of engine and storm unnerved us all as the plane violently rocked side-to-side. I watched and prayed, my nose pressed to the window as we approached the runway lights.

The approach seemed interminable. Then suddenly, it was over. We landed. Rather smoothly, I thought, under the conditions. The noise lessened—both the engine noise and the silent scream in our heads—as we taxied to the gate. As I surveyed the cabin, I saw several passengers crying with relief, their shoulders shaking. I believe we all felt a collective sense of safety and thankfulness.

I didn't know it then, but I would fly for another twenty-one years, and never again would I be that frightened aboard a plane.

I deplaned. The rain pelting my face felt good as I walked across the tarmac to the terminal. Through the rain, I heard my father reminding me, "Any landing you can walk away from is a good landing."

Since that day, I've always wondered if there wasn't someone aboard clutching a wooden Madonna.

Q is for Quiet

You want to be a writer?...Find a quiet place, use a humble pen.
—Paul Simon

THE TRAVEL WORLD is a noisy world.

Airport concourses are noisy spaces with their incessant PA announcements broadcasting in the background; thousands of shoes clicking, shuffling, scraping, and pounding along miles of corridors trailing rumbling wheeled luggage; the perpetual song of belts and beeps at security checkpoints; and the continuous stream of low-level noise coming from ubiquitous television monitors. We mustn't forget the non-stop hum of conversation, laughter, tears, coughs, wheezes, sneezes, and the occasional barking dog in the mix.

It's always amusing to see someone calmly snoozing amidst the chaos.

At some point, one leaves the noisy concourse and boards the plane. The plane pushes back, roars down the runway, and lifts off. Planes are noisy, too, despite Boeing's once-upon-a-time "whisper-jet" propaganda.[63] And anyone who has flown often enough knows the reality of "crying baby airlines."

Arrival means another noisy airport concourse, accentuated by the distinct thud and thunk of luggage dropping onto the baggage carousel even as reunions ring with happy shouts and laughter, amusing all of us who are simply standing and waiting for a familiar suitcase.

After checking into my hotel—usually the end of my travel day—I

---

63 "Whisper-jet" was a name given to Boeing 727s. [See: J is for Jumping Ship]

often craved the quiet. That's when I would sit quietly in my hotel room reading a book. No TV. No radio. No CD. Just the quiet. These days, the road warrior can find the quiet by the simple application of headphones, shielded from the diabolical decibel assault called the "outside world."

I suppose being a member of the "baby-boomer" generation helps me deal with noise. When I attended high school during the sixties, my mother would loudly lament that the Beatles were "Nothing but a bunch of noise." I'd always reply with an impertinent grin, "One man's noise is another man's music." My mother seldom agreed. Of course, I must confess I've offered the same "bunch of noise" verdict to my own children about grunge, rap, and hip-hop. I can only conclude that either my taste in music has failed to evolve, or I've turned into my mother. The jury is still out.

My mother, born in 1919, is still a living breathing aphorism. She apprises situations through the filter of her acquired folkloric wisdom, offering neat little nuggets of knowledge like "Don't speak unless you can improve upon the silence." She's always uttered these aphorisms as if they were indisputable truths, settled law.

My mother had good reason to make such pronouncements because no member of the Scannell family could ever be described as "a person of few words." I grew up in a family of talkers, each of us sure we could improve upon the silence. We were—and are—a noisy bunch. Not as bad as an airport concourse, but close. Holding the floor and getting words in edgewise were skills each of us carefully developed. My speaking ability certainly enabled me as a teacher, and served me well as a national textbook consultant. I laughed one afternoon when my middle-school daughter Amanda was asked by a teacher, "What kind of work does your father do?" Without missing a beat, Amanda said, "My daddy talks for a living."

Amidst all the talking I did in my careers, I developed a great appreciation for "the quiet."

A significant part of my life was spent in quiet discussion. As a textbook consultant, I chiefly explained the advantages of selecting my company's textbooks to committees of teachers—usually in a quiet comfortable setting. These presentations typically occurred in the late afternoon when all the students had gone for the day. I'd meet with teachers in a classroom, a school library, or a conference room in the school district's administrative offices. At this time of day, and in these places, the world was relatively quiet. Typically.

But this day, and this presentation, would prove atypical. On this gray, blustery January afternoon, I was selling literature textbooks in the East St. Louis School District in southwest Illinois. East St. Louis enjoys the company of the mighty Mississippi River which flows just west of the town.

The mid-West regional manager and I arrived at the school district offices just as we had been instructed, and the curriculum director's secretary walked with us to the presentation room in the rear of the building.

When you read the words "presentation room," what do you visualize? At minimum, I think floors, walls and ceilings. I might also think windows, but many interior rooms lack windows. I think furniture—probably tables and chairs—and maybe a bookcase or two. And I think lights—probably florescent—but I seldom think about lights in detail. After all, what are lights except the flick of a switch and voila!—let there be light!

Whatever you've just imagined as a presentation room, ignore it. This "room" was quite different.

The secretary unlocked the door to our presentation room, and without stepping inside herself, turned to us and said, "If you need anything, I'll be at my desk."

Ed and I walked into "the room." Our first impression was that the room was both chilly and quite bright. It was immediately apparent why.

Replace your imagined room with the reality of an unfinished space. The beige concrete floor had been poured, but neither linoleum nor carpet had yet been laid. The walls were simply wooden studs—no drywall. Worse, there was no exterior wall—no brick siding, no wooden siding—to keep the winter at bay. Nor was there any insulation between the studs. The room was under construction. And chilly.

Ed and I could see all the plumbing and the insulated electric wires running horizontally around the room ending in outlets screwed into the vertical studs. Above our heads, there were wooden joists without any ceiling tiles or florescent lights. There was no roof—nor anything that anyone could call a roof. Instead, the entire room was encased?—surrounded?—covered?—you can see I'm struggling for the right word—in a translucent, thick-mil plastic sheeting.

"Looks like we've just stepped outside," I said to Ed as we moved toward the center of the room.

"I'm not big on camping out in the middle of the winter," Ed responded. "Do you think we have enough light in here?"

"Plenty of light, but not much heat," I said. We stood there in our overcoats and gloves and debated whether we should remain dressed as we were. A mid-January light poured in directly through the plastic-covered ceilings and walls.

"Don't you love rooms with natural light?" Ed asked. It was a rhetorical question. About twenty student desks were scattered about the room in no particular order, and standing in the exact center of the room stood an eight-foot tall, metal monstrosity.

"What the hell is that?" I asked Ed.

He walked around the "monstrosity," bending and looking, and placing his hands against the metal monolith. "This is just what we've been looking for," he said. "It's a giant space heater. And here's the 'on' switch."

Immediately the "monstrosity" began to hum. Thirty seconds later, it began blasting hot air from four huge ducts—each duct was situated at a different height from the floor and each pointed in a different compass direction. Clearly, this monstrosity was intended to heat the entire room from floor to ceiling.

When I say "blasted," I am not exaggerating. The noise from the monstrosity obliterated all sound and all thought. It was like standing next to a jet engine—in this case, four jet engines—as the heater filled the room with thunder and hot air. After five minutes of deafening noise, the heater fell silent. The room was now bright and warm, but the temperature fell rapidly because the plastic sheeting provided scant insulation against the January winter outside.

Ed and I had come early to prepare for our literature presentation, and as I began to set up my computer and projector, Ed left our inside-outside-nowhere-near-finished room to talk to the secretary who had said we should see her if we needed anything. What we needed was a room. Ed returned and reported simply, "Looks like this is where we're presenting."

"Honest to God?"

"Honest to God."

No sooner had he confirmed the bad news, when the "monstrosity" kicked on full blast again, loudly laboring to return the room to a temperature "fit for human habitation." We stepped outside the room to avoid the conversation-cancelling noise, to decide on a plan for that afternoon.

"We have an hour for our presentation," Ed said.

"Come on, Ed. Would you want to sit in that room for an hour?" I asked. It was a rhetorical question. "I wouldn't. Jesus, who can even think in there?"

"So what do you propose?" Ed asked.

"It appears the space heater kicks on whenever the temperature drops below a certain point. I'm sure it has a thermostat that regulates its on/off cycles. I'm guessing it's on for about five minutes and then off for five. We should get in there and time the on/off cycles, because I don't plan to spend an hour with that damn contraption, and I'm not torturing the teachers with it either. When it's on, no one can hear anything. Let's be sure about the timing."

For the next twenty minutes we timed the on/off cycles of the monstrosity. It was almost five minutes of mind-boggling noise followed by five minutes of sweet silence. We decided that after the teachers had assembled, we wouldn't begin until after the machine quieted down. Then I'd speak for five minutes, and tell the teachers what I'd like them to review during the five noisy minutes which were sure to follow. At the end of the third talk cycle—talk/noise, talk/noise, talk—I'd bid them "farewell and keep warm" just before the obnoxious monstrosity drowned me out. My standard one-hour presentation would become a fifteen-minute spiel—with some unexpected, noise-filled, textbook perusal time for the teachers. Anyone who wanted to remain for an additional five minutes, as the monstrosity bellowed its heating presence, would have my undivided attention--for about five minutes.

As I said, traveling is a noisy business. Presentations, on the other hand, were designed to be quiet, except for those moments when I managed to evoke various verbal and non-verbal responses—oohs and aahs, laughter, head nods, and questions. If there was to be "noise" during my presentations, I always hoped it would be when the teachers became visibly—and audibly—excited by something I'd shown them.

I never anticipated this monstrosity.

My Dad always told me I should, "Expect the unexpected," and today was the day when I would realize just how right he was.

At about 3:40, the teachers began arriving for the 4:00 p.m. literature presentation. There were fourteen English teachers on the committee—thirteen women and one man—and they came bundled up. Quilted jackets, knit caps, scarves, gloves, mittens, heavy slacks, and fur-lined boots. Bundled up as they were, several had to wedge themselves into the desks that Ed and I had moved into rows so I could see all their faces as I spoke. No one seemed inclined to remove any outer clothing.

As Ed and I watched our bundled-up teachers assemble, Ed said, "I think they've been here before."

"Do you think that maybe they're being punished for something?" I asked.

Ed shrugged.

As teachers arrived, Ed and I thanked them for coming and handed each a literature textbook appropriate to their grade level. There were moments when we felt like mimes because our noisy monstrosity drowned out any possible verbal communication.

In the midst of the monstrosity's roaring, and a bit before 4:00, the chairperson of the committee pushed out of her desk and handed me a note. "We are all here," the note said. "We can begin any time." She'd signed the note, "Rose."

I nodded at her and turned the note over and scribbled, "We'll start as soon as the noise stops, okay?" I signed my name, too. I walked to her and handed her my written response. Speaking was not an option. She read my note, mouthed the word, "Okay," and then circulated my note among her fellow committee members. There seemed to be agreement. We'd begin when the noise stopped.

Suddenly the room and the world fell silent. There is something palpable, something visceral, when loud noises cease. Tension dissipates, muscles relax, and rational thought returns. I could see they were all ready for my presentation.

"Thank you for coming," I said as quickly as I've ever said those words before. I wanted to be sincere, but I wanted to be fast. Time was of the essence. "I can see that you've all been here before." It was a lame attempt at humor, but being in that room was really no laughing matter.

"Here's my plan. I'm not going to use the whole hour." Faces brightened. "That damn monstrosity comes on every five minutes, runs for five minutes, and then is off for five minutes. I'm going to take three five-minute talking periods—three quiet periods like now—and when that monstrosity begins its third interruption, we'll be done.

Regardless of what I've said or haven't said, we'll be done. We'll have fifteen minutes for me to talk and ten minutes for you to peruse the tabbed books while that"—I pointed at the space heater—"that monstrosity bellows. How does that sound?"

Honest to God, there was applause. Muffled, of course, because clapping mittens don't make a lot of noise, but they were clapping. Simply knowing they wouldn't have to endure the unendurable racket for an hour energized them. I could see it in their eyes

"Okay, let's start. If you'll open your textbook to the first blue tab…" And away we went. Ed kept an eye on the time, giving me a thirty second heads-up before the space heater would roar into action. On his signal, I quickly told the teachers what I wanted them to review during the tumultuous interruption.

And so it went.

I talked until the monstrosity roared. When the monstrosity fell silent, I talked again…until the monstrosity roared…again.

Toward the end of my third five-minute period of uninterrupted silence I said, "That's it. If you have questions, I can answer them after Mr. Monstrosity settles down." I looked over at Ed wondering about the wisdom of what I was about to say. I looked back at the teachers. "I'm sorry you had to put up with this. This is an awful room, but you came anyway." I looked deliberately at each of them. "Thank you for coming. Please take our books home and study them," I paused for a moment, "in silence." Even as they began laughing at my parting remarks, the Monstrosity returned to full voice.

The East St. Louis monstrosity story was one of my oft-told tales, one that I invariably offered while training new consultants who had yet to learn about the noisy world of travel and the potentially even noisier world of textbook presentations. It was the quintessential way to explain my father's simple admonition: "Expect the unexpected," the corollary of which is "Be ready for anything."

My father was always a man capable of offering simple advice. Pithy advice. Wise advice. One of his maxims was, "Treat people with kindness." If my father had walked into that impossible presentation space with me, I know exactly what he would have said.

"Get these teachers out of here as quickly as you can."

My father was ever a wise man.[64]

---

64 We got the business. I used to tell fledgling consultants that "You are the company. When you walk into the room, you are *McGraw-Hill*. If you treat the teachers well, if you treat them respectfully and with kindness, they'll respect *McGraw-Hill*. They'll think, '*McGraw-Hill* hires good people.'" I hope that's what happened here.

R is for Rules

Any fool can make a rule, and any fool will mind it.
—Henry David Thoreau

Fear changes the rules.
—Kenneth Gable

WHEN I WAS a kid, there were some basic rules. Be home for supper. Say your prayers. Do your homework. Be nice to Mrs. Hillpot, a wizened, grumpy octogenarian who kept chickens in her backyard. There weren't a lot of rules.

Since my younger days, though, it feels as if all the rules have changed. Or perhaps the world has just become rule happy.

Once upon a time—in my younger days—bike riders weren't required to wear helmets. We just jumped on our bikes and pedaled away.

Once upon a time—in my younger days—mobs of hitchhiking kids could hop into the beds of pick-up trucks and get a ride to the local swimming pool or football game. My childhood was filled with free rides to wherever I was going. All I needed was my thumb. No one needed Uber.

Once upon a time—in my younger days—cars didn't have seat belts. Making out with one's girlfriend was much easier—once upon a time.

Once upon a time—even in my not-so-younger days—airline passengers weren't expected to show up two hours early. They could walk uninterrupted to their gates without worrying about their belt, their shoes, or that pair of scissors or can of soda in their purse. And their families could bid them farewell at the gate.

Once upon a time airline passengers weren't expected to go through a massive and sometimes intimate security search whenever they wanted to board a plane. They weren't expected to doff their jackets, empty their pockets, take off their shoes, or be frisked like common criminals.

Yep, once upon a time disrobing in public was discouraged,

Once upon a time...sounds like the beginning of a fairy tale, doesn't it?

Where There's Smoke

Once upon a time, airline passengers were permitted to smoke. Yes, smoke. While the plane was 30,000 feet above anywhere. Inflight smoking was quite fashionable. No rules forbade smoking. Nothing—and no one—prohibited anyone from lighting up.

But times changed. As cigarettes became increasingly vilified for their cancerous properties, many airlines offered designated smoking and non-smoking areas in deference to the growing numbers of non-smoking passengers. I always found the airlines' "solution"—non-smoking zones—to be an illusion. More accurately, it was a delusion, especially for those non-smoking passengers seated at the intersection of Smoking and Non-smoking. I guess those passengers were expected to stop breathing for the duration of the flight.[65]

Non-smoking areas in airliners were predicated on the fiction that once the smoke has escaped the lungs and mouth of the smoker, the smoke would simply stay put, like an obedient dog. It doesn't. Just try blowing some smoke into a tin can and hope it stays on the bottom. It won't. On a somewhat larger scale, airliners are very large tin

---

65 The U.S. ban on inflight smoking began with domestic flights of two hours or less in April 1988, extended to domestic flights of six hours or less in February 1990.

cans with air recirculation systems—and that includes recirculating the smoky air.

My weekly air travel schedule began around the same time that non-smoking regulations were implemented for U.S. domestic flights. The smoking prohibition commenced in April 1988, and I began traveling regularly three months later, in July 1988. Like many people, I'd flown prior to 1988, and had suffered the smoky fiction of the airlines' non-smoking area solution. But now—dare I say, finally?—new FAA non-smoking rules had been put in place. *Hallelujah!*

Those new FAA rules, however, were not universally loved, and the habitual smoker loathed them.

My first encounter with an unhappy smoker occurred while I was standing in line at the Delta Airlines counter at Sea-Tac International. It turned out to be the man immediately in front of me—a broad-shouldered gentleman—who did not strike me as anyone out of the ordinary. There was no sign across his back declaring: BEWARE: I'M A SMOKER. He was wearing a suit—so was I. Back in 1988 business people typically wore business attire when they traveled. Why not? Those were the days when no one was going to ask you to undress on the way to your plane. The check-in line constituted the only potential inconvenience and the longest wait that any of us might have to endure—except for using the bathroom on the plane.

A Delta agent motioned to Mr. Smoker that he was next, and he went to the counter.

I was close enough to hear their conversation—eavesdropping is one of a road warrior's genuine pleasures.

"I want a seat in the smoking section," he said.

"I'm afraid that's no longer possible, sir," she said in a tone both practiced and conciliatory. She wore an "I-understand" smile. Clearly, she had dealt with "I-gotta-smoke-on-the-airplane-or-I'll-die" customers before.

I watched as he grew increasingly agitated. He ran his hand through his neatly combed hair before he spoke again. He seemed confused.

"What do you mean, no longer possible?" His voice was polite but edgy.

The Delta agent looked down at his ticket to get his name. "Mr. Cummings, Delta is now smoke-free on all domestic flights. The entire aircraft is non-smoking."

He looked at her as if she'd slapped him.

"Since when? Come on. I'm a smoker for Christ's sake." I could hear the growing frustration in his voice. "Who came up with this stupid rule? I made this same trip in March, and I could smoke."

"That's correct, Mr. Cummings. The new FAA rules were put into effect in April. Since then all our flights are non-smoking." Her tone was even.

"I've always been able to smoke. It calms my nerves."

He pleaded as if his arguments would persuade her to magically create an on-board smoking area just for him. But they didn't.

"What am I supposed to do if I need a cigarette?" he blurted angrily. He made it sound as if smoking was his God-given constitutional right.

The patient agent behind the counter didn't answer his unanswerable question. Over the years, I've learned a great deal about positive human interactions by watching seasoned airline agents in action. They are experts in human psychology.

This seasoned Delta agent looked at Mr. Cummings, giving him a very parental, raised-eyebrow look—the look she'd give a child who had just asked, "But what if I don't want to go to school?"

She waited patiently, never averting her gaze, never speaking, letting her look work its magic. Mr. Cummings took a deep breath, ran his hand through his hair for the umpteenth time, and then mumbled, "I guess I won't be able to smoke, will I?"

She nodded. "Sorry, Mr. Cummings. I really am. I understand." She paused but only for a moment. "Now, let's find you a seat. Do you prefer window or aisle?"

This woman deserved a medal.

The Ruling Class

That was 1988.

The real rule changes began right after 9/11, and even for frequent flyers, it was difficult to keep up with the next evolution of security requirements. What we knew for certain was that TSA was the new ruling class—and they made the rules even when they had no class. Those rules seemed to perpetually change.

Road warriors saw these changes in real time. One week there was nothing, the next there were x-ray machines and scanners…and longer lines.[66] I remember when they first began using the x-ray machines to scan brief cases and any technology—computers, projectors, etc.—that passengers were carrying aboard.

Over more than twenty-five years of traveling, I checked my luggage rather than use carry-on. I realize many frequent flyers abhor checking luggage, and prefer carry-on only. Yes, they avoid the waiting at the baggage carousel at their destination, and, yes, their luggage is never misdirected, like mine once was when it vacationed in Florida while I froze my butt in a wintry Pittsburgh. But many all-carry-on folks tend to be "bin hogs," a pet peeve plaguing many frequent flyers. Ironically, "bin hogs" tend to aggravate each other the most. I only ever needed a small space for my technology—sometimes under the seat, sometimes in the overhead bin.

Checking clothing and toiletries is one thing, but I always kept my indispensable technology close at hand. They were my carry-on. I could undoubtedly make a sales presentation to teachers wearing a hotel bath towel, but I could never present without my technology. As a publishing consultant making group presentations, I always traveled with my laptop computer and my LED projector—and, of course, all the cords, power packs, and connecting cables that accompanied them.

That meant that every time I checked in for a flight, I'd have to take

---

66 The curse of airline travel is waiting, the feeling one is "wasting time" in one line while waiting for the next line.

my computer and my projector out of my roller-bag so they could be x-rayed when I passed through security. Anyone who has flown has seen these x-ray scanning machines at the security checkpoints. They're really just large boxes with a small rubberized conveyer belt running through them. Passengers are expected to place their belongings on that conveyer belt—the projector and the computer had to be taken out of the carry-on bag and scanned individually—and a technician seated behind the machine reviews images on a monitor. The x-rays are expected to reveal any forbidden items like guns and knives. Watching the never-ending parade of items and bags has to be a mind-numbing job.

On one trip, the security folks became inordinately concerned about a roll of quarters that I'd unthinkingly thrown into the bottom of my bag. They wondered, "Could that be a gun barrel?" After that I carried only loose change.

Needless to say, those of us who travel with expensive electronic equipment need it to be handled carefully—a fact not always appreciated by bored and overloaded security technicians.

I particularly remember one encounter at a checkpoint at LAX—Los Angeles International Airport. Instead of placing my computer and projector directly on the moving belt, each security area had plastic trays, much like your typical flat, low-lipped cafeteria tray. Following the example of people in front of me, I knew I was expected to put my electronics on those trays. That seemed reasonable.[67]

Just ahead of me in the security checkpoint line were three uniformed flight attendants. Unlike me, they had all carry-on, and each of them placed their pieces of luggage on the rollers leading to the conveyer belt. I imagine everyone knows how it works, but just in case...

---

67 These trays were the predecessors of the larger plastic bins that passengers now use. The large bins are better.

*Once on the conveyer belt, the luggage is scanned, the image
is viewed for forbidden items by the technician watching the
x-rayed images on a computer screen, and the conveyer belt
then pushes those items out the other side where they reach
another roller belt. After the individual owner of the luggage
walks through a metal detector—security scans both the luggage and passenger—luggage and passenger are happily reunited on the secure side of security.*

That's the way it's supposed to work. But as I said, boredom and
fatigue from endless, mindless repetition sometimes undermine the
"supposed to" part. That's what happened on this day at LAX.

The young female technician running the conveyer belt seemed
particularly off her game. The conveyer belt could be run slowly or
quickly depending on the technician watching the scanned images—and this young lady seemed to be in a hurry. The conveyer belt
seemed to be moving unusually fast, which is strange, especially if
you want to competently scan any of the items passing through.

Making matters worse, the three flight attendants in line in front
of me hadn't taken off their overcoats, even though they'd walked
through the metal detector without a problem. All their luggage was
waiting to be picked up from the roller belt on the secure side of the
x-ray machine—essentially clogging the exit—but the three flight attendants had been asked to come back through the metal detector,
remove their overcoats, and place them on the belt to be scanned.
In the meantime, my projector and computer were on trays being
scanned. I had just walked through the metal detector, when I noticed the young technician running the conveyer belt as if she were a
NASCAR driver.

Clearly when my computer and projector exited the x-ray machine on the racing conveyer belt, there would be no room on the
roller belt, currently clogged with the fight attendants' luggage. My
computer and projector were about to come flying out at me on those
low trays with no place to go. I imagined them colliding with the

luggage, or worse, falling and crashing to the floor.

"Stop!" I yelled. "Stop the belt!"

The young technician took her hand off the button that activated the conveyer belt. She glared at me. "Did you just yell at me?" she asked. Her voice overflowed with contempt.

"The belt's moving too fast," I complained. "I have some very expensive equipment here. You need to go more slowly. Please, go more slowly," I said, as I pulled the tray carrying my computer off the stopped conveyer.

She kept glaring at me as if my request to go slowly were pure insolence on my part. Her hand punched the "go" button and the conveyer resumed its breakneck pace. Standing there with my computer in one hand and the tray in the other, I tossed the tray along the metal top of the x-ray machine. It skidded and stopped about a foot from where she was seated. She released the button and the racing conveyer stopped, again.

She seemed startled. "Did you just throw that tray at me?" she demanded.

"I said please go slowly. Didn't I?" *What was she thinking? Hell, what was I thinking? Dammit, I'm in trouble.*

She stood up from her monitoring screen and yelled, "Security."

Yep. I'm in trouble.

I avoided looking at her as I gathered my projector and computer and slipped them into my luggage carrier. I began walking to my gate.

A tall, slender gentleman, wearing a jacket identifying him as "Security," came up from behind me as I walked to my departure gate.

I felt him walking to one side but ignored him, keeping my eyes straight ahead. From my right side I heard him say, "Sir, you need to come with me." His voice was very calm.

"No, sir," I heard myself reply, "I need to get to my gate." *Should I keep on walking? What if I keep on walking?* We continued walking side-by-side. I kept talking. "That young woman could have destroyed my equipment. That's my livelihood. She's running that x-ray belt at a hundred miles an hour, and people's belongings are crashing into stuff that hasn't been picked up. I asked her to stop and she ignored me. Deliberately ignored me. If you want to have a talk with someone, talk to her."

"She said you threw a tray at her."

"No, sir. Not true. If I'd thrown a tray at her, I would have hit her. I threw that tray to get her attention." *Isn't that a distinction without a difference?* "Saying please doesn't seem to work with her."

We continued walking side-by-side. And my heart was sinking.

And then he was gone.

I felt that great emotional release when you've been granted a huge favor. He could have made a federal case out of my tray throwing—literally, a federal case. But he didn't. Perhaps he saved us both unnecessary grief.

If the Shoe Fits

One quickly becomes accustomed to the TSA rules. *All metal in the tray. Take off your shoes.* And then someone throws a curveball.

I was waiting in line at one of the security checkpoints at Sea-Tac International, feeling self-assured because I knew the drill. The people around me who traveled infrequently needed lots of direction, but not me. During our slow wait in the security line, the woman in front of me admitted to being a novice flyer. I told her what she needed to do. Then she asked the TSA woman on the other side of the x-ray scanner, "Do I have to take off my shoes?" I expected the answer to be the TSA's typical mantra, "Please place your shoes in the bin for scanning."

But that's not what I heard. The TSA agent said, "You can leave your shoes on. Just step through the scanner, please." The young woman stepped through, glancing back at me and smiling.

Wow! That's new, I thought. *Last week, we had to remove our shoes, and this week we can leave them on.* As I stepped toward the scanner, I asked the TSA woman, "I can leave my shoes on?" She nodded and I passed through.

"If you'll please step over there, sir," she said to me as I moved to collect my computer and projector. She was directing me to some kind of "waiting pen" fifteen feet away. I'd lose sight of my electronic equipment which had already cleared the x-ray machine and waited on the roller belt.

"Okay, but I need to get my equipment," I insisted. My face surely registered confusion.

She spoke to me more sharply. "Your things must stay where they are. Please step over here."

"No. Not until I retrieve my equipment," I said.

"You can get your equipment after the search."

I didn't budge. "Sure, if it's still there."

"It'll be safe," she said. We were clearly at an *impasse*.

"Forgive me if I don't take your word for that. If something happens to my equipment nothing happens to you. That's my life on the belt. Nope. I'm getting my equipment."

I could see she was struggling with what to say next.

"Why do I have to go over there?" I asked.

"You didn't take off your shoes." Did I detect a scowl?

"What? You said I didn't have to take them off."

"No," she replied, "you asked if you could leave your shoes on."

There's that distinction without a difference again, I thought. My annoyance meter was registering bright red.

"Jesus," I said, "Are you a lawyer or an English teacher?" She didn't comprehend my sarcastic comment. "Why didn't you tell me I'd be subject to additional search if I kept my shoes on?"

"We're not permitted to tell you that."

"That's bullshit," I said. She wasn't pleased with my words or my tone. "I'm collecting my equipment before I go anywhere." I could feel myself beginning to shout. Now she wasn't pleased with my volume.

We'd just begun arguing when a supervisor arrived. I immediately pleaded my case with him. "This woman says I have to have another search because I kept my shoes on. I don't get it. I asked her if I could leave them on just like the woman in front of me did. She said yes. So I left them on. Now I'm being told you want to search me again… because I left my shoes on. She never asked the woman in front of me to step over for a second search."

"The search will only take a few moments," the supervisor assured me.

"I don't care about the search," I replied. "Search me all you want. I care about my equipment sitting there on the belt. I'm not going anywhere for another search until I have my equipment safe in my roller bag and next to me."

The supervisor looked at me, then looked at the TSA woman who'd taken issue with my size 10½ cordovan loafers remaining on my feet. He quickly decided what had to be done. "After you collect your things," he said to me, "please come over for that secondary search." Which I did.

I never left my shoes on again.[68]

On Closer Inspection

Yes, there are rules. And TSA folks are fond of barking them out—some less politely than others. *Stand here. Go there. Wait in that line. Not that line…that line. Take that jacket-hat-shoe off. Empty all your pockets. Place everything in the tray. Touch your toes. Touch your nose. Do the hokey pokey.*

Soon after the 9/11 attacks, I concluded that the TSA adopted a simple philosophy: the more people are inconvenienced, the safer they'll feel. It's largely an illusion, of course—that correlation between safety and inconvenience—but many travelers take some comfort in believing their government is protecting them. Remember Richard Reid, the Shoe Bomber? After he decided to pack his shoes with explosives on an international fight from Paris in December 2001, all airline travelers have been asked to remove their shoes to have them x-rayed.

---

68 That's not entirely true. Please see the last section entitled **PreCheck Saved My Life**.

And everyone dutifully obeys. Including me. I won't discuss the variety of dirty, crazy, hole-filled—did I mention smelly?—socks I've witnessed scuffling through security checkpoints, nor will I render my opinion of the numerous folks who wore no socks, walking barefoot through the checkpoint. Could there possibly be any germs?

Since I flew more than 45 weeks each year, and often several times in one week, you can imagine how concerned I became when the Underwear Bomber—a Nigerian named Umar, with an unpronounceable last name and plastic explosives in his underwear—attempted his own terrorist attack on Christmas Day 2009. What piece of clothing would I be expected to take off now?

Of course, the TSA must abide by certain rules as well, a fact I became particularly aware of one day in 2003 when I was flying Southwest Airlines from Oakland, California, to Phoenix. My midweek schedule had changed, so I was flying to my next destination on a one-way ticket purchased the night before. Apparently one-way tickets raise red-flags in TSA-land, as do tickets purchased the night before. Red-flags earn a passenger an even closer look.

As I checked in for my flight, I was told that my luggage had been selected for its own personal, in-depth inspection. That is, my bag would be taken to a small inspection kiosk, opened with me present, and its contents closely examined. All I could do was be slightly annoyed…and go to the kiosk with the young man tasked with inspecting my baggage. There were four unoccupied inspection kiosks—they looked just like library nooks—and the young TSA employee placed my suitcase in one.

With my luggage on the desktop, he turned to me, pointed to a chair a few feet away, and gruffly said, "Sit down."

"Excuse me?" I asked.

"Sit down," he repeated.

"You mean, 'Please sit down, sir,' don't you?

"What?"

"You asked me to sit down. I'm happy to sit down, but only when I'm treated with respect. So let's try this again. You say, 'Please sit down, sir,' and I'll sit. It's really quite simple."

He glared at me, clearly frustrated that I was making demands of him. The stare-down continued briefly with me adamantly standing beside him while he pointed at the chair. Finally he relented and said, "Please sit down, sir."

"Thank you," I said as I sat.

He turned and unzipped my suitcase. I could clearly see what he was doing—reaching into my bag, opening up my toiletry kit—and that's when I noticed that he wasn't wearing any latex gloves.

I stood up and approached him. "What are you doing?" I asked. "Why aren't you wearing gloves? Stop pawing through my things right now! Stop!"

After two years of obeying TSA edicts—no matter how unnecessary or pointless or gratuitous—I was now confronted by a TSA employee who wasn't following his own protocols.

My approach must have surprised him. All he said was, "I'm not done, yet. Sit down."

"Oh, you're done alright," I said. "Where are your gloves?" I asked again.

I think he began to say, "I don't need them." I'm not sure, because I interrupted him before he had a chance to finish his sentence.

"*You* may not need them, but I do," I shouted. I was angry. "God only knows where your hands have been. And now you're touching my clothes." I turned toward the distant check-in counter and bellowed that four-syllable word: "Security!"

In post-9/11 airports, few words garner attention more quickly.

In no time, a TSA supervisor arrived. "What's the problem, here?" he asked casting glances at both of us.

"This man was inspecting my luggage *without* wearing gloves," I said. "I may have to put up with additional searches, but I don't have to put up with that."

The senior TSA agent looked at his younger colleague and realized I was right. After a moment, he turned to me with an apology. "I'm sorry, sir, that shouldn't have happened." He turned back to his young cohort and said, "Please, zip up this gentleman's suitcase... now...and put gloves on before you do." The young man did as he was instructed.

"Thank you," I said.

"Again, I apologize. Have a good trip, sir."

I didn't reply. For thirteen years, from 1988 until 2001, travel had been a waiting game. After the September 11th attacks, however, travel morphed into an even longer, far more annoying and intrusive, waiting game. The rules had changed.

PreCheck Saved My Life

My traveling life improved immeasurably when various airlines invited their frequent flyers to be approved for PreCheck—a system that allows frequent flyers like me to walk through the security checkpoint with my shoes on, my jacket on—do I need to mention my underwear?—and all my electronic equipment still snugly encased in my roller-bag carry-on. With PreCheck, a lengthy process was reduced to moments. For PreCheck flyers, the rules were suspended.

I've laughingly referred to PreCheck as "The Good Guys Line" because everyone else was required to trek through "The Bad Guys Line"—because everyone was a suspected terrorist until reaching the other side of security. Everyone. Even my four-foot-eleven 95-year-old mother. No doubt she was the quintessential Bad Guy. After all, my dad used to say Mom could be "a holy terror." Maybe TSA was listening.

S is for Sideshow

*It can hardly be a coincidence that no language on earth
has ever produced the expression, "As pretty as an airport."*
—*Douglas Adams, The Long Dark Tea-Time of the Soul*

There is truly no other place bearing so much love as airports.
—*Ioana Cristina Casapu*

ROAD WARRIORS ARE privy to the amazing sideshow that is life—
particularly in public spaces like airports—and I have spent much of
my life in public spaces watching that sideshow. Airport concourses
are unique public spaces, because they afford an incredible range of
feelings and emotions for all to see. I frequently found myself watching the human parade of comings and goings, of new adventures and
happy returns, of tearful departures and triumphant arrivals.

I've watched celebrations as a passel of children unfurled a huge
"Welcome Home, Grandpa" banner painted with flowers and fire-
works. The youthful entourage cheered and jumped and hooted when
Grandpa made his appearance at the top of the escalator, and they
flooded toward him when he beamed his thousand-watt smile and
opened his arms. I could hear the poet Robert Browning[69] whisper,
"God is in his heaven. All's right with the world."

What a lucky man, I thought.

Airports are osculation central for those both coming and leaving.

---

69 Hearing apropos quotations is one of the benefits of having been an English
teacher. They bubble up unbidden to meet the particular occasion.

228

I've watched as lovers blew farewell kisses to one another, and as khaki-clad soldiers turned back for a final glimpse of loved ones before disappearing down the jetway. Once while waiting at a Delta gate in Cincinnati, I watched a young man fall to one knee and slip an engagement ring on the finger of a very surprised, but very happy, young lady. She screamed and cried and jumped into his arms and everyone waiting to board the plane broke into unbridled, spontaneous applause. As I watched and applauded, I thought I heard Robert Heinlein's voice reminding me "Love is that condition in which the happiness of another person is essential to your own."[70]

Yes, airport concourses are sideshows without peer. Every aspect of life is on display—from ennui to excitement; from fear to hope; from the ordinary to the amazing; from new beginnings to sad endings. Of course, every sideshow has its share of the comedic.

Two particular occasions at security checkpoints struck me as quite amusing. In one instance, a family was undergoing the routine search—take off all jackets, take off your shoes, empty your pockets—when one TSA person held up a small gym bag and asked, "Whose luggage is this?"

A youngster slowly raised his hand—he couldn't have been more than seven or eight years old—and Mr. TSA asked him to step over to a separate inspection station.

"Let's see what we have in here," Mr. TSA began, pulling out three t-shirts that had been wrapped around a large ceramic container of some kind. I looked over the shoulder of the woman in front of me.

"It's a piggy bank," she chuckled. "Kid's taking his bank with him."

As Mr. TSA handled the bright blue piggy, it slipped from his grasp and shattered on the airport's unforgiving tile floor. Mr. TSA had dropped the youngster's piggy bank and hundreds of quarters, nickels, dimes, and pennies bounced and rolled in every direction. Immediately, dozens of waiting passengers, at various stages of the security check-in process, jumped in to intercept the traveling coins, even as Mr. TSA commanded everyone to stay where they were. His

---

70 *Stranger in a Strange Land.*

commands were futile, comic…and ignored.

As the little boy was scooping up his scattered loot, a zip-lock bag appeared out of nowhere. All the coin-rescuers patiently lined up to return the recovered coins to the little boy. Handful after handful of coins tinkled into the bag, and he thanked everyone who had made the effort to retrieve his fortune.

In a few minutes, the boy and his bulging plastic bag had cleared security. As he walked away, he hoisted his bag and turned to wave to everyone who had helped. Everyone waved back.

Certain comedic moments are what we typically call embarrassing moments—and they are only comedic if they happen to someone else. If you spend enough time at airports, you'll witness the occasional embarrassing moment, usually ones that you'll happily relate to friends and relatives when you get home.

TSA rules may be partially, if not entirely, the reason for such funny, embarrassing moments. Let me explain.

The TSA rules for moving through the security checkpoint are remarkably simple: everyone is expected to take off their coats, take off their shoes, take off their hats, and empty their pockets. Oh, yes. They must take off their belts, too, if those belts have a metal buckle. It's a known fact that men wear belts because belts keep their pants from falling down. And it's also a known fact that, sometimes, removing one's belt facilitates the falling down of pants.

Several of my fellow consultants have speculated that the real reason the TSA has passengers remove their belts is for their own amusement. TSA security jobs must be suffused with monotony and tedium. Until someone's pants fall down to the embarrassment of one and the amusement of all.

Once when flying out of Denver International Airport, a young man—probably in his early twenties—removed his belt and put it in the bin for scanning with his other items, then walked to the scanning gate. When he raised both arms for scanning, his pants fell to the floor. It was the boxer shorts with Sesame Street's Big Bird on them that caught everyone's attention.

"Now there's something you don't see every day," the woman in front of me said. She turned and looked at me as I put my own belt in the bin. "I'm betting you don't wear Big Bird boxers," she said.

All I could do was smile. She was right. I've never been a boxer guy—and as for Big Bird—well, I think I'll offer one more thought.

I can't say if anyone has ever attempted to walk through the security checkpoint naked, an act that would seemingly be in compliance with all the TSA requirements. Such a person might be arrested for public lewdness, but it would be the local constabulary not the TSA that puts on the cuffs. I'm certain the TSA agent would simply say, "You're good. Thanks."

The third instance of sideshow comedy has much to do with human behavior.

When people act rudely or stupidly in public, they violate one of my mother's premier rules of conduct. *Don't make a spectacle of yourself!* It was one of my mother's favorite phrases. By contrast, my Dad's advice took the opposite tack. *Make us proud,* he'd say. Yin and yang.

It's true that rude people often inconvenience others, but they can also inconvenience themselves. Call it poetic justice. During one layover in Atlanta, the gate for my Charlotte, North Carolina, flight was just across the concourse from the departure gate for a Phoenix flight. I sat in one of those molded plastic chairs that face directly onto the broad pedestrian avenue alive with passengers going somewhere. Some were in a hurry, weaving in and out of the not-so-in-a-hurry folks who were ambling to their gates; some were struggling with bags or companions; and some were lost and surveying the overhead signs for help. There truly are few places as alive with human drama as airport concourses.

While I sat reading my book and amusing myself by watching the passers-by, I heard a boarding announcement from the Phoenix gate area. It was broadcast throughout concourse B.

"Delta Flight 1546 to Phoenix is looking for passengers Hackett, Steinkamp, and Zigner. Once again, that's passengers Hackett, Steinkamp, and Zigner. Please report to Gate B7 for an on-time departure."

The gate agent repeated the same announcement a few minutes later, and I watched as he walked to the middle of the concourse and looked both ways. Apparently, he didn't see "passengers Hackett, Steinkamp, and Zigner," and as he walked back to the gate, he shrugged his shoulders and motioned for his colleague to close the door to the jet bridge.

That's when the excitement began.

"Wait! Wait! Wait! Wait!"

From somewhere up the concourse, a voice shrieked one word. "Wait!" Shrieked it repeatedly, insistently, loudly. Everyone seated at my gate heard it, and every head turned toward the sight of three young women—perhaps forty yards distant—running down the concourse. Burdened with large purses and small roller bag carry-ons, they struggled toward their finish line: Gate B7.

I made a mental note: *Hackett, Steinkamp, and Zigner, I presume.* Dressed in brightly colored shorts and tank tops, they stumbled toward the gate agents who were standing in front of the now-closed jet bridge door. Two brunettes and a blonde, all in ponytails and large bracelets, arrived out of breath, clearly discombobulated, and clearly inebriated.

"Wait! We're here. We're here. That's our flight," the blonde said. "We're here." She looked over her shoulder to confirm that they were all there. All three stood there, swaying unsteadily.

I made a second mental note: *Hackett, Steinkamp, and Zigner, have knocked back a few stiff drinks, I presume.*

The male gate agent, possessing remarkable patience, asked one question. "May I see your boarding passes?"

The three women looked at one another.

The taller brunette turned to the blonde and loudly said, "You have the boarding passes."

"What?" The blonde seemed baffled and confused. "What boarding passes? Don't you have the boarding passes? I don't have the boarding passes." Everyone could hear the distress in her voice.

Another mental note: *That's the liquor talking, I presume.*

"Yes, you do. We gave all the boarding passes to you. After security. Remember? Are you too drunk to remember that? We gave you the goddamn boarding passes after security."

The blonde looked confused. "I don't remember you giving me the boarding passes!?"

The brunette was ready to blow. "Shit," she said.

Without warning, the brunette snatched the blonde's enormous purse and dumped its entire contents on the floor at the feet of the gate agent. She stood there shaking and shaking the purse.

"What the hell are you doing!" screamed the blonde.

"The boarding passes are in your goddamn purse!" screamed the brunette. "We gave all the boarding passes to you. What the hell did you do with them?"

The purse-dumping phase was followed immediately by the mutual pushing-one-another phase while the non-yelling second brunette dropped to her knees and commenced the find-the-boarding passes phase, sweeping her hands through a sea of loose change, perfume bottles, eyeliners, lotions, brushes, combs, Kleenex, and the amazing assortment of detritus that inhabited the blonde's purse.

The kneeling brunette added to the cacophony. "I can't find the boarding passes!" she screamed. "I can't find the boarding passes."

Still involved in the wobbly pushing match, the blonde pulled the brunette's suitcase-sized purse off her shoulder and dumped its contents on the already littered floor.

Another eruption of high-pitched yelling filled the concourse with the most un-lady-like language. Fifty feet of air cannot purify such angry epithets.

Additional mental notes: *Tit for tat. Hell hath no fury.*

The chaos at Gate B7, amidst a torrent of curse words and foul language, was strangely amusing. Two angry, drunken women were on the floor, frenetically searching through the spilled contents of two purses for the phantom boarding passes that would take them to Phoenix.

Sitting as we were, across the concourse from the unfolding drama, we had only moments to wait to find out how this melodrama would end. During all the dumping and shoving and screaming, three Delta agents had been summoned, and they politely but firmly insisted that the women accompany them to…well, none of us knew where. Someplace other than Gate B7.

"It's all your fault," the blonde screamed at the taller brunette as they were escorted up the concourse. "You just had to have a drink before we left, didn't ya? Just had to have a fuckin' drink, didn't ya?"

Fortunately, the Delta agents kept them all apart even if they couldn't keep them quiet. The loud, angry voices faded in a few moments, and all we knew was that they'd gone someplace else. As they departed, the two gate agents swiftly swept the purses' scattered contents back into one purse, and the male agent, purses in hand, went off in hot pursuit.

I traded glances with the waiting passengers seated around me. We were all smiling as if to say, *That's not something you see every day.* But even as I smiled, I could hear my mother admonishing me, *Don't make a spectacle of yourself.*

T is for Tragedy

There is a saying in Tibetan,
"Tragedy should be utilized as a source of strength."
—*Dalai Lama*

There are two tragedies in life. One is to lose your heart's desire.
The other is to gain it.
—*George Bernard Shaw*

I WAS SIX-YEARS-OLD when Hurricane Diane used the rampaging Delaware River to destroy the Northampton Street bridge that connected my hometown of Easton, Pennsylvania, to Philipsburg, New Jersey. I have a vague memory of the event. In that memory, I'm standing beside my father and staring down at that broken bridge from the heights of Easton's south side.

Fast forward seventeen years to early summer 1972, the year my wife and daughter and I left for Seattle so I could attend graduate school at the University of Washington. It was late June, and we were living in central Pennsylvania when Hurricane Agnes converted our little town of Millersburg into an island. Days of relentless rain had turned the normally shallow and sluggish Susquehanna River into a wide-ranging behemoth, cresting thirty feet over flood stage along the west side of town.

Several Susquehanna tributaries, with bucolic names like Shippens Run and Wiconisco Creek, helped complete Millersburg's isolation. SR 147, the major north-south road in and out of Millersburg, succumbed to Hurricane Agnes' watery charms when a swollen Shippens Run flooded any northbound exit. If one hoped to escape south, a rampaging Wiconisco Creek collapsed the southbound bridge, making escape impossible. The normally sedate Wiconisco Creek also became a macadam-chewing machine preventing any traffic trying to flee Millersburg to the east.

The flooded streams churned roads into impassable rock-strewn ruts. North, south, east, and west, there was no escape. This was Samuel Taylor Coleridge country: "Water, water, everywhere."

We lived on the bluffs above the Susquehanna, and although our apartment was high and dry, we lacked power and water. Fortunately the US Army delivered clean water in army water wagons, and our enforced isolation lasted only a few days.

Seldom do catastrophes unfold directly in front of you, and I remember standing with other curious onlookers on a sodden hillside overlooking the Susquehanna River, the rain pelting our faces, as we watched in perverse fascination. A white, two-story house floated downstream at an eerily strange angle. A dwelling become houseboat. A floating tragedy. Was anyone aboard? What hopes and dreams and memories were literally floating away to oblivion?

Hurricane Agnes was my first experience as an adult with a massive weather-related tragedy,[71] and it taught me several truths about tragedies: most of us are simply along for the ride; one must rely on the kindness of strangers; and tragedies can unmoor more than houses from their foundations.

Not all tragedies are large. On two occasions, my cross-country flights diverted to the nearest airport because a passenger suffered a medical emergency. While I typically refer to such instances in my best faux Latin as *travelus interruptus,* that is nothing compared to a life

---

71 I was a sixteen-year-old high school junior when JFK was assassinated. And 9/11 was still in the distant future. [See: N is for Nine-Eleven.]

interrupted. Once between Atlanta and Seattle, our transcontinental flight detoured to St. Louis when an older gentleman suffered a massive heart attack. Paramedics quickly came aboard, assessed the man's condition, and rolled him off on an amazingly narrow gurney built for skinny jetliner aisles. After a ninety-minute delay, we resumed our flight. As I deplaned in Seattle, I asked our flight attendant if she knew how the man was, and she simply sighed and flashed me a sad look. He hadn't made it. Cruising aloft at 30,000 feet may be lovely, but those who fly above the clouds share a special type of vulnerability, especially when emergent medical problems require immediate attention.

Individual deaths are tragic for families and friends, but communities often experience larger tragedies caused by floods, forest fires, mudslides, earthquakes, tornadoes, and hurricanes. Occasionally I was asked to go work in those communities shortly afterward. For instance, I flew into Charlotte, North Carolina, in early October 1989, just after Hurricane Hugo's winds turned noble heritage trees into kindling. Clean-up was underway, but mountainous piles of debris still crowded many street corners.

When I landed in Charlotte, I was surprised to find there were no rental cars—despite my reservation. Hurricane Hugo's winds and rain had claimed many personal vehicles, and naturally the citizens of Charlotte turned to the rental companies. Compounding the problem, many of the rental cars had been damaged by the hurricane as well. In twenty-six years of traveling, this was the only time that rental cars were not available.

For the next few days, Marie—the McGraw-Hill rep—and I drove together to various schools, witnessing along the way the damage to some of Charlotte's famous tree-lined streets. So many beautiful trees were gone with the wind. With a sigh, Marie lamented that part of Charlotte's soul had been lost.

But as bad as the damage was in Charlotte, I've never experienced anything like the aftermath of Joplin's F5 tornado for sheer destructive magnitude. That tornado had flattened a mile-wide swath of Joplin, Missouri.

The Joplin tornado was the deadliest in the United States since 1950—when modern record-keeping began. The toll was breathtaking: 8,400 houses, 18,000 cars, and 450 businesses—all flattened or blown away. The tornado narrowly missed the downtown area. St. John's Regional Medical Center was damaged, and ultimately demolished in 2012. The local high school, Joplin High School, was totally destroyed, as well. A total of 161 people died from tornado-related injuries and more than a thousand were injured. And I arrived in Joplin—several weeks afterward—blithely unaware of their horrendous May 22, 2011 tornado.

I don't know why I didn't know about the Joplin tornado. The tragedy had filled the nightly news for weeks, and I've always prided myself on my situational awareness, both macro and micro. Traveling requires situational awareness because it encompasses not only the planned work, but the weather, the history of the community, and the "special" offerings a particular destination might have—essentially what it means to be there in that place. Some call it the "character" of the place.

But I was blindsided by Joplin.

I landed in Joplin after dark, and drove to my hotel. The airport is north of the city and my hotel was in the south end. During my drive I started picking up cues about a tale of two cities. As I drove south, I drove from light to darkness to light, as if I'd driven out of the city, and then re-entered. It was very strange. I asked the hotel desk clerk if there was a North Joplin and a South Joplin. She looked at me uncertainly.

"I don't think that's funny," she said in a calm, even voice. Her eyes flashed a warning.

Her comment and look gave me pause. "I wasn't trying to be funny, Miss," I said hesitantly. "I was just wondering why a long stretch of Main Street is dark. It's really noticeable as you drive here from the airport."

Her whole demeanor changed in an instant.

"You really don't know?" she asked.

"Know what?"

"That dark area? No street lights? That's where the tornado came through. Nothing's left. It was a huge tornado. Cut Joplin in half." I could hear the pain in her voice. "It destroyed my parents' home... they lost everything...everything...except their lives." Tears welled up. "They're living with me now. Thousands of people lost everything."

Sometimes a kind word is the only remedy. Sometimes there is no remedy, but kinds words are the only tools available. Sometimes all you can do is acknowledge the pain.

"I am so sorry, Miss. Forgive me. I didn't know. I wasn't trying to be funny." I looked around at the empty lobby. "It must have been awful...truly awful...tell me about the tornado." We stood and talked for quite some time and that's when I realized that regardless of how many people are victims, every tragedy is individual and personal. During the few days I spent in Joplin, every teacher I spoke with had their own personal version of "The Day the Tornado Swept across Joplin," and while the stories shared remarkable similarities, they were all incredibly different. Overnight, the world had been converted into two camps: victims and survivors...and all survivors were victims, too.

The next day during lunch, I walked around the ruined high school with one English teacher. "We're going to recover," she said. "We'll rebuild...but it'll take time. Best of all, the citizens of Joplin have already shown they know why there's a 'common' in community. We are all struggling together."

We all must rely on the kindness of strangers.

My Joplin trip proves that I've suffered occasional failures of my own situational awareness, but I've generally been rescued by a colleague or good luck...or a hotel desk clerk.

It was a hotel desk clerk in Key Largo who, years earlier, rescued me when I had another lapse in situational awareness. I should have been alert to the arrival of Hurricane Andrew—an incredibly compact Category 5 storm that swept ashore in the early morning hours of Monday, August 24, 1992.

During the week preceding Andrew's arrival, my family and I had vacationed in Orlando enjoying Disneyworld and Epcot Center and the Florida sunshine.[72] I think the highlight of the trip was my children's easy, daily access to the hotel swimming pool.

As scheduled, my family flew home to Seattle without me on Saturday morning, August 22nd. My company was having its national sales meeting in Orlando beginning the following Wednesday on one of the Disney properties, and I wouldn't be able to check in until Tuesday evening. This gave me three days to roam.

I decided that this would be the ideal time to drive to Key West and visit Ernest Hemingway's haunts. Yes, that's the way English teachers think. It would also be the ideal time to disconnect—no radio, no television, no newspapers. Just tool along in my rental car listening to music, then relax and read books at the hotel. I would spend Saturday evening at the Key Largo Holiday Inn, and then on Sunday take Highway 1 to Key West—a peaceful, two-hour drive in the glittering embrace of the Atlantic's blue waters.

What could be better?

An early riser, even on vacation, I went for a walk in the Sunday morning sunshine. Walks invigorated me, and this walk helped me plan my Key West side trips. As I returned to the hotel, I noticed that all the deck chairs that had been neatly arranged around the edge of the pool were now in the water.

Wow, they had one hell of a party here last night, and I never heard a thing. So much for situational awareness.

---

72 As a blue-eyed redhead, I seldom enjoyed sunshine. My childhood is rife with stories of sunburns and blisters. By 1992, I never went outside without a hat, sunscreen, or a long-sleeved shirt...even in Florida.

I returned to my room, made myself a cup of coffee, and propped my feet on the bed to read a few chapters of *The Old Man and the Sea* when someone knocked on my door. I thought it was the maid. I answered the door to let her know I'd be leaving in a half hour or so. But it wasn't the maid; it was one of the hotel desk clerks.

"Yes?" I asked.

"Why are you still here?" She sounded concerned.

Although I thought it was a strange question, I responded cheerfully, buoyed by the prospect of visiting Key West. "Check out isn't until noon, right? I'll be out shortly. I'm driving to Key West." Her look of disbelief was impossible to ignore. "Is there some problem?"

"Yes," she said with undisguised befuddlement. "There's a hurricane coming. A really strong hurricane. I'm afraid you won't be going to Key West. Everyone has been ordered to evacuate."

"Evacuate?" I asked. In retrospect, I must have sounded like an idiot.

"Haven't you been watching TV?" she asked. "Hurricane Andrew will hit here late tonight. Everyone in Key Largo is evacuating. Highway 1 is strictly one-way…north."

"Oh. Oh my God. Oh my." I was stammering. "No…no, I didn't realize that. I haven't been watching any TV at all."

"Well, you need to check out of the hotel immediately," she said. "Most of the staff have already started north, and the rest of us are ready to leave. You're the last one here."

As I walked to the lobby, I noticed the empty parking lot—except for my Chevy sedan sitting by its lonesome. The hotel had already boarded the lobby windows with sheets of plywood, and except for me, only two staff members remained. I apologized profusely.

I vacated my room in record time, wondering exactly how this day would play out. Hemingway would have to wait for another trip. Should I go back to Orlando? If I did, how long would that take? When I got there, would there be any room in any of the inns?

It was time to stop disconnecting, and I turned on the car radio as I drove north on Highway 1. Every station was tracking the storm and warning everyone to evacuate or batten down the hatches. Hurricane Andrew was going to be a doozey—a Category 5 storm. The airwaves counseled the hundreds of thousands of evacuees—all of us headed north in our cars—to be patient. Tough advice when I-95 traffic was moving at a snail's pace.

Apparently, everyone had known Hurricane Andrew was on its way—except me. Fortunately, I was unable to join the 30,000 tourists who had to hunker down in the Keys. Unfortunately, I was among the 1.2 million who drove north in a seemingly endless traffic jam, hoping that when I stopped driving, there might actually be a hotel room available.

An exhausting ten hours and 300 miles later, I arrived in Orlando, with the dreary realization that my full-size Chevy might be the only place I would find to sleep that night. The trip to Key Largo had taken me less than five hours the previous day.

I worried that numerous hotels would have posted "No Rooms Available" outside their front doors—but I needn't have worried. *Every* hotel had that sign. As I approached the lobby door of each hotel, I noted the sign, and continued on. After more than a dozen attempts, I concluded there were no rooms. I was one stranded man among thousands of stranded Floridians.

I can't remember exactly where I ended up on Sunday night—a Hyatt? an Embassy Suites?—but I remember walking into the lobby and being astonished by the crowd of unregistered guests—men, women, and children—who planned to camp out until Hurricane Andrew had passed. If there were no rooms, the floor would do.

I approached the desk clerk and asked the question to which I already knew the answer. "Do you have any rooms?"

The woman behind the desk smiled, practicing patience in the face of my stupid question.

"I'm afraid not." Then she brightened as if she could make my day with a comic aside. "Unless you want to stay in the Presidential Suite."

"How much is the Presidential Suite?" I asked.

"Six hundred dollars," she said with an apologetic look.[73]

"Oh, well," I said and turned to walk away. *Too rich for my blood,* I thought. But then I turned back. "How many bedrooms in the Presidential Suite?" I asked.

"Three," she said. "And two sofa beds in the commons area."

I turned and looked at the sea of people crowding the lobby. *Homeless for a night,* I thought. *If I take the Presidential Suite, I can accommodate quite a few people—besides myself.* "I'll take it," I said. I think I surprised her.

As soon as I registered, I turned to face the lobby. At the top of my voice, I yelled, "I've secured the Presidential Suite, and I can take three families. Anyone interested in staying in the Presidential Suite tonight can split the costs with me."

There was no shortage of volunteers. Six adults and five children—eleven strangers—volunteered to spend the night with another stranger in the palatial Presidential Suite to wait out Hurricane Andrew. Six hundred dollars split four ways. Everyone pitched in to make this a fun evening. One dad made a liquor run while another ordered pizzas of every description. The other adults figured out the sleeping arrangements, while the younger kids ran from room to room, laughing and getting acquainted.

After pizza, the kids watched TV in three different bedrooms while we seven adults gathered in the commons room drinking, sharing stories, playing poker, and laughing until well after midnight. Each of us felt fortunate to have met the others, knowing we would probably never see one another ever again. Life…and a hurricane named Andrew…had thrown us together. A simple matter of humans in need of mutual support.

We all must rely on the kindness of strangers.

---

73 Remember, this is $600.00 in 1992.

U is for Unexpected

We could never learn to be brave and patient,
if there were only joy in the world.
—Helen Keller

He that can have patience, can have what he will.
—Benjamin Franklin

All things come to him who waits.
—Woodrow Wilson[74]

"EXPECT THE UNEXPECTED," my father always said. "Someday you'll have a flat tire. Someday someone will come out of nowhere and hit you, or step hard on the brake in front of you. It happens. Expect it."

My father's pithy advice always felt like the corollary to the Boy Scout motto, "Be prepared." While every road warrior I've known always preferred incident-free travel, the norm was often upended by "the unexpected"—long lines and long waits at airports, weather delays, snarled highway traffic, crowded hotel lobbies, overbooked restaurants, cancelled reservations, and the occasional surly, overworked clerk.

(I could add "towns without hotels and restaurants," or "mollifying angry but mistaken customers," but that will come later.)

---

74 This was one of my father's favorite sayings. He frequently used these exact words to counsel me.

Soon after I joined the publishing world, John Toft, a wise and thoughtful colleague at McGraw-Hill, warned me "the unexpected should never be unanticipated." His *basso profundo* voice resonated with divine authority, and his pronouncements always felt as if they'd come from the throne of God.

When I asked him what tools I might need to effectively deal with the unexpected, he held up a single index finger and boomed, "Patience."[75] Helen Keller would have agreed.

As a youngster, I learned about patience because my father was an extraordinarily patient man. I also learned about impatience because my mother's legendary impatience provided a vivid contrast. I use that duality to assess my patient—or impatient—response to the many unexpected twists and turns of road warrior life. The bottom line is that sometimes I was my Dad, and sometimes I was my Mom.[76]

To this day, I remain impatient to be patient.

Over the years, I found that The Unexpected came in two varieties—unexpected circumstances and unexpected behavior. A flat tire while traveling to a presentation is an unexpected circumstance. Being denied a hotel room at 1:00 a.m. by an uncooperative desk clerk despite a reservation and a confirmation number is probably a little bit of both.

Sometimes, it doesn't matter if you are patient or impatient. Sometimes, circumstances truly trap you—so it matters very little if your reaction is patient and calm...or impatient and irrational. When you're stuck, you are stuck. That's the way it was on one of my last trips to Alaska in the early fall of 2013. I flew to the village of St. Mary's in an Era Airlines nine-seat Cessna Caravan to help train several teachers who had purchased our programs. And I found myself stuck...truly stuck in the village of St. Mary's—a tiny Alaskan village[77] built about 50 miles shy of the Yukon River delta. I mean no disrespect when I

---

75 Patience might well deserve its own chapter, but *P is for Prayer*, and patience might well be unexpected.

76 I am reminded of The First Law of Sociology found in Paul Dickson's *The Official Rules*: "Some do, some don't."

77 Perhaps "tiny" and "village" are redundant.

call St. Mary's tiny, but a town without hotels and restaurants, a town inaccessible except by air or water,[78] ends up in my "tiny" category. I completely misunderstood what my company meant when they told me St. Mary's had "a lack of amenities."

Without question, it was a long trip to a tiny village for very few people; to a village with few roads and no phone service. It was one of the only times in my twenty-six years of traveling that I was truly isolated, virtually incommunicado.

When I landed, I was greeted by the school's principal. He threw my bag in the back of his pick-up truck and drove from the airstrip to the village. He asked me where my sleeping gear was.

"Do I need bedding for the hotels here?" I asked. I felt a bit confused.

"You wouldn't if there were any hotels."

"You don't have any hotels?" I asked. After a long flight over a watery but barren Alaskan landscape, I suspected I knew the answer.

"We don't get many visitors or tourists here. In fact, except for people like you, we don't get any. My wife says that's because St. Mary's is Alaska's best-kept secret." He laughed as we bounced down the road. "You're one of the lucky ones. I hope you take lots of pictures to make everybody jealous in the lower forty-eight."

"I didn't bring a camera," I admitted. I could feel my confidence waning.

"Your loss," he said. I could hear the amusement in his voice. "You may never pass this way again."

I stopped myself from saying, *That's a safe bet.*

"I'll bet you didn't bring any food either, did you?"

"Are you going to tell me St. Mary's doesn't have any restaurants?"

"You catch on quick," he said, again in that amused tone. A treeless, hilly terrain flanked both sides of the road as we descended toward St. Mary's. I could see the Andreafsky River, a Yukon tributary, in the distance. The principal scratched his head.

"Didn't your company's representative explain what you'd find

---

78 Let me be explicit. St. Mary's is not an island.

here in St. Mary's?"

I shook my head. "I usually don't work for this division of the company. Your rep called me from the national offices in New Jersey. She told me what you wanted, and I volunteered to come."

"Well, thanks for volunteering," he said. "I know you're accustomed to hotels and restaurants. Sorry." We continued toward town. "I've got a room next to the gym in the rear of the high school. It's an unused equipment room with a bunkbed and a microwave. No one is using it now. Sometimes the custodian stays there overnight during the winter, especially when the weather gets nasty. Do you think that'll work for you?"

"Thanks," I said. "I'm happy to lay my head anywhere that's warm and dry."

"Good." He stopped in front of St. Mary's grocery and motioned for me to jump out. "Let me suggest you get something here for dinner. You can warm it up in the microwave. I'll be back in ten minutes."

As I closed the truck door he suddenly interjected, "But we do have the internet."

"Great. Now all you need are hotels and restaurants," I said smiling. "See you in ten."

I walked into St. Mary's only grocery store. I didn't know that for certain; let's just call it a hunch. Now all I had to do was ask myself what I was hungry for...and what I could prepare using a microwave in the custodian's room. I grabbed some frozen enchiladas, a package of chocolate chip cookies, and some ginger ale and went to checkout. *That's not a very good diet, John,* I told myself. Even as I gently berated myself for my dietary indiscretions, I wondered where someone would go for a really good salmon meal in St. Mary's. Probably somebody's house.

I might be able to get a good salmon dinner in Bethel, the next closest town, almost one-hundred air miles to the southeast. I know there's a restaurant in Bethel because I dined there when my homebound flight was delayed after we landed there.

By the time I walked out the door with my groceries, the principal had returned. He drove me to the high school and toted my luggage back to the custodian's bunk room. It was spartan, reflecting the Alaskan landscape that surrounded St. Mary's. Bare beige walls. No pictures. No posters. No calendars. No decorations. A bunkbed with one pillow, a wooden chair, and a small, scarred wooden table for the dented, but working, white microwave.

Nothing in the room said, *Someone lives here.* Nothing even whispered it. I looked around and decided I would not be improving the decor. I put my groceries on the table to give the room some color.

"This will be fine," I told the principal. I hoped he didn't hear the resignation in my voice.

"Boy's shower room is right around the corner. There are thirty shower-heads, so you have your choice of any one of them."

Well, all is not lost, I thought. *At least I can shower.* "Maybe I'll turn them all on and do laps around the shower room. Get my exercise while I clean up."

"Just make sure you turn them all off when you're done," he said. "We'll meet tomorrow in the office at eight. I'll have donuts and coffee. So get some sleep. Hope you have a good book to read."

I did, but that wasn't the problem. Calling home was the problem. My cellphone and their cellphone carrier were incompatible. I'd like to be able to explain why, but I just don't really care that much. That night I resorted to communicating via computer with my wife. We Skyped.

I provided the teacher training the next day, and the principal said his folks were so pleased that they'd like me to come back—probably in a few months. However, a little more than a month after I traveled to St. Mary's, an Associated Press article dated November 30, 2013, caught my attention. Apparently an Era Airlines Cessna, just like the one I'd flown, had crashed while flying from Bethel to St. Mary's. Four of the ten people aboard had been killed—including a child. The article didn't say how old. It took two hours for rescuers to reach the site after the aircraft went down in freezing rain.

I found the article strangely unsetting. *Wow. That could have been me.*

I wondered if that was the same plane I'd flown—it was the same route.

Decades earlier, when I was about eight-years-old and ready to take my very first plane ride, I'd asked my father—who had been a World War II bomber pilot—"What makes airplanes fly?"

Without hesitation, he said, "Bird wings."

"Bird wings?" I asked.

"Well, son, do you see the shape of the plane's wings? The air flows faster over the top of the wing than it does under the wing. Just like it does for birds. The faster air creates suction, pulling the wing upward. That's what makes birds fly. Airplanes, too."

I was eight. He was my dad. That answer worked just fine. When I was eight.

Now I was sixty-five, and I wondered, *So, what happened to this airplane? Broken bird wings? Metal fatigue? Mechanical failure? Pilot error?*

My thoughts returned to 2003, when my daughter Amanda was getting married. I had assured my very nervous 80-year-old aunt—a woman who had never, ever previously flown—that "Every plane I've ever boarded has landed safely." So she boarded the plane…and arrived safely.

I was loathe to break my record. *A fatal plane crash? Now that would be unexpected.*

I never returned to St. Mary's. Retirement seemed safer.

St. Mary's represented, in every possible way, an unexpected circumstance. But on a few occasions, I encountered unexpected behavior from the teachers I was attempting to serve.

When school districts purchased my company's textbook programs, they often asked a consultant to spend time training their teachers—helping them become familiar with all the support materials and the internet-based components. When I wasn't selling books,

I was training teachers.

Wheeling Park High School in the Ohio County School District—which, curiously, is in West Virginia—had asked a consultant to come to their high school and train their social studies teachers who were about to begin the school year. Specifically, they wanted training on their new textbooks for World History, Economics, and Government. I was scheduled to spend the day with them—Government and Econ in the morning, and World History after lunch.

There was just one slight glitch. The Wheeling Park Social Studies chair was seething because his textbooks hadn't arrived. He'd called the rep a few days before my scheduled training, and, between curses, he'd explained that they'd spent $75,000 for new books. Books that had not been delivered.

The rep had called to give me a courtesy warning. "You're walking into a hornet's nest," she said.

"How angry would you say he was? On a scale of one to ten?" I asked.

"An eleven."

"That mad, huh?"

Mending fences was part of the job. "I'll see what I can do to track down the books," I said. "I'll let you know what I find out." So tomorrow I'd doff my training hat for my deerstalker cap, and track down those books.

The training was scheduled to begin at 9:00 a.m., and I arrived at about 8:15 a.m. Extreme punctuality has plagued me all my life. Some people find it admirable; others find it annoying. I remember feeling relieved when my brother Bill, who served in Vietnam with the United States Marine Corps, said his sergeant was fond of "Getting up in our grills and shouting, 'On time is late, Scannell. Early is on time.'" I love being early. Perhaps I'm a Marine at heart.

When I arrived at the high school office, I asked to see the Social Studies department chairman, who, for the purposes of this story, I've decided to call Mr. H. The secretary paged him, and I watched from the office as he came down the hall. The rep was right. He hadn't stopped seething. Dare I say the Mendenhall Glacier would have afforded me a warmer reception?

Extending my hand, I said, "Hello, Mr. H, I'm John Scannell. I'm a consultant with McGraw-Hill." He ignored my hand. *Not a good start.*

I'd been a consultant for a decade, and knew the wisdom of handling problems immediately. Seldom has anyone refused a handshake, but that simply reinforced what the rep had said: He was an eleven.

Mr. H clearly struggled to get himself under control.

"Mr. H," I said as quietly and calmly as I could, "My colleague and I spoke last evening, and I realize you're upset because the books haven't arrived."

His words burst like a broken dam. "Damn right, I'm upset. None of your books are here. None of them. Not Government. Not Econ. Not World History. We ordered back in June—and your rep told us the books would be here within a week after we ordered. A week! We're going to have kids here the day after tomorrow, and we don't have textbooks to give them."

My company called delivering textbooks "fulfillment," and clearly Mr. H was feeling unfulfilled. I couldn't blame him. He was angry with McGraw-Hill, and I as I stood in front of him, I was McGraw-Hill.

"We jumped through all sorts of damn hoops before we left for summer break to make sure we had board approval for your books." He slapped his hand on the office counter even as he pronounced the word "your" with a dismissive sneer. It was clear that I needed to solve this problem before conducting any training.

I could have been offended by his tone—delivering books isn't part of my job description—but I understood his dilemma. I knew what it was like to be a teacher wanting everything to be ready and in place before school began. Students would be arriving on Thursday, and he had no idea if or when his books might end up on his doorstep.

"I don't blame you, Mr. H. Not at all. We promised you that those books would be here, and you promised your social studies colleagues that they'd have their new books to begin the school year."

I watched him calm a bit—his anger was maybe a nine—but understanding his problem wasn't enough.

"So let's put first things first. Let me make a phone call to my secretary, okay? Let me find out what's going on with your order." My secretary, Barb Smith—actually the secretary to my boss, the National Sales VP—picked up. I put us on speakerphone.

"Hey John, what's up?"

"Hi, Barb, I've got you on speakerphone with Mr. H here in Wheeling, West Virginia. Mr. H is the Social Studies chair. I'm here for a teacher workshop, but we've got a problem. Our books were never delivered." Mr. H's face softened a bit when I stated the problem as directly as possible. "I could use a little bit of your magic to track down Mr. H's order." Barb always chuckled when I called her my personal magician. "School starts on Thursday, and the Government, Econ, and World History teachers were planning to issue those new textbooks to their students. As things stand now, that can't happen. The books never showed up."

"I understand," Barb said.

There were two things I loved about Barb. Because she knew every facet of textbook delivery, she knew how to solve delivery problems, and she loved solving delivery problems—mine anyway.

"Here's what I want you to do, John. Get the Purchase Order numbers for the books—there's probably a separate P.O. number for each title—and call me back. When I have those numbers, I'll call the warehouse, and I'll be able to track down the status of the order." Mr. H's anger was on the decline—maybe a four or five now.

"You heard what she said. Barb's my pipeline to the warehouse. All she needs are the P.O.s for your book order."

"I'll bet those P.O. numbers are in Jan Hodges office," Mr. H said, making a beeline to the back of the office. Apparently, Jan Hodges was responsible for ordering anything that Wheeling Park High School needed. From toilet paper to textbooks, all orders crossed her desk. In the educational universe, high school purchasing agents are gods—or goddesses.

We walked into Jan's office. The woman sitting behind the desk was busy thumbing through a pile of papers in a manila folder. She looked up and asked, "Can I help you?"

"Is Jan here?" Mr. H asked. "I need to see the textbook purchase orders we submitted last spring. The books have never been delivered."

"I'm sorry," she said, standing up. "I'm new here. I'm the new Jan. You probably know she retired?"

"Retired? No, I didn't know. I've been here nine years, and Jan was a fixture in this office. Whatever anyone needed, Jan delivered."

"Well, I'm going to do my best to live up to her reputation."

"I'm sorry. We've never been introduced. I'm Bill H, Social Studies department chair." They shook hands.

"I'm Pam Fortunata," she said. "As you can see, I'm new. Tell me again. How I can help you, Bill?"

"I've got to figure out why our new textbooks haven't shown up. Mr. Scannell here is from McGraw-Hill, and he thinks we should start with the purchase order numbers."

"Well, let's start there," Pam said, skillfully pushing her wheeled desk chair toward a bank of four-drawer filing cabinets. "Let's see...I think textbook purchase orders are in here." She opened one drawer and reviewed a few files, pulling out a thick folder. She scooted her chair back to her desk and opened the manila folder. "Those P.O.s should be in here."

She shuffled through the stack and pulled out three paper-clipped documents.

"Here you are," she said, handing the documents across her desk.

Mr. H studied the purchase orders. "Yep, 275 Government." He flipped to the next, "275 Econ and 450 World History. Yep." As he inspected the P.O.s, his brow scrunched, and he reddened considerably.

"All Barb needs is the name of the high school and the P.O. numbers," I said.

Without saying anything, Mr. H motioned for us to leave Pam's office.

"What's up?" I asked.

Mr. H took a deep breath before he spoke. "The books were never ordered."

"What?"

"All the paperwork is here. Everything's been approved. But the orders were never sent." He met my eyes, then dropped his head, incredibly embarrassed. For a moment, we stood in silence. "The books aren't here because no one ever sent in the order." He took another deep breath. "I'm really sorry, John. Really sorry. I've behaved like a complete ass."

That was true. He'd treated me like a pariah from the moment we met that morning, but I could see his pain and embarrassment. All I could do was look at him and smile. "You have no idea how glad I am that this screw-up wasn't our fault—because sometimes it is. You don't want to know how much crow I've eaten."

Embarrassment had replaced anger as Mr. H tapped the P.O.s on the palm of his hand.

"Listen," I said. "Now we know why the books aren't here, right? We have the P.O.s, and our warehouse is in Westerville, Ohio…no more than 150 miles from here. If we get all your information to Barb, I bet we can have the books here in a few days."

"I have an even better idea," Bill said. I trailed him back into Pam's office and he asked her if a district truck could drive to Westerville and pick up the books. Today.

As it turned out, the answer was yes. I called Barb, gave her all the information, and she told us that the books would be on the shipping dock that afternoon. "Just like magic," she said.

I'd gone from villain to hero in the blink of an eye.

"My magician just pulled your textbooks out of her hat, Mr. H," I said.

"And I am grateful," he said.

He left the office and bounded upstairs for the training. His mood had swung from a minus eleven to a plus ten. He turned on the landing. "Can we start in ten minutes?"

"Ten minutes, it is," I said as I followed him up the stairs. I didn't know what his happiness quotient was, I was just happy that he was happy.

How to deal with unexpected behavior? I could hear John Toft speaking in his God-like voice, "Patience!"

V is for *Veritas*

Whoever is careless with the truth[79] in small matters cannot be trusted with important matters.
—Albert Einstein

Honesty is the first chapter in the book of wisdom.
—Thomas Jefferson

If you tell the truth you don't have to remember anything.
—Mark Twain, Notebook (1894)

POLLS SHOW THAT an overwhelming percentage of people trust teachers. Only nurses and military officers score higher.[80] The paying public may be reluctant to compensate teachers well, but teachers' trustworthiness remains unquestioned. In stark contrast, salespeople fare less well in the trustworthiness department. No, that's an understatement.

Salespeople fare abysmally.

I failed to consult the trustworthiness polls as I shifted from high school teacher to textbook sales consultant, but during my first sales campaign, I became acutely aware that my triple-A trustworthiness rating had fallen through the floor.

Accustomed to being believed, I was bowled over by one

---

79 *Veritas* is Latin for truth...or Truth is English for *veritas*.
80 Gallup Poll, 2017: http://news.gallup.com/poll/1654/honesty-ethics-profes-sions.aspx

audacious comment made by a Texas teacher. "You're a salesperson. Everyone knows you're paid to lie," she said with neither apology nor accusation in her voice. "We take everything you say with a grain of salt."

Everyone knows? I thought. *Everyone?*

It wasn't meant to be an insult. No, it was worse. It was stated as a fact, something that "everyone knows." I felt insulted, probably because I still viewed myself as an English teacher—not an ex-English teacher, or a salesperson.

How can I prove to teachers that I am one of them, especially when I appear before them as a salesman? I wondered. *Simply asserting, "I'm a teacher, too," won't suffice.*

In the sales world, it's all about trust.

I had to show them that I truly understood what they were expected to know; truly understood the complexities of their jobs; and truly understood the complexities of their clientele—their students. If they perceived that in me, they might accord me the trustworthiness that I knew I deserved.

I resolved that whenever I spoke to English teachers, I would *be* an English teacher—not simply *appear to be* an English teacher. The difference may seem abstract, but I assure you, it is very real. I was successful selling textbooks because I was an English teacher—who happened to be selling textbooks.

Perhaps a parallel situation will clarify my point. My daughter, Amanda, is a practicing physician. Even if she never puts on her white coat, she *is* a doctor, but if I put on a white coat, even one with Dr. Scannell embroidered across the breast pocket, I only *appear to be* a doctor. Worse, I faint at the sight of blood.

I was always happy to speak with English teachers because English teachers are a breed apart. For instance, English teachers are not Math teachers. I know this to be true, because I once pinch hit for a math consultant who had taken ill. I foolishly stepped in at the last minute to present McGraw-Hill's Algebra textbook.

The problems were obvious from the beginning.

1. I had never taught Math.
2. I was never terribly good at Math. Computation, yes; abstract math, no.
3. I had no idea what was really important to Math teachers. Or Algebra teachers.
4. I had no idea what Math teachers might talk about when they discussed Math.

I should have refused the assignment, but my desire to help and a foolish bravado that "I can sell anything" placed me directly in front of a committee of seven high school Math teachers. Although they were very attentive, I know I lost their vote from the moment I began talking.

I decided to begin with a touch of humor, something that invariably worked with English teachers. I decided to use Algebra's love affair with "finding for 'x'" as a starting point. As we all know, "x" is the unknown, a mystery. Perhaps a mystery novel opener would capture their attention.

Big mistake.

"I am very pleased to be here, today," I began, looking at each of the Math committee members. "And I want you to know I've read this book from cover to cover"—dramatic pause while holding up the Algebra text—"and I can tell you this: the quadratic equation did it."

No reaction. Not even the glimmer of a smile. A few confused grimaces that seemed to be saying, "What the hell are you talking about."

My mistake was telling an English teachers' joke to a group of Math teachers. Math consultants, if they introduce their presentations with any kind of humor, probably tell Math jokes, math stories. Perhaps they would have responded more energetically to *Old Schrödinger's Book of Paradoxical Cats*?

I had relied on my vast knowledge of English teachers while foolishly reducing Math teachers to "those folks who are always looking for 'x'." All I know about "x" is that it is the 24th letter of the alphabet.

Need I tell you we didn't win the business?

I never made that mistake again. I *am* an English teacher, and I can talk intelligently about literature and writing. But Math? I'm afraid not.

The quest for *being* an English teacher selling textbooks consumed me. To establish trust, I devised several openers that appealed to the core instincts of all English teachers. For instance, I'd read a poem, one that I knew they liked. One of my favorites was T. S. Eliot's *Macavity: The Mystery Cat*, a poem in our ninth grade anthology.

Macavity's a Mystery Cat: he's called the Hidden Paw—
For he's the master criminal who can defy the Law.
He's the bafflement of Scotland Yard, the Flying Squad's despair:
For when they reach the scene of crime—Macavity's not there!

I'd recite Macavity in a faux British accent, and after the final three words—*Macavity's not there*—I'd assure them that Macavity "Is right here in our anthology, accompanied by an incredible array of wonderful poems and short stories. Stories and poems that your students will love. And isn't that what we want for our students?"

One of my favorite openings employed a delightfully recognizable Billy Collins poem called "Introduction to Poetry." Teachers loved it because it speaks volumes about what English teachers call "poetry resistance." Poetry resistance is the phenomenon when poetry is simultaneously too easy or too hard. I remember hearing students alternately dismiss poetry as being "kids' stuff" or accuse it of just being "too damn hard to understand." I'd laugh and tell them poetry was just another kind of language—another artistic avenue for expression. But like the English teacher in Billy Collin's poem, I had students who wanted me to unlock the door for them. "Mr. Scannell," they'd say, "tell us what the poem really means." They resisted the careful investigation that would unlock the beauty of the language. Instead, they wanted "to tie the poem to a chair with rope and torture a confession out of it." Whenever I'd recite the Billy Collins poem to teachers, they'd laugh long and loud—for they understood the delightful but difficult task of "selling poetry to teenagers." That simple act of sharing a poem—sharing the experience—built a rapport with English teachers because I was talking English teacher to English teacher rather than salesman to English teacher.

Occasionally I'd borrow a tactic from my own ninth-grade English teacher who had mastered the art of "selling poetry." She relied on "titillation." I recall one morning when she came into class looking a bit perplexed. She told us she wasn't sure if she should read a particular Shakespearean sonnet to us because it was "slightly dirty, a bit obscene." Naturally we begged her to read it to us, declaring we'd never turn her in to the principal. She then proceeded to read Shakespeare's delightful "Sonnet 138."

> *When my love swears that she is made of truth,*
> *I do believe her, though I know she lies,*
> *That she might think me some untutored youth,*
> *Unlearnèd in the world's false subtleties.*
> *Thus vainly thinking that she thinks me young,*
> *Although she knows my days are past the best,*
> *Simply I credit her false-speaking tongue:*
> *On both sides thus is simple truth suppressed.*
> *But wherefore says she not she is unjust?*
> *And wherefore say not I that I am old?*
> *Oh, love's best habit is in seeming trust,*
> *And age in love loves not to have years told.*
> *Therefore I lie with her and she with me,*
> *And in our faults by lies we flattered be.*

Granted, the poem wasn't nearly as dirty or obscene as we ninth-graders might have preferred, but we listened, and some of us even caught the possibly-obscene, sexual reference in line thirteen.

Beginning my sales presentations with the story of my clever ninth-grade English teacher, accompanied by a recitation of "Sonnet 138"—performed with my faux British accent, of course—achieved my purpose. I wanted my teacher audience to see me as the English teacher I knew myself to be.

If I didn't recite poetry, I'd sometimes begin my literature presentations with a quiz.

"As an English teacher," I'd say, "I think I know a good deal about English teachers. I know their tendencies, their foibles, and their eccentricities." I'd emphasize every syllable of "ec-cen-tri-ci-ties," and they always found that amusing. "So let me have a show of hands. How many of you have a shelf of books at home dedicated to 'Books I plan to read?'"

Lots of hands.

"Alright," I said. "Raise your hand if that list of books grows every year?"

Lots of hands. And laughter. They knew what I was talking about.

"How many of you have books double-shelved—you know, one book in front of the other—because you haven't the heart to part from the books you've read and loved, and long ago you ran out of shelf space?"

Lots of hands. Lots of laughter. Lots of nodding heads.

"Me, too," I said. "How many of you have books that are so old, but so loved, that you use rubber-bands to hold them together when the binding failed?"

Lots of hands. Lots of laughter. Lots of nodding heads. And the names of the much-beloved books that are rubber-band-bound.

"Finally, how many of you have ever tossed a book in the trash, and then in a fit of shame and regret, retrieved the book from the garbage, saving it from the awful fate of being discarded?"

Lots of hands. Lots of laughter.

"Well, just as I suspected, you really are English teachers." More laughter. "So it's okay for me to talk to you like the English teachers you are. I'm happy to say I'm one of you. My copy of *The Hobbit* is bound by rubber-bands, and probably missing a dozen pages, but I've kept it since I read it as a freshman in college. That's 1965. I've thought about getting a new copy, but somehow, I can't. I'm *connected* to that particular copy of *The Hobbit* that fascinated me decades ago."

What I didn't tell them was that copy of *The Hobbit* was hopefully still nestled into a comfortable niche on a bookshelf of the home now occupied by my ex-wife. When I divorced, there were some things I simply forgot to retrieve. And even though I know I could go to any bookstore to get a new copy, my dog-eared, falling-apart *Hobbit* still holds me in its thrall.

If I happened to be talking to a committee considering our Writing text, I'd begin with student bloopers gleaned from my teaching days.

"I saved a lot of these," I said. "It would be hard to make them up. I'm sure you've seen your share of what I call the *Three M's*: mangled, mistaken, and massacred English." I'd show them problem sentences crafted by my former students. Some were aspirational:

Maybe I'll have a couple of kids or a dog.

I have to be aware of my mistakes, so I can perfect them.

Invariably, I'd remark that there is nothing quite so wonderful as a perfect mistake. Then, of course, there were student sentences that were curiously comic.

I was seeing an illusion that wasn't there.

Suddenly, a voice appeared.

Someday, I want to live in the ruins of an old castle or chapeau.

My listeners laughed when I read that last one.

"I think we all know what she meant to say, but she hadn't said it. I called that young lady to my desk and pointed to the word 'chapeau.' I had circled it in red. She smiled and proudly announced, 'It's French.'"

More laughter from my teachers.

"I said, yes, you're right. But is it the right French word? When she realized that she wanted to live in a hat and not a house, she agreed to change that word. Nevertheless, *chapeau* was incredibly amusing."

This was all quite familiar territory. Every writing teacher has encountered the *Three M's*, as well as poor penmanship and dysfunctional grammar. Such are the lives of English teachers laboring in the vineyards of language. When I acknowledged the daily reality of the teachers sitting in front of me, it established my *bona fides*—showing them I was an English teacher talking to fellow English teachers. Their truth was my truth, too.

Then one day, just a few months after assuming my role as consultant, I was asked to lie to my English teacher audience. The sales rep wanted me to tell the English teachers on the selection committee something that I knew to be false. Worse, they'd know I was lying the moment they opened our anthology to review it—especially if they'd been taking notes.

Macmillan Literature, like so many other high school literature programs in the late 1980s, had succumbed to the demands of censorship because William Shakespeare, that awful Elizabethan, had dared to have his characters speak lines freighted with sexual innuendo.

Much to my dismay, Act I, scene i, had been excised from our version of *Romeo and Juliet* because it featured two horny teenage boys standing on a Verona street corner talking dirty. Act I, scene i, was gone. My company euphemistically labeled our sanitized version of Shakespeare's masterpiece as the *Standard High School Abridgement*—something that actually meant, "All sex has been removed." Our textbook planned to teach teenagers to appreciate great literature with a sexless love story.

In fact, there was no *Standard High School Abridgement*, not really. That was a euphemistic phrase that meant someone had spoiled a great Shakespearean play.

Our textbook also deleted many of the lines uttered by the play's bawdiest character, the Nurse. Her lines, full of sexual references— "Women grow by men"—had been removed wholesale in a bowdlerization to satisfy the prudes who populated textbook selection committees, like the one In Texas. It's important to realize that a textbook frequently must pass muster with the members of State Textbook Commissions before it can be sold to any individual school districts. Literary tastes and moral predilections may cause committee members to declare a book unsuitable if they personally find something objectionable. With textbook review committees like that, it's easy to see how publishers arrived at a neutered *Romeo and Juliet*.

True, some English teachers preferred the bowdlerized version so they would never have to conduct a discussion on the evolution of the dirty joke or pun, but most English teachers loved the play in its entirety. Unfortunately, my company didn't offer the complete, unexpurgated play.

The rep and I met before my presentation to the literature selection committee.

"You've got to assure the committee we have the complete version of *Romeo and Juliet*," she said.

"But we don't," I countered.

"That doesn't matter. One committee member specifically asked me if our books censored anything, and I told her absolutely not. If she sees that we don't have the complete version of *Romeo and Juliet*, she won't vote for us."

"Well, you shouldn't have told her that. If I lie to the committee, they'll have no reason to trust anything else I tell them. I can't lie. I won't lie. I'd rather say nothing about *Romeo and Juliet* than lie about it."

I could see the frustration in the rep's face. This was her Texas territory. She wanted to win the business, and I was sales support. According to my job description, I worked for the representatives.

"You are working for me," she said emphatically. "And this is what I want you to do." She was adamant. "This is what I need you to do."

There they were—the very real horns of the dilemma. I want to win, but I will not lie. I want my job, but the person I'm working for is asking me to be unethical.

"You do understand that we've removed the entire first scene of Act One, don't you? It's gone. It normally comes in right after the Prologue and it's meant to set the tone, to be playful, to introduce us to some sexually-charged Elizabethan teenagers. But someone higher up on the editorial staff said we had to sacrifice that scene, in the name of purity, or sanctity, or something. God knows who did it and why."

"I don't care why it's gone, John. We've got to assure them that we have the whole play."

"Well, I'm sorry," I said, feeling genuinely apologetic. "I can't do that. We don't have the whole play. I'm sorry." I'd said I was sorry twice in the same breath. My wife calls that "being Catholic." Guilty as charged.

She became angry. "If you won't, I'll just have to do the presentation myself," she said.

And she did. I never entered the presentation room, but I did give her my overhead transparencies and my notes—notes that I'd long ago memorized and adapted and re-memorized and re-adapted and…

She didn't get the business…that is, *we* didn't get the business. I never knew why. Perhaps the committee perused *Romeo and Juliet* immediately after she falsely assured them that we offered the entire play. If a teacher had asked me if we had the complete *Romeo and Juliet* in our anthology, I would have answered quickly and candidly with a simple, "No."

I can imagine the best English teachers wanting the entire,

unexpurgated play. "Either give us Shakespeare, or don't. No half measures. No gap-toothed smiles."

Or perhaps she did a terrible presentation. I really don't know. She'd never been an English teacher, and she didn't talk the talk. That's what consultants were for.

Worst of all, she didn't mind lying to her customers. In my experience, that's never a wise choice. We never worked together after that.

I don't want to give the impression I couldn't walk close to the line where truth bumps up against falsehood. I could. Every teacher...no, every parent...knows where that boundary is. Whenever I got close, I chose silence. All textbooks—even those of our competitors—have their blind spots, important issues that editorial never addressed at all, or addressed inadequately, usually for economic or deadline reasons. I never talked about our weaknesses. I focused on our strengths, hoping they'd carry the day and be sufficiently persuasive.

I always felt better talking about *our* book, selling *our* book, rather than denigrating the competition. My job was to make *our* book shine. Because textbook presentations were all about our program's strengths, lies never served that agenda. Teachers scrutinized the books before and after we presented, and they'd know if we were attempting to pull a fast one. They invariably selected the book that solved the problems and challenges they felt needed to be solved.

Telling the truth. Veritas.

That's one of the secrets that helped me survive for twenty-six years as a consultant. Truth served my cause...and my career.

W is for Weather

Climate is what we expect; weather is what we get.
—Mark Twain

Go to Heaven for the climate—Hell for the company.
—Mark Twain

A great, great deal has been said about the weather,
but very little has ever been done.
—Mark Twain

Conversation about the weather is the
last refuge of the unimaginative.
—Oscar Wilde

MARK TWAIN WAS right. Everyone talks about the weather...particularly at airports...even though there is still nothing that anyone can do...except watch and wait. I've already written about the weather under *P is for Prayer* and *T is for Tragedy*, but road warriors drive as well as fly, and the weather can have a deleterious effect on cars as well as planes. When dark clouds gather and wind shear threatens, when blizzards close airports, when hailstorms rivet the wings of parked planes, all anyone can do is watch. And wait.

Weather fits into one of several "Misery loves company" categories for road warriors. It goes along with the "Sorry-sir-there-is-no-room-in-first-class" category and the

"It's-spring-break-and-there-are-150-middle-schoolers-on-board" category, and the ever popular "Sorry-we-are-out-of-liquor" category. Whenever the last three categories combine, a road warrior's woes increase dramatically.

Of all the things that can interrupt a trip—whether for business or pleasure—weather is the number one culprit. Complicating matters, it's not always the weather where you are, it's the weather where you're going. You may be sitting amidst sunshine, blue skies, and puffy clouds but your destination has been red-flagged for uncooperative weather. Snow, thunderstorms, and a variety of wild weather patterns can stall the beginning of a trip with a delightfully-named delay called a "ground hold." "Ground hold" is synonymous with "You are stuck where you are for now. Be patient and wait."

Every road warrior with a wealth of traveling experience has tales to tell when the subject turns to weather. Sometimes the gathering storm means it's time to "Get outta' Dodge." Sometimes the gathered storm can scare the hell out of passengers in a plane dodging the angry thunderheads. And sometimes the weather simply turns a trip into a prolonged waiting game...with a dash of danger.

Get Outta' Dodge

I was fast asleep in Denver, not Dodge, when my phone rang. The digital clock beside my bed assured me it was only 4:00 a.m., but the ringing phone overruled the glowing face of the clock.

"Sorry to call so early, John," said a recognizable voice. It was my boss, Rich Sayers. He lived in Fort Collins, Colorado, just north of Denver.

"That's okay," I said. "I had to get up to answer the phone." Comedy at 4:00 a.m. is my specialty. "So what's up?"

I could hear my boss chuckling. "Have you looked out your window?"

"Should I?"

"I wouldn't be calling otherwise."

Typically, I keep my curtains drawn when I stay in a hotel room. Years of habit, I guess. I rose and drew back the drapes. Snow was already piling up in the parking lot—three or four inches at least. "Wow!" I said. "I suppose this means I won't be talking to the Aurora teachers today, will I?" I generally stayed near the airport, but the falling snow obscured seeing much beyond the parking lot.

"They've already closed most of the Denver area school districts, John. I've had my TV on most of the night and Aurora announced just a while ago. This is supposed to be an all-day storm along the Front Range, and they expect at least a foot of snow. Probably more." Rich paused for a moment. "If you can get a flight home right now"—he emphasized *right now*—"you'll probably be able to get out before they close the airport. If you don't, you'll be stuck here for at least a day, maybe more."

"Good to know, Rich." I thanked Rich for giving me the heads-up and lighting a fire under me. "I can be out of here in fifteen minutes. Anything else?"

"Nope. That's why I called. Travel safely."

Rick traveled almost as much as I did, and he knew time was of the essence when the Colorado snows began piling up at Denver International. Without a shower or shave, I quickly packed my bag and checked out, trampling through four-inches of cold, dry, parking-lot powder to get to my rental car. My fingers numbed as I wiped off the windshield. As I climbed into my car, I wondered if I should refuel. *Now that's a stupid question*, I thought, *just get to the terminal*.

Which I did. As quickly as possible. End of drama.

I actually got a seat on the next Alaska Airlines flight to Seattle scheduled for 6:00 a.m. Denver International Airport closed at eight o'clock that morning, just about the time my flight was touching down in Seattle.

Elevator in the Sky

If you fly almost every week—and sometimes several times in the same week, or even several times on the same day—the words that every road warrior loves hearing are, "We are ready to board."

It deserves to be said that boarding on time is the norm. Airport horror stories all revolve around endless waiting, but as my Dad used to say, "Better to wait for a while than to die forever." Leave it to my father, a man with infinite patience. In that respect, I am not my father's son.

I used to love flying United Airlines because I could plug in my headset and listen to the cockpit talk with the tower on Channel 9. I always found the rhythm of the terse talk between pilots and air-traffic controllers fascinating. Once while climbing to altitude out of New Haven, Connecticut, the plane encountered wind shear[81] and that caused the plane—a Boeing 737—to feel like an express elevator headed down. Despite wearing a small United Airlines headset to eavesdrop on pilot chatter, I could hear screams from somewhere in the cabin. The plane certainly felt as if it were headed straight to the ground.

The radio crackled to life immediately. The cockpit reported the plane-wide elevator experience to someone on the ground with uncanny calmness. "Severe wind shear northeast of the airport at 1,500 feet."

"Roger, that," the ground responded.

That was all. No commentary deserving or requiring exclamation points. I'd like to say that experienced road warriors are inured to such occurrences, but that would be mere bravado…aka, a lie. Still, I have supreme confidence in the pilots during moments like these. These men and women have "flown" dozens of hours in simulators before their airline grants them the privilege of turning left rather than right when they board the plane. Additionally, pilots usually have two annual simulator training cycles where they once again deal with both the unusual and the unthinkable. My son-in-law, a floatplane pilot, once told me that "Flying is hours of tedium, interrupted occasionally by a few moments of sheer terror. I'll take the tedium any

---

81 Wind shear: a radical shift in wind speed and direction that occurs over a very short distance.

day." Me, too.

Nevertheless, when the plane and a down elevator feel synonymous, I always hope that there is sufficient air between the airliner and the ground. When that elevator stops its precipitous drop, I want the plane to proceed uneventfully to its destination. It always has.

Dark Clouds Over Idaho

There are those times in the lives of veteran road warriors when we are the ones behind the wheel—an automobile wheel, of course. During twenty-six years as a national textbook sales consultant, I drove at least 25,000 miles annually in my company car...and that's when I was home. I drove many more miles than that in rental cars—in big cities and tiny towns, in suburbs and rural areas, in good weather and lousy weather. I drove more than 600,000 miles, much of it over largely unfamiliar roads.[82] Sometimes I wish I'd kept a careful log of all my travels.

Unfortunately, there are no automobile simulators that might prepare us for every weather contingency. I've changed a flat tire on the Jersey-barrier side of a busy Illinois interstate. Detoured for flooded roads in Missouri—driving an additional eighty miles. Been stopped by Idaho state police because brush fires and dense smoke ahead made navigating the road impossible. Performed a graceful 360-degree pirouette in my rental car on the downhill side of a Colorado highway. Let me say that I hit nothing, and nothing hit me, but life did seem sweeter when my car came to a complete stop. Finally, on one trip back to Denver from Grand Junction, Colorado, I came to

---

82 Of course, we all now use GPS—or as I like to call it, "the voice of the Travel God"—to direct us wherever we go. That wasn't always the case. A few months after I retired, I finally sorted through a large bin of alphabetically arranged state and city maps that I had accumulated over almost three decades of traveling. I had maps of all fifty states, and bundled together with each state map were maps of cities in that state. For instance, bundled with the state map of Tennessee, I had city maps for Memphis, Nashville, Murfreesboro, Knoxville, and Chattanooga. Texas and California were neck and neck as the thickest stack of maps. Added up, I had more than 375 maps. [See: M is for Math]

an unexpected halt while a herd of elk surrounded my car. My car sat in the road as one giant brown-eyed stag with an impressive rack stared at me, his black nose steaming up the outside of my passenger window. Only after the elk herd had ambled across the highway did I realize I was only one of dozens of cars halted in amazement. And awe. Nature tends to do that.

Flat tires, fires, and elk don't really count as weather problems, but did I mention that I changed that tire in the rain, or that the elk seemed to be enjoying the snow flurries falling as they headed wherever they were heading?

But sometimes the weather creates unique problems—especially if the car experiences an equipment malfunction. Let me offer a brief, humorous example of what I mean.

On one trip to San Antonio, Texas, I was riding along with my colleague, Ysau Flores. He was driving his company van on I-410, one of the major ring roads allowing drivers easier access to the San Antonio suburbs. He and I were watching an approaching thunderstorm as we drove toward the Northside Independent School District. We could see the gray curtain of rain as it swept west toward us. It was no surprise when it hit, but we were both surprised when his windshield wipers failed. They simply wouldn't turn on. The deluge blinded us as we sped along at sixty miles per hour. Ysau didn't seem inclined to reduce his speed.

"Whoa, Ysau, slow down and pull over. Pull over." My voice was full of panic. The volume of rain on the windshield had obliterated any ability to see where we were going—much less know where we were. I quickly rolled down my window, the driving rain soaking me and my suit.

At least Ysau can use the passenger-side rearview mirror, I thought, *and we can both see where the shoulder of the road is.* Otherwise, we were driving blind.

But Ysau didn't slow down. At least not noticeably.

"Don't worry, John," Ysau said as he gripped the wheel and squinted fruitlessly through the rain-cloaked windshield, "I know the road."

Know the road? I said to myself. I was not about to play interstate blind-man's-bluff.

"Know the road?" I shouted. "Know the road? What the hell does that mean, Ysau? You can't see anything. Slow down and pull over, man. You can't see anything...and you certainly can't see where other cars are. Pull over. Pull over, now." I was scared. And loud, because I was scared.

At first, Ysau seemed just as perplexed at my response as I was at his, but then he slowed down and pulled over. My open window helped him navigate to the shoulder. I rolled up my window as we came to a stop. I was soaked, but we were safe.

"Sorry, John," he said, as he listened to the heavy rains pelt the outside of the car. He looked a bit sheepish as we sat there waiting for the squall to pass, but he managed a smile when he said, "You need a hair dryer, my friend." What could I do but laugh?

Those who travel for a living are expected to use common sense behind the wheel when weather-related problems crop up. The temptation to go, or keep on going, when one should stay put, is often irresistible.

Fortunately, I have knowledgeable colleagues like Rich Sayers, the supervisor who warned me to depart Denver before the snows made that impossible. More than once, a knowledgeable colleague has helped me avoid difficulty and grief.

I remember driving south from Boise toward Twin Falls, Idaho, with the local Idaho representative, Joyce Sutter. Once again, I was the passenger, and we were cruising along at 75 mph along I-84 in her Toyota Sienna. Joyce pointed to the eerie black clouds of a distant storm approaching from the south.

"See those clouds, John?" she asked as we zipped along.

"Sure, there's a storm coming north."

"Oh, you got that right, Johnny boy, but this is going to be a real doozy of a storm." She seemed quite calm despite what she'd just said. "Those aren't just dark clouds, those are black clouds...low-slung, black clouds. We're gonna get a hailstorm in just a few moments."

"I take it you've see this kind of thing before?"

"Oh yeah," Joyce said, "and you don't screw around with it."

As you may already know, storms are a lot like rivers. They tend to take the path of least resistance, and Joyce and I could see the storm moving northwest toward us following the Snake River Valley. The Sawtooth Mountains to the northeast and the Owyhee Mountains to the southwest flanked the Snake River Valley and provided a comfortable avenue for the storm to steer itself to the northwest. Joyce and I were in the middle of that avenue.

At first, nothing seemed unusual. But as soon as Joyce could see the hailstones dancing on the distant roadbed, she pulled her van to the shoulder and came to a complete stop. When the hailstones reached our parked car a few moments later, the din was deafening, and all the windows soon darkened under inches of accumulating ice. We sat saying nothing. The storm did all the talking.

Perhaps ten minutes passed, and then it was gone. The interior of the van was dark. It took considerable effort to open our car doors because they were encased in ice. The entire landscape— our car, the highway, and the scrub-brushed plains flanking the highway, glittered in the sunlight. I looked to see the black clouds moving off to the northwest.

"What now?" I asked.

"This will all melt pretty quickly," Joyce assured me. "Pretty cool, huh?"

She was right. Bathed in sunshine, the car and the landscape warmed rather quickly, and the hailstones began melting.

"We'll be able to leave in a few minutes," Joyce said. "I bet we'll see some accidents as soon as we get back on the road. It always happens. People don't know that you can't drive in a hailstorm. It's not like snow."

Joyce's prediction proved spot on. As we resumed driving south, it was clear more than a half-dozen cars failed to realize that the highway had become a veritable skating rink—and that they had tires and not skates on their cars. Most of the accidents were cars that had ploughed down the slope of the wide grass median. The worst wreck was a car that had skidded into a bridge abutment. In many cases, other drivers had already stopped on the shoulder to lend assistance.

At that moment, I realized that I probably would have been one of those unlucky drivers now stuck in the grassy median. I'd seen the same black clouds that Joyce had, but it never occurred to me that they signaled danger. Joyce's experience with these hailstone squalls kept us both out of harm's way.

When I asked her how she had learned about the effect of a hailstone roadbed, she simply gave me a broad smile and said, "Don't ask."

Smugness Cometh Before the Fall

As I said earlier, sometimes it's the weather where you are going rather than where you are that stalls your trip or creates real problems. Road warriors everywhere are confronted with problems they've never had before, and they do their best to improvise a solution.

For instance, I once arrived in Charlotte, North Carolina, just after Hurricane Hugo had hit in September 1989. My flight arrived on time—always a good thing—but I discovered that there were no rental cars—probably never a good thing. I had a reservation with Hertz, but enough local cars had been mangled or destroyed by Hugo that local rental car dealerships felt they had an obligation to the local residents. Ergo, no rental cars for out-of-towners. I was the out-of-towner—which translated into the out-of-lucker. Fortunately, the local representative loaned me her car, while she used her husband's.

In another instance, I had boarded a plane at the Nashville International Airport after two days of presentations to the Tennessee Textbook Committees. My 4:00 p.m. departure to Dulles International was about to push back. When I landed, I'd have a ninety-minute drive north to Martinsburg, West Virginia, to participate in the *West Virginia Council for the Teachers of English* where I would be the featured speaker tomorrow morning. Everything seemed to be going smoothly.

"Seemed" was the operative word. We'd been sitting in our aircraft waiting for pushback when the captain addressed us over the intercom. "Ladies and gentlemen, if you're wondering why we haven't pushed back, it's because we are currently on a ground hold. Thunderstorms in the Washington, DC area. We don't know how long this hold will last, but we'll do our best to keep you updated."

They did keep us updated. Every half hour or so they moved the departure out another half hour, and that's when I began to worry that they'd push our departure so far out that we'd finally be confronted with a cancellation. I needn't have worried. About 6:00 p.m. they cancelled the flight. When I asked them when I could be rebooked, they told me they could get me to Dulles by 1:00 p.m. tomorrow. Clearly, that wouldn't work for my 9:00 a.m. speech in Martinsburg.

I quickly decided that if I couldn't fly, I'd drive. I rented a car, estimating that Martinsburg was about 300 miles away. There were only two highways to navigate: I-40 and I-81. It would be high-speed interstate all the way. If I left Nashville by 7:00 p.m., I could make Martinsburg by 1:00 a.m., maybe 2:00 a.m. at the latest. After more than twenty years on the road, I was skilled in contingency planning. Having traveled around the US as much as I had, I felt fairly smug about my geographical knowledge. I could tell you the distance between San Francisco and Los Angeles, between St. Louis and Kansas City, between Jacksonville and Tampa. Name two cities: I trusted the map in my head. I felt I knew pretty much where various cities were—and could gauge distances between points A and B.

That's when I learned that "smugness cometh before the fall." The map in my head was wrong. By 327 miles. More than a 100% error.

As I pulled onto I-40, I called my wife Wendy to let her know what I was doing. "I'm driving from Nashville to Martinsburg."

"How far is that?" she asked.

"I'm guessing it's about 300 miles," I said, trusting that the map in my head would be accurate within a few miles.

"Let me look," Wendy said.

She was on her computer at home. The Tennessee local time was about 7:15 p.m. but she was at her desk at home where it was 5:15 p.m. I didn't have to wait long because one of Wendy's fortes was navigating the computer keyboard.

"How far did you say it was?"

"Three hundred miles…give or take."

"Well, you'd better be ready to give," she said, "because it's 627 miles. All interstate, but 627 miles. You must have been using your English-teacher math again."

It took me a moment to compute that number in my head. "Jesus," I said. "Damn, Wendy, how did I get that so wrong?"

"I don't know, but I just looked up the weather in Knoxville, and you're going to be driving through some crummy weather, too. Looks like thunderstorms."

I must have fallen silent because Wendy broke in and said, "Are you sure you want to do this?"

I took a deep breath. "Yeah. I'm going to keep on driving. I'm guessing eleven hours—twelve if I take a nap along the way."

"Make sure you stop the car before you take that nap," Wendy helpfully suggested. "You could always cancel and just fly home from Nashville, you know."

"I know. I thought about cancelling, but this is what I do," I said.

That was true. Besides selling books and talking to teachers about pedagogical methods, I traveled. And I was good at it. In fact, viewed from a time perspective, traveling was probably 70% of my job. Sometimes more. If one considers that the average daily commute is 25.5 minutes each way—or 51 minutes every day—most people working a forty-hour workweek spend about 10% of their time traveling. As I used to say, "Others commute, I travel."

"Don't forget," Wendy pointed out, "if it takes you twelve hours, it will actually be thirteen. Nashville is central time and Martinsburg is eastern."

"Well, I'm scheduled to speak at 9:00 a.m.—so we'll see. I can sleep all day tomorrow."

From her office in our Sammamish home, Wendy had often helped me solve traveling problems. Once, I needed to know where I could find a Radio Shack in south central New York State. She looked it up online and guided me. More than once I wanted to know where I could get my morning caffeine fix. She'd calmly open a new browser window and send me off in the right direction to the nearest Starbucks.

But tonight I would be doing all the driving—for 627 miles.

"Call me whenever you need to," Wendy said. "If I can't get you to cancel, I want to get you there alive, okay?"

"Okay," I said, as I drove east across Tennessee on I-40. In the gradually failing light, I could see thunderstorms gathering in the distance. "I'll call you along the way."

I drove, night fell, thunder and lightning crashed around me, and I felt the full weight of my dubious decision to drive. My mind seized on the postman's creed: "Neither snow nor rain nor heat nor gloom of night shall stay these couriers from the swift completion of their appointed rounds."

I thought to myself, *I notice the creed doesn't mention thunder and lightning*. Perhaps I wasn't a postman, but I was going to get to Martinsburg and give my speech. *I can do this. I travel for a living.*

At 7:45 a.m. EDT, after more than ten hours behind the wheel, four phone calls to Wendy, a full bag of black licorice, two Dr. Peppers, and two twenty minute naps at roadside rests, I pulled into the parking lot of Martinsburg's Holiday Inn.

As I registered, the desk clerk said that he had expected me to arrive last night.

"Me, too," I said. "Me, too. Long story, longer drive."

As soon as I got to my room, I shaved, showered, and dressed, only briefly debating whether I should risk taking a quick nap before going to the conference. I abruptly answered myself. *What the hell are you thinking?*

278

I went downstairs, asked the desk clerk for directions, and headed off to make my speech.

I'm pleased to say that things went off flawlessly. I'd made a similar speech to English teachers before, but as I began to speak, I remembered the advice I'd often given to my own students when they said they "didn't have anything to write about." I'd tell them that almost everything is a story, if you can just find the best way to tell it.

"Thank you for inviting me to speak to you this morning," I began. "I always enjoy speaking to English teachers, and I am glad to be here."

I paused and looked at the faces in the auditorium.

"Let me tell you just how glad I am. You see, yesterday evening at 7:00 p.m., I was in Nashville, Tennessee. I'll bet many of you know just where Nashville is, and I'll bet many of you would laugh at me if I told you that last night I was sure Nashville was only a three-hundred mile drive from Martinsburg."

They laughed.

"It isn't. Last night I discovered it is six hundred and twenty-seven miles, not three hundred."

They laughed, again.

"Six hundred and twenty-seven miles from Nashville International Airport to the Holiday Inn off Interstate 81, if you can believe the odometer of my rental car. I had intended to fly, but thunderstorms and a cancelled flight required me to rethink my travel plans. And therein lies a story."

Heads nodded. Faces smiled. And I knew that driving that six hundred and twenty-seven miles was a good choice.

"Isn't that what we are all about? Stories? What is life, all of life, if not a series of stories that we want to share?"

I loved talking to English teachers. We could talk about nouns or verbs or dangling participles, but if you wanted to get them really excited, talk stories.

So now I had another story to tell. The trip from Nashville to

Martinsburg.

And, I assured myself, *I will definitely never do that again.*

Famous Last Words

Rebecca Powell was a consultant colleague who lived in Ft. Lauderdale. When she joined McGraw-Hill in 1991, she suggested we divide the country for all future assignments. I thought she meant that we find the imaginary centerline of the United States—she'd take the east and I'd cover the west. But that's not what she had in mind. Instead, she was suggesting that we cut the US in two with a line traveling east-west—a line located along the 50-degree isotherm. She'd be happy to work in the warmer climes, those places south of the 50-degree isotherm. As for the colder climes north of the 50-degree isotherm, those would be mine.

"I'm warm-blooded," she said. "I live in Florida, and I simply don't have the clothes." She was teasing me, of course, but working in the colder climes during the winter frequently offered travel challenges that every road warrior has to deal with, and I'm not talking about wardrobe.

It was a Monday in late January 2011 and, like all my fellow passengers, I was a bit miffed by the announcement that our Seattle to Chicago flight was on a ground hold for at least two hours because of a Chicago snowstorm. The weather in Seattle was overcast and relatively warm, but Chicago's nasty weather would keep us on the ground here in Seattle—for a few hours, anyway.

My work during this trip included an 8:00 a.m. presentation to English teachers the next morning in Livonia, Michigan, a city just northwest of Detroit. I'd connect to a Detroit flight when I got to Chicago. That was my plan...but plans change.

My plane took off two hours late and landed at a snowy O'Hare International Airport two hours late. Funny how that works. Only then did I learn that all connecting flights to Detroit Metro Airport had been cancelled. The snowstorm that had caused our delay into

Chicago had moved off to the northeast—to a place called Detroit.

This is Nashville all over again, I thought.

Well, that's only partly true. A drive to Detroit would be less than half the distance—282 miles—but it would be nighttime driving all the way with a blustery snowstorm thrown in for good measure. Should I attempt to drive to Livonia for my Tuesday morning sales presentation, or should I simply find a local hotel room in Chicago and skip Livonia? I was scheduled to make a sales presentation in Elgin, Illinois, on Wednesday afternoon.

My thoughts were always, *I don't want to let the representative down. If I can do this, I'll do it.*

Flying to Detroit was out, so driving was my only option. I rented a car, and at 6:00 p.m. I headed out of O'Hare and drove southeast around the southern reaches of Lake Michigan. Once again, I questioned the wisdom of this journey.

What the hell, John, are you out of your freakin' mind? I thought. *It's snowing, it's blowing, and you could get stuck somewhere and then what?*

Road warriors have these quiet debates with themselves when their best instincts warn them against the very actions they are taking.

I kept driving. The trip north on I-94 along the eastern shore of Lake Michigan proved to be the snowiest and windiest, with huge gusts buffeting the car. I doubt that I ever drove faster than 35 miles an hour along that stretch of highway, but I kept driving. Clearly, I arrived in Livonia alive and well, but I didn't arrive until about 4:30 a.m.—3:30 a.m. Chicago time. It had taken nine and a half hours to drive 282 miles.

As I said, *Nashville all over again, but with snow.*

As I climbed out of my car into the frigid air of the snow-filled hotel parking lot in Livonia, I shook my head in disapproval. *Dummkopf,* I thought. *You could have killed yourself. You might get ninety minutes of sleep before you have to be up and off to the Livonia School District central office.*

Fortunately, the district office was only a mile away.

After an unsatisfactory ninety-minute snooze—hardly getting my money's worth—I showered, dressed, and drove to the Livonia School District offices.

That's when I repeated the comment I'd made to myself earlier that morning, only louder as I pounded my steering wheel.

Dummkopf! Dummkopf! Dummkopf!

Except for my car, the snow-filled district parking lot was empty. Completely empty. I was flying solo. Did I have the wrong day?

I called the local representative—she had set up the sales presentation—and apparently my call got her out of bed. She seemed surprised to hear from me. "Oh, hi John," she said in a sleepy voice. "School is cancelled in Livonia today. There won't be any presentation, but you probably know that, don't you. Where are you anyway?"

There was a long pause before I answered.

Don't we have voicemail? I thought. I was steamed, but there was that small voice telling me that I should have suspected something like this after my driving-through-blinding-snow marathon last night.

"I'm in the district parking lot," I said.

It was the rep's chance to fall silent for a moment or two. "Oh, John," she said with genuine sincerity, "I'm so sorry. I called the airline last night and they said your flight into Detroit had been cancelled. So I figured you wouldn't be here. And I already knew the district had cancelled school." I could hear something rustling in the background. "You didn't drive through that storm, did you?"

"All night," I said.

"Oh, John," she fell silent again. "Well," she said, "that's clearly above and beyond."

Beyond? I thought. *Beyond stupid. I could have died on the way here.* But my annoyance at her evaporated when that small voice wagged its finger at me. *You know, John, she never asked you to drive almost 300 miles through a snow storm. You did that all on your own.*

"Okay," I said. "I guess we'll reschedule." I hung up and immediately felt an overwhelming weariness wash over me. I needed sleep.

I drove back to my hotel room and set my alarm for 11:45.

Check-out was at noon. As I dropped into bed, I vowed to never again pull a death-defying, late-night, snow-filled marathon like that. *Never again*, I said to myself. *Never again.* Again that small voice whispered in my ear before I drifted off. It sounded suspiciously like my mother.

Never again? Sure. Famous last words.

X is for X-rated

*The difference between men and women is that, if given the choice
between saving the life of an infant or catching a fly ball,
a woman will automatically choose to save the infant,
without even considering if there's a man on base.*
–Dave Barry

*Always remember that you are absolutely unique.
Just like everyone else.*
—Margaret Mead

*Why does a woman work ten years to change a man,
then complain he's not the man she married?*
—Barbra Streisand

IT'S MY UNDERSTANDING that men and women are different. Why else would the French have an expression for it? *Vive la différence!* When those differences are exposed for all to see, we move into X-rated territory.

That's how I came to name this chapter *X is for X-rated.* The title is probably misleading because a reader looking for salacious material will be sadly disappointed. Sorry. The very last episode in this chapter comes closest to a conventional x-rating, but after rereading it, I found it more comic than titillating. Again, my apologies.

When the discussion turns to the differences between male and female road warriors—men and women who spend more than fifty percent of their work lives on the road—all I can say is this: They travel very differently. Women worry about things that seldom worry men.

During the first few years of my consultant career, my McGraw-Hill consultant colleagues were all women. That never struck me as unusual because, for more than a decade, I'd been an English teacher, a position where most of my fellow English teachers were not fellows at all—they were women. As I traveled around the country speaking to committees of English teachers, I quickly realized that English departments are female domains. Male English teachers were decidedly the minority.

While attending my first McGraw-Hill national sales meeting, the topic of traveling safely sparked a lively discussion among the consultants. We each understood the extent of the required travel—150 to 160 days on the road—but until that conversation, I never realized how differently we organized our travel—physically and psychologically. When I said I'd never given the idea of traveling safely much thought, my fellow consultants responded in unison—"That's because you're a guy."

They explained their "rules for safe traveling." The rules could all be summarized with the single exhortation: You can't be too careful.

Rule number one for female road warriors: Travel in daylight. They knew, of course, that they would be traveling occasionally at night, checking into hotels late, gassing up their rental cars beneath garish gas station lights, but whenever possible, do everything during the day. Walking alone in the dark was not high on their list of smart things to do. You can't be too careful.

Rule number two: Always be vigilant. Be vigilant in parking lots, at airports, in hotels. Be vigilant everywhere. Their sense of being perpetually "on guard" surprised me. They all spoke about trusting their intuitive feelings. If something felt off—one colleague used the word "strange," while another used "hinky"—they avoided it. The anecdotes flowed freely as each of my female colleagues explained situations which felt "off," "strange," or "hinky."

"I pulled into a gas station one night and something just felt hinky," Brenda explained. "So I drove away. I just had a bad feeling about that place." All the women said they knew exactly what she meant. I didn't, possibly because I hadn't yet learned that you can't be too careful.

As they traded tales, I was flattered to hear that I was actually the hero when Nancy related her safe travel story. My colleague Nancy and I had checked into a hotel in Portland, Oregon. About a half hour after I'd gotten my bag unpacked—that is, after I'd hung up my suits—she phoned and urgently asked me to come to her room.

When I arrived, she walked over to her partially open window and explained that she couldn't get the window closed. Her sash-style window—something common in older hotels, and this was definitely a vintage hotel—wasn't open more than five inches, but she'd had no luck closing it. Closing stubborn windows is a guy thing, right? So I tried to shut it, practically standing on the top rail of the bottom window. Still no luck. Then we tried together, unsuccessfully. That was one stubborn window.

We were both staring at the window when she declared, "I can't stay in this room, John. It's not safe. I called the desk earlier, and they said they're full tonight. When I told them to send up a repairman, they said that could take more than an hour." I could see she was upset.

"Don't worry," I said with mock gallantry, "we can trade rooms." It seemed like the simplest solution. "Gather your things and come up to my room, and we'll swap. Okay? But don't forget, if they find my lifeless, bludgeoned body tomorrow morning, it's your fault." It took her only a moment to see that I was kidding. As she gathered up her belongings and walked out the door, she remarked, "You can't be too careful."

That stubborn open window was an annoyance to me, but for

Nancy it was clearly a safety issue. And the repairman never showed.

Rule number three: Get a room in a hotel that has interior corridors—not outside entrances facing the parking lot. If possible, stay on the second floor or above. When possible, make sure the hotel has its own restaurant and room service. If it doesn't, find a hotel with a nearby restaurant, preferably a two-minute walk or less.

Among the women, there was general unanimity about the rules, none of which had ever occurred to me. Even now I can hear the refrain, *That's because you're a guy,* tap-dancing in the back of my brain.

Additionally, several of my colleagues had certain safety rituals they observed, and I found Melanie's Entering-the-Hotel-Room ritual fascinating.

"I unlock my door," Mel explained, "and place my luggage against the door so it stays open. Then I walk into my room, turn on the lights, open the blinds, check the bathroom—make sure the shower curtain is pulled completely back—check the closet, and check under the bed." All of my female colleagues nodded in agreement. "Only then do I remove my luggage from the door, close and lock the door, and attach the safety latch." More agreement. "I always worry some guy will jump out. You can't be too careful."

I had listened carefully, realizing just how seriously these women took traveling safety. Far more seriously than I did. The only serious traveling issues for me were extreme punctuality [See: U is for Unexpected] and filing my expense reports on time [See: C is for Credit Card]. It had never occurred to me that I should be on alert when entering my hotel room. I decided to lighten the conversation.

"When I get to my hotel room," I explained, "I don't hold the door open with my suitcase or anything else. In fact, I open the door as quickly as possible, shut it behind me just as quickly, and launch myself immediately onto the bed, hoping some beautiful woman will burst out of the bathroom or the closet and take advantage of me."

They all flashed me that disparaging look: *You're such a guy.*

If you travel often enough, you will experience a few startling—perhaps even scary—moments. These moments will be exactly that—just moments—but they will remain in memory for a long time. I've had several such moments, and I began internalizing what my female colleagues had been reciting: You can't be too careful.

Once in an Oklahoma City hotel room, I had just unpacked my suitcase when the phone rang. It was quite late—after midnight, but any time after 9:30 p.m. is late for me. I assumed the desk clerk was calling for some reason, so I picked up the phone.

It wasn't the desk clerk. The voice on the other end was definitely male, and that voice was asking me in quiet, sultry tones if I wanted some company for the evening. As hard as I tried, I couldn't identify the voice, and I didn't know anyone in Oklahoma City.

I'm sure I said something stupid in response like, "What are you talking about," but truthfully I can't remember. It took me only a few moments to realize I was being solicited before I said, "No. No, thank you." Then I hung up.

I found my own reaction a bit baffling. *You said 'thank you,' John?* I asked myself. *Why the hell did you say 'thank you?'*

This is one of those internal conversations you have when confronted by an entirely novel situation. I was neither gay nor promiscuous, but my response almost sounded as if I was saying, *No, I'm not in the mood for gay sex tonight, but thanks for asking. Maybe next time.*

As I thought about the call, a vague uneasiness replaced my curiosity. Whoever called my room knew my room number. Whoever it was had probably seen me arrive, and was probably close by. I immediately lowered my blinds, locked my door, put on the safety latch, and jammed the top of my desk chair under the door knob—a move I hoped was actually an authentic method for stopping an intruder and not just some Hollywood gimmick. I even looked under the bed.

You can't be too careful.

Sometimes these moments are more comic and awkward than startling. On one trip early in my publishing career, I attended a book conference in Vancouver, British Columbia. After our exhibit had closed for the day, several of my colleagues and I went to dinner, and one of the things I found I liked about the French influence in Canada is their penchant for leisurely dining. Dinner commenced at 6:00 and we pushed back from the table about 10:00.[83]

Back at my hotel room, I changed clothes and prepped everything for the next morning. Sleepwear for me was a t-shirt and a pair of loose jogging shorts. No pj's. When I was a child, my mother would buy me pajamas for Christmas—I know because there is photographic proof that I used to wear pajamas. But I gave up pajamas after high school. I often joked that I wore jogging shorts so that I could jump out of bed and zoom down the road without interruption.

The TV was on—I've always been a news junkie—when I heard a knock at my door. It was late, close to midnight. But I was attending a conference, so I had several colleagues staying in the hotel, and a few teachers who I knew were there as well.

If I'd been an adherent of Melanie's Opening-the-Hotel-Door-Late-at-Night ritual, I could have avoided what followed.

First of all, Melanie would probably be wearing pajamas—or a night gown—and she'd probably put on a robe, go to the door, and look through the peep hole. She might even conduct a conversation through the closed door. "Who is it?" "What do you want?" "Do you realize how late it is?" When, and only when she was satisfied that the person in the hallway presented no threat, would she open her door. The safety latch would remain chained the entire time. You can't

---

83 I had considered writing a chapter on food—or about the best restaurants I encountered over a quarter century on the road. But my tastes are quite pedestrian and I seldom made note of the restaurants where I dined. Over the years, I found myself far more interested in people and the way they behave.

be too careful.

Me, I went to the door, and opened it.

Before me stood a very attractive woman, while I stood in my t-shirt and jogging shorts. Despite my earlier braggadocio, I did not invite her in to take advantage of me.

However, that is precisely why she had knocked on my door.

"Are you John?" she asked.

I knew the answer to that question. But I didn't know who was asking or why. I was looking at a smiling brunette, maybe five-eight in heels, possibly in her mid-twenties, wearing a fitted wool jacket with a fur collar, and a fairly tight skirt. She held a black clutch purse against her bosom. She had striking dark eyes and amazingly red lips. I knew immediately what she was selling...and it wasn't Girl Scout cookies.

"Can I help you?" I asked.

"I don't know," she said in a quiet, hotel-corridor voice while smiling coquettishly. "You called, and here I am."

"I called?" It was a question. "I didn't call. Who did I call?" I felt very nervous. My mind was racing with the realization that the young lady standing in the corridor was a call girl. A prostitute. A hooker. My English teacher's mind drifted to the Elizabethan synonym—strumpet. Maybe if I had declaimed, "Thou art a strumpet," she might have run off and solved my problem, but that was just another missed opportunity.

Rather than answering my questions, she asked, "May I come in?"

Another simple question.

"Uh...who are you?"

"I'm Gabrielle. May I come in?"

A third simple question.

I should have had simple answers to her simple questions, but I stood stupidly in the doorway. I should have said *No*, but I was curious. "Do I know you? How do you know my name?"

I watched as this sweet coquette began morphing into an impatient woman.

"You're wasting time, you know?" Her head dropped to one side as if she were trying to look over my shoulder into the room.

"Look, I'm not sure what's going on here." I tried smiling at her as if that would somehow persuade her that I was in earnest. "I didn't call you. I'm afraid you have the wrong room. You definitely have the wrong person."

"I know *you* didn't call *me*." She stopped for a moment and then began explaining as if I were a two-year-old. "You called my service... *they* called me...and here I am." Her voice tinged with annoyance.

"I'm sorry, miss, I...I...I didn't call you, and I'm certain I didn't call your service." A wave of embarrassment swept over me. A call girl was standing at my door, and I was thoroughly unaccustomed with late-night, call-girl etiquette.

I decided I needed to be more emphatic. "I wouldn't call your service."

"Look." She spoke with growing volume—the coquette had disappeared. "You called, and now I'm here. My time is valuable. I could be somewhere else, except you called and asked for a girl."

Apparently, we were having two completely different conversations. She was frustrated, certain that I called, and I was embarrassed and knowing full well that I hadn't.

She pulled a small piece of paper from her pocket. "You're John Scannell, right?"

She'd mispronounced my last name, but half the world does that. What confused me was that she seemed sincere enough. She had the right name and the right room number in the right hotel—and then the light came on.

"Miss....Gabrielle...I'm afraid someone is playing a trick on you...and me, too. Someone's playing a prank on both of us. I don't know who called your service, but it wasn't me. I'm sorry you've come here for nothing."

Now I was facing an angry woman.

"What the hell." She spat the words like a bad taste.

Her quiet do-not-disturb-voice escalated into a shout as the two of us stood in my open doorway.

"You owe me a hundred dollars," she said at the top of her voice.

"What? No. No, I don't," I insisted. I failed at keeping my voice low.

"Well, I'm not leaving until you pay me," she said.

I didn't know what to do. A friend told me I should have just shut the door in her face. Another said I should have called hotel security. I did neither.

"Wait here," I said.

I hurriedly rescued a twenty-dollar bill from my wallet and handed it to her as she stood in the hallway. Whatever I thought might happen, didn't.

She snatched the twenty from me but made no move to leave. "I need more."

It's difficult to look authoritative in a t-shirt and jogging shorts, but I had grown angry as well. "Well, good luck getting it. That's all I have."

That was a lie, but I just wanted this indelicate encounter over.

"I'm sorry you came for nothing, but I didn't ask you to come here. I don't know who did, but it wasn't me." I began closing my door. "I gave you all my money," I said repeating the lie. "That's the easiest twenty dollars you'll ever make."

I watched her turn and walk angrily toward the elevators.

Why did you give that woman twenty dollars? I asked myself. *You know you should have immediately said, "No," don't you?*

I hate it when I can't win an argument with myself.

Upon further reflection, I realized I should have followed Melanie's Opening-the-Hotel-Door-Late-at-Night ritual. That is, Melanie would never have opened the door. I can see her wagging her finger at me and saying, "You can't be too careful."

The following morning, a representative from one of my company's competitors—one of the guys with whom I had dined the previous evening—asked me if I'd had a good time last night. I said I loved the leisurely dining, and he gave me an impish smile.

"I mean later. After dinner. Did you have a good time?"

It took me a moment to realize he'd been the one who phoned the call-girl service and set me up.

"What? A good time? No." I looked at him as if I'd never seen him before. "What the hell were you thinking?"

"It was a joke."

"It wasn't funny...not to her...and not to me. I sent her away," I said.

"You sent her away?" He sounded surprised.

"Yeah, I did. I'm no angel, but..." I couldn't think of anything else to say. He ignored the look on my face.

"Was she good looking?" he asked.

I shook my head. "None of your business." I turned to walk away. "Next time you pull a stunt like that, just make sure you pay the fee in advance, so I can enjoy myself on your dime. By the way, you owe me twenty bucks."

It was his chance to say, "What?"

I love New York City. I always loved attending textbook conferences there because NYC means great food and great theatre. Sometimes I'd even skip dinner with colleagues, and snag a single ticket to a Broadway show—usually a musical. Single tickets were easily available.

Early in my publishing career, when I was still a practicing Catholic, I enjoyed attending Sunday Mass at NYC's most inspiring cathedral—St. Patrick's on Fifth Avenue. The time had long passed since I was religious about attending Sunday Mass when I was on the road—and yes, the pun is intended. For years, I often traveled on Sundays and attending Sunday Mass was simply not possible.

So, here I was, in New York City on a brisk November Saturday evening. Many of my colleagues had decided to go to Little Italy for dinner, but, on a whim, I decided I'd go to see my favorite musical,

Les Misérables—probably for the fourth or fifth time. And yes, I was once again reduced to tears. *Les Miz* does that.

I returned to my hotel happily humming *Bring Him Home*. As I watched the late news and readied for bed, my mood persuaded me to attend early Mass at St. Patrick's. Both St. Patrick's and *Les Misérables* are solemn, spiritual, and uplifting, each in its own way.

Attending seven o'clock Mass meant I should leave the hotel by 6:30 a.m., so I set my alarm for 5:30 a.m.

I woke up one minute before my alarm went off and turned on the TV to find out if I should bundle up. At 6:30 a.m., I set out for St. Patrick's, dressed against the frigid November morning. By my reckoning, I was about nine blocks from St. Patrick's: two-and-a-half east-west blocks—those are the longer blocks—and seven shorter north-south blocks.

It was very cold—the wind burned my face and made my eyes water—but my overcoat and knit cap kept the rest of me warm. I pulled up my collar and tucked my chin into my overcoat and walked along quickly, wishing I'd worn a scarf…or hailed a cab. My hands were shoved deep in the pockets of my overcoat.

Official sunrise wouldn't be for another fifteen minutes, but it would be well past sunrise before the sun warmed NYC's concrete canyons.

There was virtually no traffic, so I crossed streets without looking at the stoplights. I'd just jaywalked and stepped onto the sidewalk, when I came to an abrupt, involuntary halt. Two women, one on each side of me, had each threaded one of their arms through one of my arms. I had a two-person escort.

"Whoa, whoa, sunshine. Where you goin' in such a hurry?" one of them said after they pulled me to a complete stop.

For a moment I couldn't see either of them, and a sense of panic seized me. Then they both stepped in front of me, standing shoulder to shoulder, keeping a firm grip on each of my arms. One tall and one short. My overcoat and hat helped keep the cold at bay, but these two women were clearly not dressed for the weather. They had gloves, but only one wore a hat. They both wore short skirts, high heels, and tight but partially unzipped jackets to show off their cleavage. *Advertising,* I thought, and *their legs must be freezing.*

"You cold darlin'?"

"Yes, I am." I didn't know if my voice quavered from cold or from fear.

"'Course you are, it's cold out. What are you doin' out here this time of the morning?" asked the tall one, tightening her grip on my arm.

"Maybe he's lookin' for us," the other replied speaking to her friend. "You lookin' for us, darlin'?"

I couldn't get a word in edgewise or otherwise.

"You like to play with girls?" the tall one asked as she massaged my arm.

"Bet he does," said the other. "He hasn't run away yet."

Running away didn't feel like an option. I was a very small mouse in the claws of two cats.

The tall one put her face close to mine. "You want to take time out of your busy morning and play with us?" I could feel her warm breath on my face, her words coming out in puffy clouds.

"I don't think he can afford us," said the short woman in confidential tones. "Can you afford us, honey?" she asked me.

Oh my God, the voice in my head screamed. *They're going to rob me.* Fear gnawed at me. If they had asked me for my wallet at that moment, I would have handed it over.

I blurted out, "I can't. I'm going to early Mass at St. Patrick's."

"You hear that? Did I hear right?" the tall woman said in mock surprise. "You goin' to church, darlin'?"

I nodded, my vision shifting by turns to each one. Their grip on my arms hadn't lessened.

"Gonna let Jesus warm you up?"

I nodded again.

"Well, honey, will you say a prayer for us?" said her shorter companion.

I nodded. Fear made me swallow my words.

"Yeah. Tell Jesus we need some warmer weather," the taller one said as she released her hold on my arm.

The shorter one pulled me closer and whispered in my ear. "Nah. You tell that Jesus of yours we want some really rich guys to take us to someplace warm. Okay? Someplace where we can take our clothes off." She kissed my cheek. "Okay?"

"Okay," I said. Suddenly I was free.

The shorter woman had released my arm, too. The two women sauntered away in the morning cold. The one who'd planted the kiss on my cheek turned and shouted, "Don't forget. You're gonna ask Jesus for some sunshine and sand."

I shouted back. "I'll remember."

The tall one waved as if I were an old friend. "You stay safe now, darlin'." And then they were gone.

What just happened? I asked myself. I could feel my fear ebbing. *Were those two working girls just playing with me after a long cold night on the streets? Was I just a pleasant diversion in the dim, unpleasant cold?*

They'd gone, and I hadn't moved.

Well, good news, I said to myself. *They didn't rob me.*

Relieved, I turned and walked as quickly as possible to St. Patrick's, knelt down quietly in the cavern of the cathedral, and said a prayer. Several prayers.

After Mass, I stepped out into a cold gray morning. New York City had begun waking up. I considered walking back to the hotel, but I took a cab.

Did I just hear Melanie whisper, "You can't be too careful?"

Y is for Yahoos! and Yikes!

Surprises are all part of life's journey.
—Steven Redhead

WITHOUT DOUBT, THE life of a road warrior is full of surprises. Surprises come in two flavors: Yahoos!—a word that requires no explanation—and Yikes!—a synonym for yuck or "Uh-oh!" As you might imagine, Yahoos! were always preferable. Here's a sampling of Yahoos!

I worked in every state, in communities large and small, talked to teachers in rich districts and poor. Best of all: I saw the USA…a significant part of it anyway. Yahoo!

I frequently upgraded to first-class because of my airline status. Yahoo!

I visited my far-flung friends and family virtually every year instead of every five?…or ten? …years. Because I could. Yahoo!

When a school district server went down just as I began my workshop with a group of high school advanced placement teachers in Georgia, one of them suggested we go to Starbucks to use their wi-fi. We had great wi-fi…and great coffee! Yahoo!

I took teachers to major league baseball games in EVERY major league city. Yahoo!

I took teachers to Broadway shows. Yahoo!

I visited every major Civil War battlefield with teachers in tow. Yahoo!

I visited more than twenty National Parks. Yahoo!

A Triple Yahoo! I was able to read all the novels and historical works I've ever wanted to read—on company time. Yahoo! And the company bought the books. Yahoo! And I gave away most of those books to teachers. Yahoo!

I was selected Consultant of the Year in 2003 and went to Bermuda as my reward. Yahoo!

A person could travel forever if the road warrior life were a sea of Yahoos!—the sun shining, everything on schedule, and the TSA folks smiling. But that's not always the case. I was once told that the typical national publishing consultant lasts five years or less. I can see why. I once considered why people might quit the road warrior life. The list was easy to concoct:

1. The travel. It is constant and wearying.
2. The time away from home. One spends too many nights in hotel rooms.
3. The lack of routine. About tomorrow: Where will I be? What will I be doing?
4. Health problems. Soldier on. Don't get sick until the holidays.
5. The loneliness. Knowing yourself is not always easy.
6. The tedium. Life is an endless succession of airports, hotels, and schools.

Or it could be too many Yikes! Too many surprises—surprises that come in an unhappy, endless array.

I arrived at airports multiple times to find that my flight was delayed...indefinitely. Yikes!

I survived a dozen missed approaches and two aborted take-offs. Yikes!

The tire of my rental went flat while I was driving in the far-left lane on Los Angeles' crowded I-110—which has five lanes. I had to fix the flat. Yikes!

A streaking foul ball hit by Mark McGwire in Busch Stadium narrowly missed my head, and I spilled my beer on the regional manager. Yikes!

I miscalculated the driving distance to my next presentation by more than 300 miles. Yikes!

My Ford Taurus was rear-ended in Salem, Massachusetts, by a teenage courier in a hurry. Yikes!

The meniscus in my left knee failed while stepping out of my rental car in Anchorage. Yikes!

My Chicago hotel elevator stalled with a couple of claustrophobics aboard. Yikes!

I got "the runs" in the middle of a critical North Carolina presentation. Yikes!

My Gary, Indiana, computer-based workshop stalled because the teacher who knew the access codes for the computer lab had retired. He was vacationing in France, and was unreachable. Yikes!

I was stuck in a middle seat on an eight-hour flight to Guam. Yikes!

I prepped to do an Indianapolis workshop for 190 teachers, and seven showed up. Yikes!

I was thirty feet from the school's front door, and the Florida rain refused to abate. I dashed through the unrelenting deluge. I got soaked. Yikes!

If traveling were all Yahoos!, there would be no stories. Any English teacher will tell you that a good story depends on conflict—a problem—the Yikes! No conflict, no story. Sometimes the conflict ends happily when the protagonist adapts or changes. Sometimes it ends unhappily when the protagonist cannot improvise or adapt. Sometimes the conflict concludes comically when people are surprised—sort of a Yahoo! and a Yikes! yoked together—as they are in the following story.

McGraw-Hill had just acquired a new dictionary that its sales force would be selling in the high schools—at least that was the story we were told. In reality, we probably would not be selling the dictionary at all. Dictionaries would be offered as a free-with-order item to sweeten the deal for districts interested in purchasing our literature and writing programs. This was standard operating procedure in the school publishing business. If a school district decided to purchase one of our high school literature programs, every literature teacher would receive a class set of dictionaries—about 30 to 35 dictionaries each. It was a great deal. Who could possibly object?

New books, like this new dictionary, were typically sent to representatives and consultants for us to "drop off" to language arts chairs or language arts curriculum directors so they could review and evaluate them.

When I received my carton of dictionaries, I immediately gave one to Terry Leister, the language arts curriculum director in the Northshore School District, my home school district. Over the years Terry had purchased numerous programs from me. He also taught Advanced Placement English, in addition to his curriculum duties. True to form, Terry scrutinized our new dictionary thoroughly. I trusted Terry's advice because when he evaluated educational materials, he was a man on a mission.

A few days later, on a sunny Friday afternoon, Terry phoned me.

"Hey, John," he began, "I'm glad I got you at home. I was afraid you might be on the road."

"Nope. I'm at home, why?"

"How about me swinging by this afternoon about 4:00? You'll want to have a six-pack on ice because there's something I need to show you. Okay?"

Terry had aroused my curiosity. "Alright, Leister. What's going on? What are you going to show me?"

"Can't tell you. It's a surprise," he said in a teasing tone. "You wouldn't want to spoil the surprise."

"A surprise? Will I like this surprise?"

"Hmmm. Good question." Terry was being very evasive.

"Will I not like this surprise?"

"An equally good question. But don't worry, we'll have a few beers, and that's the best way to end the week, don't you think?"

"So, you're not going to tell me, are you?"

"Nope." He paused. "Can't." He paused again. "Won't." He was toying with me.

"Okay. See you at four."

"Don't forget the beer," he said as he hung up.

I didn't forget the beer, and Terry showed up at my front door at precisely four o'clock. My kids were outside playing, and my daughter, Mandy, shouted into the house, "Hey, Dad, Terry's here."

Terry, a tall, lanky, long-limbed guy, walked into my kitchen and settled onto a stool at the kitchen counter. He plunked the dictionary

I'd given him on the counter-top, while I opened two bottles of beer.

"Okay, Dr. Leister," I said, handing him his beer. "What's your surprise?"

"Got it right here," he said, patting the unopened dictionary.

"Our dictionary?"

"McGraw-Hill's brand new and improved high school diction-ary," he said with a smug smile. "McGraw-Hill's brand new and im-proved, *surprising* high school dictionary."

"What could possibly be surprising?"

He opened the book and thumbed through till he reached the page he wanted. He looked up, and sipped his beer. "Let me ask you a question. Is sixty-nine simply the number that follows sixty-eight?"

I took a moment to consider what he'd just said. "That's one definition."

"Maybe. But it's not the definition that your dictionary provides. McGraw-Hill's definition is far more exciting, way more explicit."

I moved around the counter to sit beside him. Terry pushed the book toward me, his long finger underlining the word "sixty-nine."

I started laughing. "You've gotta be kidding. Honest to God."

"Oh," Terry said, "it gets better. Lots better. Mr. Scannell, your new dictionary has all the words in it." And he laughed uproariously. "All the words."

We spent the next hour drinking beer and finding "all the words"—words normally excluded from dictionaries out of prudish-ness or modesty. Each new taboo word caused another eruption of laughter, and I don't think we stopped laughing that entire afternoon.

"I'll tell you this," Terry said. "If my students have this dictionary, they'll never misspell 'motherfucker' ever again. That's a real plus."

"Do you think the Northshore School District would purchase this dictionary?" I asked him.

"Only if you smuggled it in through the back door at midnight," Terry said. "These folks blush when you say 'poopy-face.' The word 'shit' is strictly *verboten*. Imagine what they'd do with all the varia-tions of 'fuck.'"

I could only imagine, until I conducted a series of literature work-shops for several dozen high school English teachers in San Diego. One of my jobs was to guide teachers through the various features of the program they'd just purchased, and familiarize them with all the support materials that accompanied the program. Workshops like this required about three hours—longer if I was working with fledgling teachers—and I'd typically do one grade level at a time. This particular morning began with a room full of ninth grade English teachers.

As I concluded the workshop, I did what I always do. I told them how they could contact me, and I asked them if there were "any questions for the good of the order," an expression I inherited from my father. One teacher raised her hand.

"You have a question?" I asked.

"Not exactly. What can you tell us about the dictionaries we are getting?" she asked.

Unsure where her question was leading, I decided to go for the comic comment.

"Well," I said, "you'll be pleased to know that all the words are in alphabetical order. A McGraw-Hill first."

Most of the teachers laughed, but the questioner would not be deterred.

"Have you looked at your dictionary?" she asked with a trace of frustration.

Comedy won't put this woman off, I thought. *I've got to treat her respectfully and professionally.*

"Yes. Yes, I have."

"Mr. Scannell, my students are ninth graders. They're thirteen and fourteen years old. They're kids."

Now I knew where she was going, and I suddenly flashed on that beer-infused afternoon, when Terry and I laughed our way through the new dictionary. I couldn't help but smile.

"You're concerned because these new dictionaries have all the words, aren't you?"

"Yes, I am."

Other teachers looked back and forth between their colleague and me, a bit confused. Most of them had not yet looked at the dictionaries their students would be using. In fact, most of them hadn't seen the dictionary until it was given to them when they arrived for the workshop.

I decided it was best if I waded into the "language appropriateness" issue before it became a problem. Perhaps it was already a problem for some teachers, but it wasn't a problem for me.

"May I be completely candid?" I asked.

"By all means," she said.

"All of you will be receiving class sets of the dictionary we gave you when you arrived today." I held up a copy. "I know we're already done with today's workshop, and it's time for you to leave, but please humor me for a few minutes more, okay?"

They all put their dictionaries on their desks.

"Recently, a good friend of mine and I went through this dictionary," I said. "I'd given him a copy—he's a curriculum director—and he brought certain facts to my attention." I could feel myself dancing around the issue and needed to get to the point. "I feel obligated to tell you…this dictionary has all the words in it. All of them."

I looked around the room, trying to read their faces. How could I drive this point home?

"Okay. Think of a word you find vile or offensive. Okay? Now, open your dictionary to see if it's in there."

Pages started turning, and giggles, gasps, and guffaws followed. Many turned to colleagues asking, "What word did you find?" And the giggles, gasps, and guffaws were repeated. Some had gone immediately to that versatile noun/verb/exclamation that television commentators politely call "the F bomb." It was there in all its variations. After a few minutes, the hubbub quieted down, they all looked to me as if I had a solution to an unnamed problem. I wasn't sure what I should say, but I was the consultant, so I must have some words of wisdom.

"Certain words have always been considered taboo," I acknowledged. "That doesn't mean we don't hear them or see them, does it? I remember hearing and seeing these taboo words almost every day in the school corridors when I was teaching."

Lots of nodding heads.

"It just means we don't consider them acceptable in polite company."

More nodding heads.

"But those words exist. Really exist. They don't simply disappear if we print dictionaries without them."

I felt a small anecdote might help. "I grew up with a mother who believed you could understand something about a person by the language he used. If someone used 'ain't,' or said things like 'he don't,' well they'd better not come anywhere near my mother. She'd correct them. She corrected me plenty of times. 'Ain't isn't a word,' she'd always say. When I visited her two months ago, I showed her our new dictionary with the word 'ain't' right there on the page…in living color. She was not amused. You can imagine what she said."

They laughed. A few "Oh, yeahs" floated to the front of the room.

"Living with my mother was a nonstop grammar lesson. However, I did NOT show her any of the other words that you've already discovered today. I needed to get out of her apartment alive."

From somewhere in the room, one of the teachers offered, "Your mother's corrections did you some good, didn't they?"

"Without a doubt. Thanks to her, I know what standard American English is." I smiled at my class. "However, if you really wanted to send my Mom off the rails, all you had to say was 'shit.' 'We don't use that kind of language, young man,' she'd say. The tone of her voice said it all. I can't imagine what she would have done if I'd ever said 'fuck' in front of her. By the way, I never did."

Some teachers laughed. Some didn't.

"This dictionary deals with the English language the way it is, not the way we might wish it to be. Some of you may choose not to use it, and I understand that. But while you're here, let me point out several things. First, this will be the first dictionary you'll ever own that will teach your students the difference between 'chickenshit' and 'bullshit.'"

They began paging through the dictionary even as they laughed. An occasional "Oh my God," or "I don't believe it," whispered across the room.

"Please notice that the word 'chickenshit' is a guide word at the top of the page." I couldn't help laughing. "That's not something you see every day, is it? The other guide word on that page is 'Chilkoot Pass.' When I was reviewing the dictionary with my friend, he said that would be a great title for a novel: *From Chickenshit to Chilkoot Pass.*"

They were taking all this in—some laughing, some grimacing, and some just wondering. They were English teachers and this was their language—and their students' language. As ninth grade teachers, they could well be teaching J. D. Salinger's classic, *The Catcher in the Rye*, a book that used the word 'fuck' three times by my count. An angry parent once told me, "That's three times too many."

I watched the teachers paging through their dictionaries and realized the effect that words have in our lives. English teachers were all about language, and there was something slightly sacred about a dictionary, and this new dictionary felt slightly sacrilegious.

But I couldn't change anything about our dictionary, and wouldn't if I could. *Sticks and stones,* I thought. The teachers' faces betrayed everything from elation to consternation.

"Do I have any lovers of T. S. Eliot here?" I asked. "Any T. S. Eliot scholars?"

A few hands shot up.

"*Macavity*'s in your anthology, isn't it?" one teacher asked. "I love that poem."[84]

Numerous voices echoed her feelings.

"Have any of you ever heard T. S. Eliot's literary concept of 'ironic juxtaposition?'"[85]

A few hands went up.

---

84 *Macavity: The Mystery Cat* is one of the poems found in T. S. Eliot's volume, *Old Possum's Book of Practical Cats*. The musical *Cats* is based on Eliot's 1939 volume of poetry. [See: V is for Veritas.]

85 Ironic juxtaposition features two ideas, objects, or words in proximity to provide a contrast to one another.

"I always think of ironic juxtaposition as 'stark contrast'," I explained. "Two ideas are juxtaposed—placed side-by-side—and the contrast between them is so dramatic that it causes an equally dramatic response in the viewer." I then directed them to open their dictionaries to the entry, 'Mother Goose.'

They did. In seconds, most of them also saw the entry immediately preceding 'Mother Goose'—another 'mother' word, the one with four syllables.

Their response was immediate—a chorus of "Oh, my God's," loud laughter, and the breathy sounds of astonishment.

"If any of you ever have to teach the concept of ironic juxtaposition, just open your dictionary and you'll have the best possible example," I said.

I waited a moment for everyone to calm down.

"Ladies and gentlemen, these dictionaries belong to you. Every word in them is part of our English language—the good, the bad, and the profane. I'm not sure what else to say. You'll have to decide if you want your students to use these dictionaries, but I think we all know there probably aren't any words in this dictionary that your kids haven't encountered somewhere…somehow."

There seemed to be universal agreement about my last remark.

"Now, once again. Is there anything else for the good of the order?"

There were no more questions. But then from the back of the room, I could have sworn I heard a solitary voice say, "Lunch is waiting. Let's get the fuck out of here."

Yikes!

Zzzzz is for Sleep

Each night, when I go to sleep, I die.
And the next morning, when I wake up, I am reborn.
—Mahatma Gandhi

There is a time for many words,
and there is also a time for sleep.
—Homer

Sleep is God. Go worship.
—Jim Butcher

SLEEPING IS A valuable skill.

When I am asked how I could survive for so many years, over so many miles, across so many time zones, in so many strange places, my answer is simple: I can sleep. The ability to sleep kept chronic *circadian dysrhythmia*—the delightful medical term for jet lag—at bay. Seated on a plane, or a train, or lying amidst pillows in some distant hotel room, sleep was never far away.

From what I've been able to discern, there are four kinds of people in the world where sleep is concerned:

1. People who need little sleep but who still function in peak form. (I was going to say they need "no sleep," but that is never the case.)

ZZZZZ IS FOR SLEEP

2. People who need sleep but find it impossible to get to sleep. Chronic insomniacs, they frequently seem to be in a state of semi-consciousness and seldom function at their best.
3. People who need sleep, but require various conditions to be perfect: the right amount of light and sound; the correct amount of mattress or pillow firmness; the correct time of day.
4. People who need sleep, and can fall asleep quickly and easily, almost anywhere. These people are what my mother used to call "bed-of-nails sleepers."

The most capable road warriors I have ever known belong to either category one or category four. Category three can be capable road warriors, but only if they've had their daily caffeine fix.

As for me, I am a bed-of-nails sleeper—a champion sleeper—a dues-paying member of category four. My mother anointed me a bed-of-nails sleeper the day she found me snoozing soundly in the living room while lying on a scattering of toy plastic soldiers and Lincoln logs.

"Good Lord, John," she said, shaking me awake. "How can you sleep with all these toys poking you? I believe you could sleep on a bed of nails." People who know me, know I can sleep almost anywhere.

In the interest of full disclosure, I've never tried sleeping on a bed of nails. Nor have I ever tried to sleep standing up—another position my mother has hypothesized from time to time. Mom was simply referring to the fact that I fall asleep quickly.

I'm proud to say I'm a champion sleeper, and always have been. Almost any space or surface will do. Time and place are largely irrelevant, but I must admit, my facility for swift immersion into the arms of Morpheus amused some and annoyed others.

Lou Serensits, my roommate during my senior year in college, was one of those folks who found it both amusing and annoying. As Lou tells the story, I once fell asleep in mid-sentence while we were having a discussion. That is, I was in mid-sentence, not Lou.

From what Lou told me—remember, this was all reported to me, because I'd fallen asleep—I was talking to Lou about one of our classes, and then I fell silent. Lou walked over to my bed and saw that I'd fallen asleep. He couldn't believe it. Lou decided the best way to deal with my impromptu, mid-sentence snooze was to drop several textbooks on my midsection. College textbooks are notoriously large and heavy.

Startled, I woke up, just as Lou hoped.

"Damn it, Scannell," he said, after he'd dropped the books on me, "at least finish your sentence and say goodnight before you doze off." His voice betrayed that mixture of amusement and annoyance.

My sleeping ability qualified me to be a road warrior, because a road warrior's life often departs from the concept of regular hours. Extensive traveling explodes—some say "eradicates"—the forty-hour work week. Not infrequently, my work week would begin early Sunday morning when I was bound for an East Coast destination. I'd fly, let's say, to Boston. Arriving in the late afternoon or early evening, my internal clock needed some recalibration. Ten o'clock Eastern time is seven o'clock Pacific, but on Monday morning I had to be up, showered, dressed, and calling on teachers before classes began at one of the local high schools. So I had to sleep. More to the point, I had to be *able* to sleep…and I could.

That's why an employer looking to hire a person who will be traveling almost every week ought to ask, "How well do you sleep? Can you sleep just about anywhere? On planes? On trains? In a car? In a strange bed?"

I've seen my share of weary road warriors who can't sleep on planes, or catch a nap during the many periods of "endless waiting."

Not infrequently, I would meet national consultants doing the same kind of work I did—let me call them fellow road warriors—and they would complain about how tired they were.

"Don't you sleep on the plane?" I'd ask.

"No. I just can't get comfortable." Or "Who sleeps on planes?" Or "There's just too much work to do on the plane."

The problems others had sleeping on planes were unknown to me. For me it was a matter of getting as comfortable as possible and falling sleep. Even if I was vaguely uncomfortable, I'd never know it once I'd dozed off. As for work, I never liked working on planes. I've seen plenty of sleep-deprived insomniacs working on planes. They work because they can't sleep, not because they want to work. If I'm going to be awake on a plane, I'll be reading books or conversing with a seatmate.

Sleeping solves other problems, too. It helped me deal with the airline phenomenon that we all abhor—the middle seat. On the rare occasion that I'd find myself in a middle seat, I'd sleep. Often to the amazement of my seatmates.

On long transcontinental flights, chances were excellent that I'd fall asleep. Sleeping in transit allowed me to rise especially early to leave for the airport and catch the earliest available flight. Any sleep lost by rising early was immediately reclaimed when I settled into my seat. I often fell asleep before the plane had even pushed back from the gate. Several times a flight attendant would nudge me awake so I could watch for the umpteenth time the seat-belt/oxygen mask ritual required by the FAA before every flight. One of my colleagues, who'd spent a great deal of time in Japan, called it "Airline Kabuki."

One final, interesting sleep anecdote that testifies to the depth of my sleeping.

When I awoke in the mornings in my always-strange-but-all-too-familiar hotel room, I would typically grab the television remote and search for the news. But on more than a half-dozen occasions, the television refused to turn on. The first time this happened, I called the front desk and reported that my television wasn't working.

"Is it plugged in?" the clerk inquired.

"Well, it should be," I said, annoyed at such a bonehead question. "The television was working just fine when I fell asleep last night."

"No problem, Mr. Scannell," the clerk said cheerfully, "I'll have someone come up and look at it shortly." I often speculated that hotel desk clerks get paid extra for being infinitely more cheerful than is normally possible.

When I hung up, the clerk's words and my own curiosity pushed me to look behind the television. I wanted to be certain it was plugged in—otherwise I would look foolish when someone came to repair a perfectly-functioning television. I bent over the bureau to see the television's plug dangling. The TV was unplugged. Unplugged? How? I stared for a moment in disbelief.

I immediately called the front desk and confessed to the clerk that her question, "Is it plugged in?" was, in fact, the problem. Boy, did I feel stupid. The unplugged television was a mystery, until it happened again…and again…and again.

Either I was being gas-lighted by a prowler following me around the country and nefariously unplugging my television set in the middle of the night to drive me insane, or something else was responsible.

That "something else" was me. This is all speculation, of course, but I prefer the "me" explanation to the nefarious prowler skulking about my hotel room in the dead of night.

Here is what I know: The television was on when I fell asleep.

Here is what I'm guessing: Sometime during the night, in my unconscious stupor, I couldn't figure out how to turn the television off with the remote. I got out of bed and did the only thing my sleeping mind could conjure: *Unplug the damn thing!*

Yes. I have a talent for falling asleep and staying asleep.

Afternoon Naps

Not only can I sleep through the night, I can nap. I've been napping since my college days when regular naps occasionally drove my roommates crazy. More than a few times, George would come back from class on his way to football practice. If I was napping, he'd shout, "Little kids nap, Scannell. Cats nap. Not adults. You're not a little kid. Drink some coffee."

True, I wasn't a little kid, and, until I graduated college and began teaching, I never liked coffee. So napping *was* my "coffee." After a twenty-minute nap, I would awaken, completely refreshed and invigorated. I've seen some of the research on napping:

> More than 85% of mammalian species are polyphasic sleepers, meaning that they sleep for short periods throughout the day. Humans are part of the minority of monophasic sleepers, meaning that our days are divided into two distinct periods, one for sleep and one for wakefulness. It is not clear that this is the natural sleep pattern of humans.[86]

I suspect I'm polyphasic, which means napping works for me. This particular ability—to briefly nap and feel restored—helped me innumerable times when I had a late afternoon presentation before a school committee.

On days when I had a scheduled presentation—typically after the end of the regular school day—I'd roll into the school parking lot earlier than anyone thought was reasonable. Arriving early and actually being in the school's parking lot meant I never had to worry about the unexpected traffic jam, the unanticipated accident, or any of a dozen contingent possibilities that could arise to make me late. I was there, and because I was there early, I could put my seat back, and take a nap. I'd awaken refreshed and ready.

I've contemplated writing "Terrific sleeping and napping ability" under *Other Skills* on my résumé.

The Gambler's Shuttle

There was one instance when my ability to sleep proved especially helpful. I did most of my own travel planning, and on this trip, I'd managed to screw up my own schedule.

Let me give the reader the twenty-five-word-or-less summary: *I was in Roswell, New Mexico, late Wednesday afternoon, and needed*

---

86 This information was gleaned from The National Sleep Foundation: https://sleepfoundation.org/sleep-topics/napping

to be in Post Falls, Idaho, for an in-service by 9:30 Thursday morning.

I think that's exactly twenty-three words. Explaining my trip will actually require a few more words.

It was June 1998, and I'd scheduled a rare[87] afternoon sales presentation on Wednesday, June 10th, in Roswell, New Mexico. Ordinarily that wouldn't pose a problem, but I'd also scheduled a teacher in-service in Post Falls, Idaho—an in-service I thought I'd scheduled for Friday, June 12th. I was mistaken. In fact, it was scheduled for Thursday morning at 9:30 a.m.

I learned of my scheduling snafu when Sylvia, the Post Falls language arts curriculum coordinator, left me a voicemail detailing the where and when of my presentation. Before I received her message, I'd anticipated an uneventful return to Seattle—I would arrive in Seattle about 6:00 a.m. Thursday morning—and then I'd go home, get some sleep, and return to Sea-Tac for a leisurely commute to Spokane on Friday.

Her message overturned those expectations. I had to be in Post Falls tomorrow morning.

I knew there were no flights from Roswell to Albuquerque after 5:00 p.m., and my Roswell presentation was scheduled to go until 6:00 p.m. When finished, my itinerary called for me to drive to Albuquerque and then take the flight from Albuquerque to Seattle called the Gambler's Shuttle. The Gambler's Shuttle was the 11:30 p.m. Albuquerque flight on America West Airlines that made stops in Las Vegas and Reno—thus the name. It would touch down in Seattle around 6:00 a.m. I had to make that flight.

Then I'd immediately fly from Seattle to Spokane, then drive the short twenty-two miles to Post Falls, Idaho, for my 9:30 a.m. session with their teachers.

The only real problem was this: Could I do an in-service after flying all night long?

The answer was, "I hope so."

---

87 Sales presentations in June were rare. Typically, all purchasing decisions were made well in advance of the end of the school year.

My Roswell work concluded, and I packed up my projector and computer and drove the more than 200 miles nonstop to Albuquerque. Night had fallen when I arrived at 10:00 p.m. for my 11:30 p.m. departure. When I boarded the plane, I asked the flight attendant just how far she was going.

"I finish tonight in Seattle," she said.

"Good," I said, "me, too. I want to sleep all the way because I'll be working tomorrow morning in Idaho."

"Really?" she asked. "You fly all night…and then you go to work?"

"No," I said, reassuring her. "With your help, I'll sleep all night."

She gave me an approving look. "You got it." She was as good as her word.

I was asleep before we lifted off from Albuquerque at 11:30 p.m., and I don't remember waking until we bounced down in Seattle just a few minutes after 6:00 a.m. I had a window seat, a pillow, and a blanket, and I slept the entire way. The two stops, one in Las Vegas and the other in Reno, may actually have happened, but I couldn't testify under oath that I ever landed in either place.

When we touched down in Seattle, the woman in the aisle seat shook my shoulder. "I think this is where we all get off," she said. As she pulled her carry-on from the overhead bin, she commented, "I got on in Las Vegas, and you slept all the way from there. Are you okay?"

"Yes," I said with a wave of my hand. "I have to work this morning just east of Spokane. I just needed my sleep."

"Well, I wish you luck."

I thanked her, followed her off the plane, picked up my suitcase at the baggage carousel, and walked to my car. I drove to the Red Lion, a hotel a few blocks from the terminal, where I shaved, brushed my teeth, changed my shirt and tie, and returned to Sea-Tac's parking lot. I boarded my Spokane flight at 7:15 a.m. and landed at 8:20 a.m. Since I had no luggage, I was in my rental car by 8:50 a.m., and drove the twenty-two miles to Post Falls, Idaho, in a half hour. I was ten minutes early.

"What can I get you?" the curriculum coordinator asked as I walked in.

"A big cup of coffee," I said.

Coffee in hand, I guided a dozen English teachers through the literature program they would be implementing next September. Coffee and momentum kept me going until the early afternoon.

"That's it," I told the teachers assembled for the in-service. "If you need anything more, I am only a phone call away."

I drove back to the Spokane Airport and returned my rental. Alaska Airlines had hourly flights to Seattle, and I would catch the next one.

Arriving at my departure gate, I spoke with the Alaska Airline representative behind the counter.

"Can I help you?" she asked.

"I am exhausted," I said. "I'll be sitting right over there. I will probably be asleep when you call the 3:00 p.m. flight. Could you please wake me up?"

She smiled. I'm sure I wasn't the first exhausted passenger she'd encountered. "I'll be happy to, Mr. Scannell. I can see that the flight isn't heavily booked...so it will be around 2:45 when we board."

I've always been grateful for people like her. We both did our jobs. I fell asleep, just as I knew I would. She woke me up just as she said she would. Then I walked aboard the plane and fell asleep almost the moment my rear end hit the seat.

I felt genuinely refreshed when we touched down at Sea-Tac International.

It was the end of a long day.

CPSIA information can be obtained
at www.ICGtesting.com
Printed in the USA
FFHW021052290319
51353459-56817FF

9 780578 216898